혁신 개정판

Just
GRAMMAR

MG
3A

혁신 개정판
Just Grammar MG 3A

지은이 신석영
발행인 조상현
발행처 (주)위아북스

주소 서울시 마포구 공덕동 풍림빌딩 304호
문의 02-725-9988 **팩스** 02-725-9863
등록번호 제300-2007-164호
홈페이지 www.wearebooks.co.kr
ISBN 978-89-6614-034-3 53740

혁신 개정판

Just
GRAMMAR

신석영 지음

MG
3A

We're
위아북스

PROLOGUE

"영어는 세계의 동서남북을 한꺼번에, 내다볼 수 있는 마법의 창문이다." – 인도 수상 네루

그렇습니다. 책이 사람의 인생을 바꿀 수 있고, 책을 통해 전 세계를 여행하며, 영어를 통해 전 세계와 의사소통할 수 있습니다. 학생 여러분들이 필수적으로 갖추어야 할 생활 도구의 하나가 바로 영어가 아닐 수 없습니다.

요즘에는 '문법 무용론'을 주장하는 사람들도 있지만, 앵무새처럼 몇 마디 따라 말하고 일상 회화 정도를 하려고 영어를 공부하지 않을 것입니다. 특히 우리나라의 영어교육의 환경이 'EFL(English as a Foreign Language)', 즉, "외국어로서의 영어" 환경임을 제대로 이해하는 사람이라면 제 2외국어로써 무엇보다도 문장을 이해하는 것이 우선되어야 한다는 것은 기본이자, 상식입니다.

모국어로 영어를 습득할 수 있는 단계가 지나버린 우리 학생들에게는 오히려 인지 능력이 덜 형성된 상태이기 때문에, 성인 학습자들보다 학습 능력이 훨씬 떨어진다는 연구 결과를 발표한 학자들도 있습니다. 그러므로 '학생들이 무분별한 학교 교육 또는 어학원 영어, 그리고 외국인이면 무조건 받아들이는 관행으로는 오히려 학습 장애를 초래하는 결과를 낳을 수도 있습니다.

문법은 필요한 학습이지만, "올바른" 학습 방법이 아니면 의미가 없다!

문법 교육에 있어서는 '어떤 교재로 가르치느냐?, 누가 가르치느냐?'하는 것은 굉장히 중요한 사항입니다. 영어 실력도 중요하지만 무엇보다도 아이들의 특성을 이해하고 인지 발달 단계와 언어 학습 원리에 맞게 가르칠 수 있는 최적의 교재가 필요합니다. 수업에 대해 좋고 나쁨을 판단할 비판적 사고가 부족한 학생들에게 단지 시간과 비용만 투자한다고 해서 실질적으로 도움을 준다고 볼 수는 없습니다.

Just Grammar(혁신 개정판) 시리즈는 대한민국 영어교육의 최전선에서 현장강의를 통해 오랜 세월동안 직접 가르치며 만들었습니다. 입시학원과 외국어 학원 그리고 MBC 방송 강의를 통해서 실제 검증된 교수법을 바탕으로 학생들에게 가장 최적화된 학습물인 Just Grammar(혁신 개정판) 시리즈를 가만히 내놓습니다.

이 책의 특징은 다음과 같습니다.

첫째, 현행 중학교 영어 교과서 문법 내용을 중심으로 실용적인 문법 사항들을 체계적으로 편성했습니다.

둘째, 각 영어 교과서를 철저히 분석하여, 반드시 알아야 하는 내용을 짜임새 있게 엮었습니다. 또한 현실감 있는 상황에서 실제로 자연스러운 문법을 구사하는 연습을 할 수 있습니다. 문법 문제 하나하나를 일상적인 상황에서 활용할 수 있는 능력을 향상시키고, 학생의 흥미를 이끌 수 있는 활동으로 구성하였습니다.

셋째, 점점 중요성이 높아져 가고 있는 학교 내신 영어시험의 서술형 문제들에 효과적으로 대비할 수 있도록 서술형 기본 대비에서 실전 서술형, 논술형 문제까지 완벽 대비할 수 있도록 하였습니다. 특히, 학교에서 출제된 기출 응용문제와 교육청 출제 경향에 맞춘 다양한 문제들로 채워 서술형에 대한 고민을 완벽히 해결하였습니다.

넷째, 문법학습의 궁극적인 목표는 스피킹입니다. Super Speaking 코너를 통해 지금까지 배운 문법 사항을 스피킹으로 마무리할 수 있게 구성하여 자연스럽게 스피킹 시험에 대비할 수 있게 하였습니다.

"Just Grammar 혁신 개정판"이 출간되기까지 더 좋은 책을 위해 헌신의 노력을 다해주신 위아북스 관계자 여러분들에게 고개 숙여 깊은 감사를 드립니다. 부디 이 책을 통해서 모든 학습자들이 영어에 대한 자신감을 얻어 내신 성적 향상은 물론, 더 이상 영어로 인해 힘들어하지 않고 이것이 문법의 마지막 공부가 될 수 있기를 희망합니다. 마지막으로 항상 옆에서 힘이 되어주는 내 가족, 힘들어도 묵묵히 응원해준 내 아내 미선이, 그리고 아빠에게 언제나 용기와 희망을 주는 서윤이와 강민이에게 깊은 감사와 사랑을 전합니다.

신석영

학교 내신 · 서술형 문제를 뛰어넘어
Speaking과 Writing을 대비할 수 있는 교재

기존의 교재들은 문법 설명을 장황하게 설명하여 이해하기도 쉽지 않고 문법 중심 객관식 문제나 단편적인 단답형 주관식 문제들만 나열하고 있어 실제 학습효과를 기대할 수 없으나 Just Grammar 혁신 개정판 시리즈는 각 학년에서 중요하게 다루고 있는 문법 세부 항목을 체계적으로 정리하였고 쉬운 문법 문제에서 서술형 기초다지기 그리고 신경향 실전 서술형 평가문제들을 담았습니다. 그 어떤 교재에서도 찾아볼 수 없는 Super Speaking 코너에서는 배운 문법 내용을 실제 원어민들이 사용하는 말하기 연습을 할 수 있도록 구성한 국내 유일한 교재입니다.

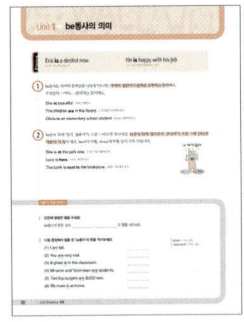

1단계　문법 해설

Preview를 통한 대표 예문만 봐도 영문법의 개념을 이해할 수 있고 예문 중심으로 설명한 문법 설명은 머리에 쏙쏙! 어려운 문법 용어와 난해한 설명 방식에서 탈피하여 새로운 방식으로 문법의 줄기와 핵심을 잡아줄 것입니다. 참신한 예문은 실제 원어민들이 자주 사용하는 표현들을 담았습니다.

2단계　기본기 탄탄 다지기

배운 핵심 문법을 올바로 이해하였는지 바로 확인할 수 있는 연습 문제, 쉽고 재미있는 기본 문제들로 구성되어 문법에 대한 자신감이 쭉쭉! 올라갑니다.

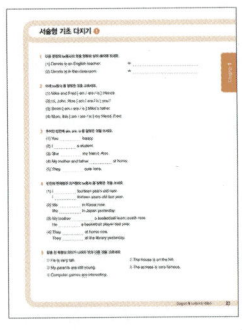

3단계　서술형 기초 다지기

앞서 배운 Unit을 다시 점검할 수 있는 다양한 문제들을 구성하여 문법 개념을 확실히 이해할 수 있도록 하였습니다. 이를 통해 서술형 문제에 대비할 수 있도록 하였으며 문제의 난이도가 한 단계 업그레이드되어 실제 시험 유형의 문제로 내신에 대비할 수 있게 됩니다. 단순한 문법 연습이 아닌 응용, 심화 과정으로 발전해나간 누적식 구성이므로 모든 앞 내용이 자연스럽게 반복되어 충분한 학습 효과를 볼 수 있습니다.

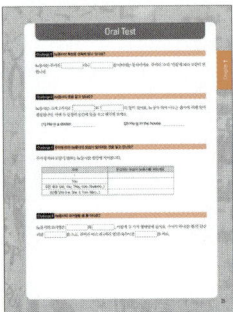

4단계　Oral Test

학습한 문법 개념을 스스로 질문에 답을 하거나 현장 수업에서는 학생들이 답을 직접 말하며 대답하는 질의응답 형식의 test입니다. 하나의 Chapter가 끝난 후 또는 다음 Chapter를 공부하기 전 복습용으로 사용해도 좋습니다. 문법 개념에 대한 질문을 정확히 답을 하지 못할 때 다시 한 번 복습해야 한다는 것을 잊지 마세요!

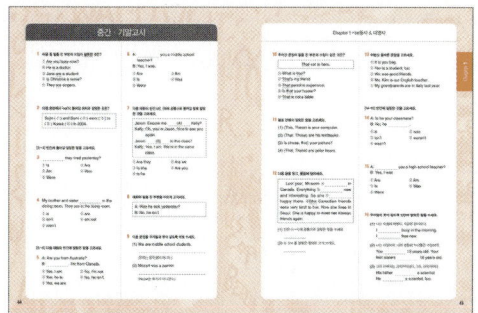

5단계 중간·기말고사

해당 Chapter 학습을 마치고 학습 성취도를 평가할 수 있는 실전 문제, 심화 문제로 구성하였습니다. 실제 학교 시험을 철저히 분석하여 자주 출제되는 필수 문법 문제들로 수록하였습니다. 다양한 유형의 교과서 기출 문제와 서술형 문제까지 해결함으로써 내신 성적 향상에 큰 도움이 될 것입니다.

6단계 Grammar in Reading

독해 지문 안에 생생한 문법이 쏙쏙, 문법에 대한 개념의 이해와, 응용력이 생긴 이때 다양한 독해 지문을 통해 배운 문법을 독해에 즉시 활용하여 적용할 수 있도록 구성하였습니다.

7단계 Super Speaking

학습한 문법 내용을 Speaking에 적용하여 스피킹 영역에도 소홀함이 없게 구성하였습니다. Just Grammar 혁신 개정판 시리즈로 리딩, 라이팅, 스피킹을 연계하여 자연스럽게 전 영역을 아울러 학습하도록 구성하였습니다.

8단계 실전 서술형 평가문제

실제 학교에서 출제된 서술형 응용문제와 교육청 출제경향에 맞춘 서술형 평가대비 문제로, 학생들의 사고력과 창의력을 길러줍니다. 해당 Chapter에서 출제될 가능성이 있는 서술형 문항을 개발하여 각 학교의 서술형 평가문제에 철저히 대비할 수 있도록 하였습니다. 단순 암기에서 벗어나 직접 써보고 생각해 볼 수 있는 코너입니다.

9단계 워크북

보충자료 워크북을 활용하여 Just Grammar 3에 해당하는 모든 문법사항을 최종 정리하며 복습할 수 있습니다. 본책에 해당하는 문법사항 중 시험 적중률이 높은 유형의 문제들을 뽑았습니다. 숙제나 자습을 통해 보충하기에 좋은 자료입니다.

해설집 + 워크북 무료!

CONTENTS

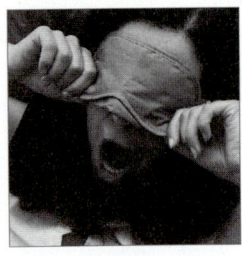

Chapter 1
to부정사

Unit 1 • 명사 역할을 하는 to부정사

To camp out under the stars is romantic.
= **It** is romantic **to camp out** under the stars.
별 아래에서 야영을 하는 것은 낭만적이다.

① 주어, 목적어, 보어 자리에 명사나 대명사를 쓰지만 동작이나 행동을 나타낼 때는 부정사를 쓰며, '~(하는) 것'으로 해석한다. 부정사가 주어 자리에 쓰인 경우, 그 자리에 가주어 it을 쓰고 부정사를 뒤로 보낸다. 이것을 가주어 · 진주어 구문이라고 한다.

To camp alone in the woods is very dangerous. 숲속에서 혼자 야영하는 것은 매우 위험하다. (주어 역할)
= **It** is very dangerous **to camp** alone in the woods.

I decided **to marry** her. 나는 그녀와 결혼하기로 결심했다. (목적어 역할)

My dream is **to live** in London. 나의 꿈은 런던에서 사는 것이다. (보어 역할)

② 부정사의 부정은 부정사 바로 앞에 not 또는 never를 쓴다.

She promised **not** to run away again. 그녀는 다시 도망가지 않겠다고 약속했다.

Can you promise **never** to repeat that? 다시는 그것을 하지 않겠다고 약속할 수 있니?

기본기 탄탄 다지기

1 괄호 안의 말을 바르게 배열하시오.

(1) _____(problem, solve, this, to) is difficult.

(2) My dream is _____ (languages, speak, three, to).

(3) We decided _____(out, not, to, go) because of the weather.

> solve v. 풀다, 해결하다
> language n. 언어
> interview n. 면접, 인터뷰

2 주어진 문장을 It ~ to부정사(가주어 · 진주어 구문)의 문장으로 바꿔 쓰시오.

(1) To write a letter in English is difficult.

➡ _____

(2) To understand why Jessica is angry is easy.

➡ _____

(3) To practice interview questions before going on an interview is a good idea.

➡ _____

> ▶to부정사가 문장 맨 앞의 주어로 오는 경우는 주로 속담이나 문학작품과 같이 문어체 문장에서 자주 볼 수 있다.
> **To see** is to believe.
> 보는 것이 믿는 것이다.(백문이 불여일견)
>
> ▶to부정사가 주어인 경우 단수 취급하여 반드시 단수 동사를 쓴다.
> **To express** feelings is good for your mental health.
> 감정을 표현하는 것이 정신 건강에 좋다.

Unit 2 • 의문사 + to부정사

Preview

Please tell me **how to get** to the City Hall.
시청에 어떻게 가는지 좀 알려주세요.

She knows **when to start** the level test.
그녀는 언제 레벨테스트가 시작하는지 안다.

1 '의문사 + to부정사'는 명사처럼 주어, 목적어, 보어 역할을 한다. 단, why는 부정사와 함께 쓰지 않는다.

how to v	어떻게 ~할지	where to v	어디로 ~할지
what to v	무엇을 ~할지	which to v	어느 것을 ~할지
when to v	언제 ~할지	whether to v	~ 할지 말아야 할지

He hasn't decided **where to stay** during his trip. 그는 여행 동안 어디서 머물지 결정하지 못했다. (목적어 역할)
I don't know **what to say** about the topic. 나는 그 주제에 관해 무엇을 말해야 할지 모르겠다. (목적어 역할)
How to do is more important than **what to do**. 어떻게 할지가 무엇을 할지보다 중요하다. (주어 역할, 목적어 역할)

2 '의문사 + to부정사'는 '의문사 + 주어 + should + 동사원형'으로 바꿔 쓸 수 있다.

Please tell me **how to solve** the problem. 내가 그 문제를 어떻게 풀어야 할지 알려줘.
= Please tell me **how I should solve** the problem.

기본기 탄탄 다지기

1 다음 괄호 안의 말을 알맞게 배열하여 문장을 완성하시오.

(1) Please tell me (to, how, get) to the City Hall.
➡ _____

(2) He let me know (say, to, what) next.
➡ _____

(3) Why didn't you ask me (when, start, to)?
➡ _____

(4) Will you show me (to, play, where) this game?
➡ _____

(5) I want to learn (how, should, drive, I) a car.
➡ _____

(6) I have no idea (I, should, what, do) for her.
➡ _____

> **have no idea** 전혀 모르다
>
> It is unclear **whether to leave** here or not. 이곳을 떠날지 말지가 명확하지 않다.
> I can't decide **whether to answer** her letter. 나는 그녀의 편지에 답을 할지 말지를 결정할 수 없다.

Unit 3 ● 목적격 보어로 쓰이는 to부정사

Preview

The doctor *told* me **to eat** more vegetables.
그 의사는 내게 야채를 더 많이 먹으라고 했다.
We *saw* a thief **breaking** into the house.
우리는 도둑이 그 집안으로 침입하는 것을 봤다.

1 목적어가 동작이나 행위를 해야 할 경우 '동사 + 목적어 + to부정사'를 써서 부정사가 목적어의 동작을 나타낸다. 이때 부정사는 '앞으로 해야 할 현재나 미래'의 의미가 내포되어 있다.

They *expected* Jane **to attend** the ceremony. 그들은 Jane이 그 의식에 참여할 것이라고 예상했다.
　　　　　　 O　　　 O.C.

Dad *wanted* me not **to hang out** with bad boys. 아빠는 내가 나쁜 애들과 어울려 다니지 않기를 원하셨다.
　　　　　 O　　　　 O.C.

2 사역동사(make, have, let)는 '(목적어에게) ~하도록 시키다(허락하다)'의 뜻으로 목적격 보어 자리에 'to' 없이 '동사원형'만 쓴다. 지각동사(see, smell, watch, hear, feel)도 목적격 보어 자리에 '동사원형'을 쓰는데, 목적어의 진행 중인 상황을 나타낼 때는 현재분사(V-ing)를 쓴다.

My father *let* me **buy** a new smartphone. 아빠는 내가 새 스마트폰을 사는 것을 허락하셨다.

The teacher *had* us **be** quiet during class. 선생님은 우리가 수업 중에 떠들지 못하게 하셨다.

I *saw* many girls **rush** into the building. 나는 많은 소녀들이 그 건물 안으로 달려가는 것을 봤다.

I *smelled* something **burning** in the kitchen. 나는 부엌에서 무언가 타고 있는 냄새를 맡았다.

기본기 탄탄 다지기

1 다음 괄호 안의 표현 중 알맞은 것을 고르시오.

(1) He advised me not (tell / to tell) a lie.

(2) The teacher made the girl (clean / to clean) the windows.

(3) She let me (have / to have) a free coffee.

(4) I heard someone (shout / to shout) in the distance.

(5) We heard some strange sounds (coming / to come) out of the room.

(6) The boy asked his mother (make / to make) some pancakes.

(7) She didn't allow us (light / to light) candles in the room.

advise v. 충고하다
shout v. 소리 지르다, 외치다
in the distance 멀리에서
pancake n. 팬케이크
candle n. 양초

▶ get은 목적격 보어 자리에 'to부정사'를 쓰고, help는 '동사원형' 또는 'to부정사' 둘 다 쓸 수 있다.
I got him **to visit** his teacher. 나는 그에게 선생님을 방문하라고 했다.
Can you help me **(to) find** my wallet? 내 지갑 찾는 것을 도와주겠니?

1 다음 문장과 뜻이 같도록 할 때, 빈칸에 알맞은 말을 쓰시오.

(1) To eat junk food is not good for children.

➡ _____ is not good for children _____ _____ junk food.

(2) To learn computer skills is very important.

➡ _____ is very important _____ _____ computer skills.

(3) To learn a foreign language is interesting.

➡ _____ is interesting _____ _____ a foreign language.

2 주어진 문장을 '의문사 + 주어 + should + 동사원형'으로 다시 써 보시오.

(1) Do you know what to do next?

➡ _____

(2) I don't know what to give her for a birthday gift.

➡ _____

(3) Do you know how to go there?

➡ _____

3 다음과 같이 부정사를 이용하여 문장을 완성하시오.

visit / my parents once a month
➡ _____ To visit my parents once a month _____ is a joy in my life.

(1) have / a baby this month ➡ My younger sister is _____.

(2) fill in / this application form ➡ It is necessary _____.

(3) get / a promotion this year ➡ He expects _____.

(4) design / a new house on the hill ➡ _____ is a good idea.

4 다음과 같이 괄호 안의 표현을 이용하여 5형식 문장을 완성하시오.

> I didn't want to stay at home. (They made)
> ➡ They made me stay at home.

(1) He arrived early. (I saw)

➡ _____

(2) She got out of the car. (We watched)

➡ _____

(3) Susan and Paul were having a date. (We saw)

➡ _____

(4) They allowed me to telephone my lawyer. (They let)

➡ _____

(5) The police officer told me to empty my pockets. (The police officer had)

➡ _____

5 우리말에 맞도록 괄호 안의 말을 이용하여 빈칸에 알맞은 말을 쓰시오.

(1) Sarah는 내 영어 공부를 도와주고 싶어 한다. (want / help)

➡ Sarah _____ _____ _____ me with my English.

(2) 그것은 너무 충격적이어서 무슨 말을 해야 할지 몰랐다. (say)

➡ It was really shocking, so I didn't know _____ _____ _____.

(3) 그는 나에게 몇 권의 책을 도서관에 반납해 달라고 부탁했다. (return / some books)

➡ He asked me _____ _____ _____ _____ to the library.

(4) 나는 그가 나머지 임무를 마치도록 했다. (make / he / finish)

➡ I _____ _____ _____ the rest of his task.

(5) 그녀는 티켓을 어디에서 구해야 하는지 잊어버렸다. (get)

➡ She forgot _____ _____ _____ a ticket.

Oral Test

Challenge 1 부정사의 명사적 용법을 알고 있는가?

to부정사는 명사처럼 문장에서 [   ], [   ], [   ]의 역할을 할 수 있다.

[   ] 역할 : **To write** a letter in English is not easy. 편지를 영어로 쓰는 것은 쉽지 않다.

[   ] 역할 : My dream is **to live** in Sydney. 나의 꿈은 시드니에서 사는 것이다.

[   ] 역할 : We planned **to go** to a movie on Friday evening. 우리는 금요일 저녁에 영화보기를 계획했다.

Challenge 2 '의문사 + to부정사'의 쓰임을 알고 있는가?

(1) to부정사가 의문사와 함께 쓰여 문장에서 [   ], [   ], [   ] 역할을 할 수 있다.

※ 현대영어에서는 주로 '의문사 + to부정사'를 목적어 자리에 쓴다.

(2) '의문사 + to부정사'는 '[   ] + [   ] + [   ] + [   ]'으로 바꾸어 쓸 수 있다.

Have you decided **what to eat** for lunch? 점심으로 무엇을 먹을지 결정했니?
= Have you decided **what you should eat** for lunch?

Challenge 3 부정사를 목적격 보어 자리에 쓰는 이유를 알고 있는가?

5형식 문장에서 목적격 보어로 명사나 대명사 그리고 형용사를 쓰지만 목적어가 [   ]을 해야 할 경우 목적어 뒤에 목적격 보어로 to부정사를 쓴다. 이때 부정사는 목적어인 명사가 앞으로 해야 할 현재나 미래의 의미가 담겨있다.

The doctor advised *me* [   ] more vegetables. 의사는 나에게 더 많은 야채를 먹으라고 충고했다.

Challenge 4 원형부정사는 언제 쓰는가?

(1) [   ], [   ], [   ] 등의 사역동사는 목적격 보어 자리에 [   ] 없이 [   ]만 쓰는 원형부정사를 사용한다.

• make : 선택의 여지가 없이 어떤 일을 하라고 강제하는 경우 (= force)

• have : 부탁이나 요청하는 경우 (= request)

• let : 어떤 일을 하도록 허락하는 경우 (= permit, allow)

(2) see, watch, hear, smell, taste, feel 등의 지각동사의 목적격 보어 자리에도 마찬가지로 [   ]을 사용한다. 단, 진행 중인 짧은 순간을 보거나 들은 경우에는 목적격 보어 자리에 [   ]를 쓴다.

We *watched* the full moon **rise** yesterday. 우리는 어제 보름달이 뜨는 걸 봤다.

I *saw* Peter **working** out at the gymnasium yesterday. 나는 어제 Peter가 체육관에서 운동하는 것을 봤다.

Unit 4 • 형용사처럼 쓰이는 to부정사

I never had *the chance* **to talk** with her.
나는 그녀와 얘기할 기회가 전혀 없었다.
We're going to order *something* **to eat**.
우리는 먹을 것을 주문할 것이다.

1 to부정사가 명사 뒤에 위치하여 앞에 있는 명사를 꾸며주어 우리말 '~할, ~하는'의 뜻이 된다. 수식을 받는 명사가 전치사의 목적어가 되는 경우에는 'to부정사 + 전치사'가 명사 뒤에 위치하여 똑같이 '~할'의 뜻이 된다.

I don't have *a friend* **to advise** me. 나는 내게 충고를 해줄 친구가 없다.

What is *the best way* **to learn** English? 영어를 배울 가장 좋은 방법은 무엇이니?

Is there *a chair* **to sit on**? 앉을 의자가 있니? (sit on a chair)

She needs *a friend* **to talk with**. 그녀는 함께 얘기를 나눌 친구가 필요하다. (talk with a friend)

2 something, anything과 같이 –thing으로 끝나는 대명사는 반드시 부정사가 뒤에서 꾸미고 형용사와 함께 꾸밀 경우 '–thing + 형용사 + to부정사'의 어순으로 쓴다.

Would you like *something* **to drink**? 마실 것을 원하세요?

Please give me *something* **cold to drink**. 마실 시원한 것 좀 주세요.

기본기 탄탄 다지기

1 다음 괄호 안의 말을 알맞게 배열하여 문장을 완성하시오.

(1) I have no house (live, in, to). ➡ _____

(2) She is the last (tell, person, to) a lie. ➡ _____

(3) I have no friends (me, to, help). ➡ _____

(4) E-mail is the easiest (contact, to, way) John. ➡ _____

(5) We have many (do, things, to) now. ➡ _____

(6) We have (something, show, to, important) you.

➡ _____

last n. 최후의, 마지막의
contact v. 연락하다

▶'It's time + to부정사'는 '~할 시간이다'라는 뜻으로 명사 time 뒤에서 to부정사가 수식한다.
It's time **to go** to bed.
It's time **to have** dinner.

Unit 5 • be동사 + to부정사

Preview

They **are to** come at five.
그들은 5시에 올 예정이다.

My phone **was** not **to** be found.
내 전화기는 찾을 수가 없었다.

1 be동사의 보어로 형용사를 쓰듯이, to부정사 역시 형용사처럼 주어를 서술하는 주격 보어 역할을 한다. 이를 'be to 용법'이라고 한다.

예정 be going to	~할 예정이다	Her speech **is to** start soon. 그녀의 연설은 곧 시작할 예정이다.
의무 must	~해야 한다	We **are to** study English. 우리는 영어를 공부해야 한다.
가능 can	~할 수 있다	No stars **are to** be seen in the daytime. 별은 낮에 볼 수 없다.
의지 want to, intend to	~하려고 하다	If you **are to** pass the exam, you'd better study hard. 네가 시험을 통과하고자 한다면, 열심히 공부해야 한다.
운명 be doomed to	~할 운명이다	He **was** never **to** see his hometown again. 그는 두 번 다시 고향에는 돌아오지 못할 운명이었다.

기본기 탄탄 다지기

1 다음 밑줄 친 부분의 의미를 보기에서 찾아 쓰시오.

the Prime Minister 국무총리, 수상
homeland n. 조국, 고국
at once 즉시

예정	의무	가능	의지	운명

(1) You are to do your homework. _____

(2) The Prime Minister is to visit Singapore next week. _____

(3) Scott was never to see his homeland again. _____

(4) If you are to be here on time, you must leave at once. _____

(5) No one was to be seen in the room. _____

Preview

Steve *went* to Korea **to learn** Taekwondo.
Steve는 태권도를 배우기 위하여 한국에 갔다.

We were *shocked* **to see** her face.
우리는 그녀의 얼굴을 보고 충격을 받았다.

1 to부정사가 부사처럼 쓰이면 형용사 수식(~하기에), 목적(~하기 위하여), 원인(~해서, ~하게 되어서), 근거(~하다니, 하는 것을 보니), 조건(~한다면), 결과(~해서 ...하다) 등의 다양한 의미를 나타낸다.

This book is very *difficult* **to understand**. 이 책은 이해하기에 너무 어렵다. **(형용사 수식)**

I *stopped* **(in order) to take** pictures of the wonderful view. 나는 멋진 풍경을 찍기 위하여 멈췄다. **(목적)**

We were *happy* **to help** the poor. 우리는 가난한 사람들을 도와줘서 행복했다. **(원인)**

She *must be* crazy **to fall** in love with him. 그녀가 그를 사랑하게 되다니 미친 게 틀림없다. **(근거)**

You *will* be punished **to lie** again. 너는 거짓말을 다시 한다면 벌을 받게 될 것이다. **(조건)**

Seo-yoon *grew up* **to be** an English teacher. 서윤이는 자라서 영어선생님이 되었다. **(결과)**

기본기 탄탄 다지기

1 밑줄 친 to부정사의 용법을 골라 쓰시오.

형용사 수식	목적	원인	판단의 근거	조건	결과

(1) I am sorry to <u>hear</u> that her mother passed away. _____

(2) She ordered some food to <u>give</u> it to the poor. _____

(3) He grew up to <u>be</u> a great doctor. _____

(4) Han-geul is easy to <u>learn</u>. _____

(5) She must be brave to <u>fight</u> with the tiger. _____

(6) You couldn't do that to <u>save</u> your life. _____

▶**형용사 수식**: to부정사가 형용사 뒤에 위치하여 '~하기에'의 뜻이 된다.
목적: 주로 동사가 이동을 나타내거나 use, need와 함께 자주 쓰인다. 어떤 행위에 대한 목적을 정확하게 나타내기 위해 'in order to부정사'를 쓰기도 하는데 일상 영어에서는 in order를 주로 쓰지 않고 생략한다.
감정의 원인: 감정을 나타내는 형용사(happy, sad, glad, surprised, amazed, disappointed 등) 뒤에 to부정사는 '~해서'의 뜻이 된다.
I was **pleased to meet** Nancy.
판단의 근거: must be, cannot be, 감탄문과 함께 to부정사가 쓰일 경우 '~하다니'로 해석한다.
He **cannot be** a gentleman **to say** such a rude thing.
조건: 조동사 will 또는 would와 함께 쓰이는 to부정사를 '~한다면(= if)'으로 해석한다.
결과: 주로 grow, awake, live 등의 동사와 함께 자주 쓰고 'only to v, never to v'도 결과를 나타낸다.
She went to the haunted house, **never to come back**.

서술형 기초 다지기 ❷

1 다음을 to부정사를 이용한 문장으로 고쳐 쓰시오.

> She was surprised. + She heard his failure.
> ➡ She was surprised to hear his failure.

(1) I was excited. + I ate such delicious food.

➡ _____

(2) Dad was disappointed. He found that I lied to him.

➡ _____

(3) Tom grew up. He became a movie director.

➡ _____

2 주어진 문장과 같은 뜻이 되도록 다음과 같이 쓰시오.

> He came early so that he could take a good seat.
> = He came early to take a good seat.

(1) I went to the library so that I could borrow some books.

= _____

(2) Some people need English so that they can get a better job.

= _____

(3) Jane is going to go to the nursing home so that she can take part in volunteer work.

= _____

(4) I hurried so that I wouldn't be late for school.

= _____

(5) We arrived early so that we could finish the given work.

= _____

(6) She turned on the TV so that she could watch the news.

= _____

3 주어진 문장을 다음과 같이 to부정사를 이용한 문장으로 바꿔 쓰시오.

> I don't have a chair. + I will sit on it.
> ➡ I don't have a chair to sit on._____

(1) I need something. + I want to drink something cold.

➡ _____

(2) They're looking for a house. + They want to live in the house.

➡ _____

4 주어진 우리말과 뜻이 같아지도록 괄호 안의 단어를 고쳐 쓰시오.

(1) 나는 어제 그 소식을 듣고 충격을 받았다.

➡ I was shocked _____ yesterday. (hear, the news)

(2) 컴퓨터를 고친다면 나는 게임을 할 수 있다.

➡ I can play _____ my laptop. (fix, computer games)

(3) 내 남자친구와 헤어져서 정말 슬퍼.

➡ I'm really sad _____ my boyfriend. (break up with)

(4) 그는 살아서 자기 손녀의 결혼을 보았다.

➡ He lived _____ his granddaughter's marriage. (see)

5 다음과 같이 빈칸에 알맞은 'be동사 + 부정사'를 쓰고 그 용법을 쓰시오.

> The President is going to speak on TV tonight.
> ➡ The President _____ is to speak _____ on TV tonight. (예정)

(1) The meeting is going to be held tomorrow.

➡ The meeting is _____ tomorrow. (   )

(2) If you want to succeed, you should work hard.

➡ If you _____, you should work hard. (   )

(3) You must come in at once.

➡ You _____ in at once. (   )

(4) Not a sound could be heard in the house.

➡ Not a sound was _____ in the house. (   )

Oral Test

Chapter 1

Challenge 1 to부정사의 형용사 역할을 아는가?

(1) to부정사가 명사 바로 [   ]에 위치하면 명사를 꾸며 주어 '~(해야) 할'의 뜻으로 형용사 역할을 한다.
People have *a right* **to enjoy** a happy life. 사람들은 행복한 삶을 즐길 권리가 있다.

(2) 수식을 받는 명사가 전치사의 목적어인 경우에는 '명사 + [   ] + [   ]'의 어순으로 쓰는데 이때 전치사를 빼면 안 된다.
They don't have *a house* **to live in**. 그들은 살 집이 없다.

Challenge 2 be to 용법은 무엇인가?

be동사의 보어로 형용사를 쓰듯이, to부정사 역시 형용사처럼 주어를 서술하는 역할을 한다. 이를 'be to 용법'이라고 하고 [   ](be going to), [   ](should, must), [   ](can), [   ](want to, intend to), [   ](be doomed to)이 있다.

Challenge 3 to부정사의 부사적 용법을 알고 있는가?

to부정사가 동사, 형용사 등을 수식하여 다양한 의미를 나타낸다.

(1) [   ] 수식 : 형용사 바로 뒤에 위치하여 '~하기에'의 뜻을 나타낸다.
The river is *dangerous* **to swim** in. 그 강은 수영하기에 위험하다.

(2) [   ] : ~하기 위하여, ~하러 (= in order to, so as to)
We *went* to the station **to see** her off. 우리는 그녀를 배웅하기 위하여 그 역에 갔다.

(3) 감정의 [   ] : ~해서, ~하게 되어(서) (주로 감정을 나타내는 형용사 happy, surprised 등과 쓰임)
We were *surprised* **to see** Susan at the party. 우리는 파티에서 Susan을 보고서 놀랐다.

(4) 판단의 [   ] : ~하다니, ~하는 것을 보니 (주로 must be, cannot be, 감탄문과 쓰임)
She *must be* angry **to say** such a word to me. 그녀가 내게 그런 말을 하는 것을 보니 화난 것이 틀림없다.

(5) [   ] : ~한다면 (주로 조동사 will, would, can 등과 쓰임)
I *can* do my homework **to fix** the laptop. 노트북을 고친다면 나는 숙제를 할 수 있다.

(6) [   ] : 그 결과 ~하다 (주로 live, awake, grow, only, never과 함께 쓰임)
Nancy *grew up* **to be** a supermodel. Nancy는 자라서 슈퍼모델이 되었다.

Preview

This book is difficult **for me** *to read.*
이 책은 내가 읽기에 어렵다.

It was careless **of her** *to go* out alone.
그녀가 밖에 혼자 나간 것은 부주의했다.

1 모든 동작에는 그 행위를 하는 주인인 주어가 반드시 있어야 한다. 부정사의 주어가 문장의 주어나 목적어와 같거나 일반인일 때 의미상 주어를 따로 쓸 필요가 없다.

She decided **to take** a vacation. 그녀는 휴가를 내기로 결정했다.
➡ take 동작의 주어(의미상 주어)는 문장 전체 주어인 She

Nicole told **me** not **to go** to a movie. Nicole은 나에게 영화 보러 가지 말라고 했다.
➡ go 동작의 주어(의미상 주어)는 목적어 me

To learn Chinese is not easy. 중국어를 배우는 것은 쉽지 않다.
➡ 일반인 we, you, people 등의 의미상 주어는 생략

2 부정사의 동작에 대한 주체를 따로 표시해 주어야 하는 경우에는 부정사 앞에 'for + 명사(대명사는 목적격)'를 반드시 쓴다. 사람을 칭찬하거나 비난하는 형용사와 함께 쓸 경우 for 대신에 of를 써서 'of + 명사(대명사는 목적격)'를 쓴다. 의미상 주어가 없으면 '누가' 부정사의 동작을 했는지 알 수가 없다.

It is dangerous **for children** *to use* the knife. 아이들이 그 칼을 사용하는 것은 위험하다.
The sofa is too heavy **for her** *to move.* 그녀가 소파를 옮기기에는 너무 무겁다.
It was stupid **of her** *to give up* her new job. 그녀가 새 직업을 포기한 것은 어리석었다.

기본기 탄탄 다지기

1 우리말에 맞도록 빈칸에 알맞은 말을 쓰시오.

(1) 나는 그가 오늘 저녁에 여기에 도착할 것을 기대합니다.
➡ I expect _____ here this evening. (he / arrive)

(2) 당신이 그의 제안을 거절한 것은 현명했다.
➡ It was wise _____ his offer. (you / refuse)

(3) 나는 그녀에게 데이트 신청하기로 결심했다.
➡ I determined _____ her out on a date. (ask)

(4) 나는 그녀가 말하는 것을 이해하기가 어려웠다.
➡ It was difficult _____ what she was saying.
(I / understand)

(5) 그런 짓을 하다니 그녀는 아주 잔인하다.
➡ It is very cruel _____ such a thing. (she / do)

> **wise** a. 현명한
> **determine** v. 결심하다
> **ask ... out on a date** 데이트를 신청하다
> **cruel** a. 잔인한, 모진
>
> ▶사람을 칭찬하거나 비난하는 형용사 kind, nice, silly, (im)polite, stupid, careful, careless, generous, mean 등은 의미상 주어 for 대신에 of를 써야 한다.

Unit 8 • to부정사의 시제

I am sorry **to have kept** you waiting so long yesterday.
= **I am** sorry that I **kept** you waiting so long yesterday.
어제 그렇게 오래 기다리게 해서 죄송합니다.

1 to부정사도 현재 또는 과거와 같은 시제를 나타낼 수 있는데, to부정사의 동작이 문장 전체의 시제와 동일한 때에 일어나거나 미래를 나타낼 때는 'to + 동사원형'을 쓴다.

Tom *is said* **to be** a brilliant boy. Tom이 똑똑한 소년이라고들 한다.
= They **say** that Tom **is** a brilliant boy.

She *seemed* **to be** happy. 그녀는 행복한 것처럼 보였다.
= She **seemed** that she **was** happy.

2 to부정사의 동작이 말하는 시점보다 더 이전에 있었던 일은 'to have + V-ed'로 쓴다. 흔히 완료부정사라고 부른다.

I *am* sorry **to have been** late for the last meeting. 지난번 회의에 늦었던 것을 죄송하게 생각합니다.
= I **am** sorry that I **was** late for the last meeting.
(회의에 늦은 것은 말하는 시점보다 먼저 일어난 일)

He *seemed* **to have studied** English in his school days. 그는 학창시절에 영어를 공부한 것처럼 보였다.
= It **seemed** that he **had studied** English in his school days.
(영어를 공부한 것은 말하는 시점보다 더 먼저 일어난 일)

기본기 탄탄 다지기

1 다음 괄호 안의 표현 중 알맞은 것을 고르시오.

(1) Beth seems (to be / to have been) ill for a week.

(2) It was late, so we decided (to take / to have taken) a taxi home.

(3) She appears (to be / to have been) rich before.

(4) I am sorry (to be / to have been) absent yesterday.

(5) It was a nice day, so we decided (to have gone / to go) for a walk.

(6) They think Jina (to have passed / to pass) the exam, but she didn't.

absent a. 결석한
go for a walk 산책하다

Unit 9 ● 독립부정사

To tell the truth, I have never been to Korea.
솔직히 말하면, 나는 한국에 가본 적이 없다.

To make matters worse, it began to rain.
설상가상으로 비까지 내리기 시작했다.

1 특정한 뜻을 가지고 문장 전체를 꾸며 주는 to부정사를 독립부정사라고 한다. to부정사가 하나의 숙어처럼 굳어진 표현이라고 생각하면 된다. 중요 표현들은 암기해 두는 것이 좋다.

To be frank with you, she is not pretty. 솔직히 말하면, 그녀는 예쁘지 않다.

Needless to say, you must keep the secret. 말할 필요도 없이, 당신은 비밀을 지켜야 한다.

Strange to say, I have had the same dream for a week. 말하기에는 이상하지만, 나는 일주일 동안 똑같은 꿈을 꾸었다.

to be frank with you	솔직히 말하면	so to speak	말하자면, 소위
to begin with	우선, 먼저, 무엇보다도	strange to say	말하기에 이상하지만
not to mention	~은 말할 필요도 없이	needless to say	말할 필요 없지만
to make a long story short	간단히 말하면	to make matters worse	설상가상으로
to tell the truth	사실대로 말하자면	to sum up	요약해서 말하면

기본기 탄탄 다지기

1 우리말에 맞게 위의 표를 이용하여 빈칸을 완성하시오.

(1) 사실대로 말하자면, Kathy가 정말 사랑하는 사람은 내가 아니고 Peter이다.

➡ _____ , it is Peter not me that Kathy really loves.

(2) 설상가상으로, 날이 점점 어두워지고 있었다.

➡ _____ , it was getting dark and dark.

(3) 그는 말하자면 걸어 다니는 사전이다.

➡ He is, _____ , a walking dictionary.

(4) 나는 김치는 말할 것도 없고 불고기와 비빔밥을 좋아한다.

➡ I like Bulgogi and Bibimbap _____ Kimchi.

서술형 기초 다지기 ❸

1 빈칸에 for와 of 중 알맞은 것을 넣으시오.

(1) It was silly _____ you to forget the car key.

(2) Baker stepped aside _____ Kelly to pass by.

(3) It can be difficult _____ young people to buy their own car.

(4) It was rude _____ your friend not to shake hands.

(5) We wanted _____ William to be the captain of our team.

2 다음에서 알맞은 말을 골라 빈칸에 독립부정사 형태로 쓰시오.

make	say	mention	tell	be

(1) _____ _____ the truth, I have never been to Europe.

(2) Strange _____ _____, I saw a ghost yesterday.

(3) _____ _____ frank with you, I don't love her.

(4) She can speak Japanese, _____ _____ _____ Chinese.

(5) _____ _____ matters worse, she got sick while I was gone.

3 다음 문장을 부정사를 이용하여 다시 쓰시오.

It seems that he forgot what to do.
➡ He seems to have forgotten what to do. _____

(1) It appears that she bought a new smartphone yesterday.

   ➡ _____

(2) I am sorry that I bothered you so far.

   ➡ _____

(3) It seems that the reporter enjoys writing on her blog.

   ➡ _____

4 주어진 문장을 'for + 목적격' 또는 'of + 목적격'을 이용하여 문장을 완성하시오.

> Students should learn standard English.
> ➡ It's important _____ for students to learn standard English _____ .

(1) I can't stay up until late at night.

   ➡ It's impossible _____ .

(2) She made me kill the flies.

   ➡ It was cruel _____ .

(3) Jessica gave up her new job although it is hard to get another one.

   ➡ It was foolish _____ .

(4) They made the same mistake.

   ➡ It is stupid _____ .

(5) Children usually can't sit still for a long time.

   ➡ It's difficult _____ .

5 두 문장이 같은 뜻이 되도록 빈칸에 알맞은 말을 쓰시오.

(1) My girlfriend appeared to have stopped smoking.

   = It _____ that _____ .

(2) He seems to have studied hard.

   = It _____ that _____ .

(3) They seem to have worked together in the past.

   = It _____ that _____ .

(4) The accident seems to have happened when I was young.

   = It _____ that _____ .

(5) Sarah seemed to have gained weight.

   = It _____ that _____ .

Oral Test

Challenge 1 to부정사의 의미상 주어는 어떨 때 쓰는가?

(1) 부정사를 행하는 동작이 문장의 [＿＿＿＿＿＿]나 [＿＿＿＿＿＿]와 같거나 일반인일 때는 따로 의미상 주어를 표시하지 않는다.

We decided not **to go** out because of the weather. 우리는 날씨 때문에 밖에 나가지 않기로 했다.
Do you want *me* **to come** with you? 내가 당신과 함께 가길 원하나요?

(2) 의미상 주어를 따로 써주어야 할 경우 부정사 바로 앞에 [＿＿＿＿＿＿]를 쓴다. 사람을 칭찬하거나 비난하는 형용사 (clever, smart, wise, cruel, stupid 등)가 to부정사의 보어로 쓰인 경우 부정사 바로 앞에 [＿＿＿＿＿＿]를 의미상 주어로 쓴다.

It isn't easy **for me** to remember phone numbers. 내가 전화번호를 기억하는 것은 쉽지 않다.
It was truly honest **of you** to admit your fault. 너의 잘못을 인정하는 것은 참으로 정직했다.

Challenge 2 부정사도 시제를 나타낼 수 있다는 것을 아는가?

(1) to부정사의 시제가 문장의 시제와 동일한 때(본동사가 현재면 부정사도 현재, 과거면 부정사도 과거)에 일어나거나 미래를 나타낼 때는 [＿＿＿＿＿＿]으로 쓴다.

Your country expects you **to volunteer** to help the poor. (to volunteer의 시제는 expects보다 나중인 미래)
여러분의 국가는 여러분이 나서서 가난한 사람들을 도와주기를 기대한다.

(2) to부정사의 동작이 말하는 시점보다 더 이전에 행해졌던 일은 [＿＿＿＿＿＿]로 나타낸다.

Jane seems **to have traveled** around Europe. (보이는 것은 현재이나 여행한 것이 그 보다 더 이전인 과거)
Jane은 유럽을 여행한 것처럼 보인다.

Challenge 3 중요 독립부정사의 표현들은 암기하고 있는가?

숙어처럼 하나의 뜻으로 굳어진 표현으로 문장 전체를 수식하는 to부정사구를 독립부정사라고 부른다.

	솔직히 말하면		말하자면, 소위
	우선, 먼저, 무엇보다도		말하기에 이상하지만
	~은 말할 필요도 없이		말할 필요 없지만
	간단히 말하면		설상가상으로
	사실대로 말하자면		요약해서 말하면

Unit 10 ● too ~ to / enough to

He is **too** young **to travel** alone.
그는 혼자 여행하기에는 너무 어리다.

She is strong **enough to carry** the box.
그녀는 그 상자를 옮길 정도로 힘이 세다.

① 'too + 형용사/부사 + to부정사'는 '~하기에는 너무 ~하다'라는 의미로 too를 형용사나 부사 앞에 쓴다. 'so + 형용사/부사 + that + 주어 + can't/couldn't'로 바꿔 쓸 수 있다.

Sandra is **too** old **to drive**. Sandra는 운전하기에는 너무 나이가 들었다.
= Sandra is **so** old **that** she **can't** drive.

This coffee was **too** hot for me **to drink**. 이 커피는 내가 마시기에는 너무 뜨거웠다.
= This coffee was **so** hot **that** I **couldn't** drink it.

② 'enough to부정사'는 '~할 정도로'의 뜻으로 형용사/부사를 enough 앞에 써서 '형용사/부사 + enough to부정사'로 쓴다. 'so + 형용사/부사 + that + 주어 + can/could'로 바꿔 쓸 수 있다.

She is smart **enough to solve** this problem. 그녀는 이 문제를 풀 정도로 똑똑하다.
= She is **so** smart **that** she **can** solve this problem.

Bob studied hard **enough to pass** the entrance exam. Bob은 입학시험을 통과할 정도로 열심히 공부했다.
= Bob studied **so** hard **that** he **could** pass the entrance exam.

기본기 탄탄 다지기

1 우리말에 맞도록 괄호 안의 말을 이용하여 빈칸에 알맞은 말을 쓰시오.

(1) 그녀는 도둑을 쫓아갈 정도로 용감하다. (brave)

  ➡ She is _____ _____ _____ run after the thief.

(2) Jennifer는 학교에 가기에는 너무 어리다. (go, young)

  ➡ Jennifer is _____ _____ _____ _____ to school.

2 주어진 문장과 뜻이 같도록 too ~ to나 enough ~ to를 이용하여 문장을 완성하시오.

(1) This smartphone is so expensive that I can't buy it.

  ➡ This smartphone is _____ .

(2) Bill Gates is so rich that he can buy whatever he wants.

  ➡ Bill Gates is rich _____ .

run after ~를 뒤쫓다

▶'enough to부정사'를 '충분히'로 해석하는 경우가 많은데 '~할 정도로'의 의미가 더 정확하다. '충분한'이란 뜻으로 쓰일 때는 enough가 형용사로 명사 바로 앞에 위치한다.
I had **enough time** to go to the party. 나는 파티에 갈 충분한 시간이 있었다.
She has **enough money** to travel around the world. 그녀는 전 세계를 여행할 충분한 돈이 있다.

Unit 11 • 대부정사

Jacob wanted **to see the scary movie**, but his mother didn't allow him **to**.

Jacob은 그 공포영화를 보길 원했지만 그의 엄마는 허락하지 않았다.

(**to** = to see the scary movie)

① 같은 내용의 부정사를 피하기 위하여 to부정사의 to만 쓰는 것을 대부정사라고 한다. to만으로 동일한 내용의 to부정사 전체를 대신한다는 의미이다. to 뒤에 나올 동사를 서로 알고 있을 경우에 쓴다.

You may call me if you'd like **to**. (**to** = to call me)
원한다면 내게 전화해도 됩니다.

You can come and see me if you want **to**. (**to** = to come and see me)
당신이 원한다면 오셔서 절 만나실 수 있습니다.

I've never eaten Kimchi, but I'd like **to**. (**to** = to eat Kimchi)
나는 김치를 먹어보진 못했지만 그러고 싶다.

She wanted to go to the concert, but Steve told her not **to**. (**to** = to go to the concert)
그녀는 콘서트에 가고 싶었지만 Steve가 그녀에게 가지 말라고 했다.

기본기 탄탄 다지기

1 주어진 문장을 읽고 생략할 수 있는 부분에 밑줄을 그으시오.

may ~해도 좋다

(1) Q: Would you like to have some coffee?

　　A: Yes, I'd like to have some coffee.

(2) I asked her to play the violin, but she didn't want to play the violin.

(3) Q: Do you want to take a break?

　　A: If you really want me to take a break.

(4) Q: Can I go out to meet Sally?

　　A: If you want to meet Sally.

(5) Q: Are you going to buy a new car?

　　A: I'm planning to buy a new car.

(6) I didn't want to take a taxi, but I had to take a taxi as I was late.

(7) Q: Can I stay here for a night, if you don't mind?

　　A: No problem. You may stay, if you want to stay.

Unit 12 ● 목적을 나타내는 so that / 가목적어 it

Preview

Jessica studies English (**in order**) **to** get a better job.
= Jessica studies English **so that** she **can** get a better job.
Jessica는 더 좋은 직장을 얻기 위해 영어를 공부한다.
I think **it** dangerous **to swim** in this river. 나는 이 강에서 수영하는 것이 위험하다고 생각한다.

1 '~하기 위하여'의 뜻인 목적을 나타내는 to부정사는 긍정문일 경우 'so that + 주어 + can/could'로 바꾸어 쓸 수 있다. 부정사 바로 앞에 not이 있는 부정문은 'so that + 주어 + won't/wouldn't'로 바꿔 쓸 수 있다.

I'm saving my money (**in order**) **to** buy a car. 나는 차를 사기 위해 돈을 모으고 있다.
= I'm saving my money **so that** I **can** buy a car.

We hurried (**in order**) **not to** be late for school. 우리는 지각하지 않기 위해 서둘렀다.
= We hurried **so that** we **wouldn't** be late for school.

2 5형식 문장에서 to부정사가 목적어 자리에 와서 길어지는 경우 그 자리에 가목적어 it을 쓰고 to부정사구 전체를 뒤로 보낼 수 있다. 주로 5형식 동사 think, find, make, believe 등이 자주 쓰인다.

We think (**to do the work in a day**) (**impossible**).
                 O   O.C.

= We think **it** impossible **to do the work in a day**. 우리는 그 일을 하루 만에 끝내는 것은 불가능하고 생각한다.
          가목적어   진목적어

기본기 탄탄 다지기

1 괄호 안에서 알맞은 말을 고르시오.

(1) Tom sat down in an armchair so that he (can / won't) rest.

(2) I went to the library so that I (could / can) borrow some books.

(3) They hurried so that they (wouldn't / could) miss the bus.

2 두 문장의 뜻이 같도록 빈칸에 알맞은 말을 쓰시오.

(1) This toothbrush will make to brush your teeth easier.
= This toothbrush will make _____ easier _____ your teeth.

(2) Western people believe to break a mirror unlucky.
= Western people believe _____ unlucky _____ a mirror.

(3) Eun-seon thinks to learn Japanese easy.
= Eun-seon thinks _____ easy _____ Japanese.

> ▶목적과 의도를 나타내는 to부정사 대신에 'for + 명사 / 동명사'로 나타낼 수도 있다.
> Let's go to the restaurant to have lunch.
> = Let's go to the restaurant for lunch.
> This knife is only to cut bread.
> = This knife is only for cutting bread.

> **toothbrush** n. 칫솔
> **western** a. 서양의
> **mirror** n. 거울
> **unlucky** a. 불길(운)한

1 주어진 문장을 so ~ that을 이용한 문장으로 다시 쓰시오.

(1) The pizza was too hot for us to eat.

➡ _____

(2) Susan is old enough to drive in Korea.

➡ _____

(3) Kevin is too stupid to understand the situation.

➡ _____

(4) The water was too cold for me to swim in.

➡ _____

(5) The girl is brave enough to speak in front of other people.

➡ _____

(6) The T-shirt is too small for you to put on.

➡ _____

2 다음 문장을 too ~ to 또는 enough to를 이용한 문장으로 바꾸어 쓰시오.

(1) The bicycle is so expensive that I can't buy it.

➡ _____

(2) She is so tall that she can reach the top branch of the tree.

➡ _____

(3) Jane was so sick that she couldn't attend the meeting.

➡ _____

(4) Sunny is so cool that she can forgive anybody.

➡ _____

(5) She was so foolish that she could trust him.

➡ _____

(6) Her grades were so high that she could get the license.

➡ _____

3 다음 밑줄 친 대부정사 to 뒤에 생략된 부분을 찾아 빈칸에 쓰시오.

(1) A: Did you see the pyramids?

B: No, I wanted <u>to</u>, but I didn't have enough time. ➡ to _____

(2) A: Who took my dictionary?

B: Jacob, but I told him not <u>to</u>. ➡ to _____

(3) A: Did you watch the movie last night?

B: Yes. My father told me not <u>to</u>, though. ➡ to _____

(4) A: Is she going to go out for dinner?

B: No, she is not going <u>to</u>. ➡ to _____

(5) A: Why did you punch your brother on the forehead?

B: It was not my intention. I didn't mean <u>to</u>. ➡ to _____

4 주어진 문장을 보기와 같이 가목적어, 진목적어를 이용한 문장으로 다시 쓰시오.

> Most Koreans think to eat Kimchi with every meal necessary.
> ➡ Most Koreans think it necessary to eat Kimchi with every meal.

(1) I make to have breakfast at seven a rule.

➡ _____

(2) They believed to answer the questions easy.

➡ _____

(3) Do you think to grow those plants in this land difficult?

➡ _____

(4) The machinery will make to increase productivity possible.

➡ _____

(5) The alphabet makes for us to read and write thousands of words with only twenty-six different letters possible.

➡ _____

_____

Oral Test

Challenge 1 too ~to 와 enough to부정사의 쓰임을 알고 있는가?

(1) 'too + ⬜⬜⬜ + to부정사'는 '~하기에는 너무 ~하다'의 뜻으로 '문제나 어려움이 있어 어떤 일을 할 수 없다'라는 부정의 의미를 담고 있다. 'too ~ to부정사'는 '⬜⬜⬜ + 형용사/부사 + ⬜⬜⬜ + 주어 + ⬜⬜⬜/⬜⬜⬜'로 바꿔 쓸 수 있다.

Lisa is **too** tough **to have** a boyfriend. Lisa는 남자친구를 사귀기에는 너무 터프하다.
= Lisa is **so** tough **that** she **can't** have a boyfriend.

(2) '⬜⬜⬜ to부정사'는 '~할 정도로 ~하다'의 뜻으로, 형용사와 부사를 enough 바로 ⬜⬜⬜에 위치시킨다. '⬜⬜⬜ + 형용사/부사 + ⬜⬜⬜ + 주어 + ⬜⬜⬜/⬜⬜⬜'로 바꿔 쓸 수 있다.

We got to the concert early **enough to get** good seats. 우리는 좋은 자리를 차지할 수 있을 만큼 일찍 콘서트에 도착했다.
= We got to the concert **so** early **that** we **could** get good seats.

Challenge 2 대부정사는 언제 사용하는가?

앞에 나온 말의 반복을 피하기 위해서 to부정사의 ⬜⬜⬜만 쓰는 것을 대부정사라고 한다.

She wanted to go to the park, but her mother told her not **to**. (**to** = to go to the park)
그녀는 공원에 가길 원했지만, 그녀의 엄마는 가지 말라고 했다.

Challenge 3 가목적어 it은 왜 쓰는가?

5형식 문장에서 to부정사가 ⬜⬜⬜ 자리에 올 경우 길어지기 때문에 그 자리에 ⬜⬜⬜을 쓰고 to부정사구를 모두 뒤로 보낸다. 이를 가목적어, 진목적어라고 한다.

I found **to stay up all night** very hard. 나는 밤을 꼴딱 새우는 것이 어렵다는 것을 알았다.
= I found **it** very hard **to stay up all night**.
　　　　　가목적어　　　　　　　　진목적어

We believe **to keep up with the latest information** important. 우리는 최신 정보에 뒤지지 않는 것이 중요하다고 믿는다.
= We believe **it** important **to keep up with the latest information**.
　　　　　　가목적어　　　　　　　　　　진목적어

1 다음 빈칸에 알맞은 것은?

> It is difficult _____ me to learn a
> second language.

① of   ② with   ③ in   ④ for   ⑤ by

2 다음 두 문장을 바르게 고친 것은?

> I saw Kevin yesterday.
> He was eating vegetables.

① I saw Kevin ate vegetables yesterday.
② I saw Kevin to eat vegetables yesterday.
③ I saw Kevin eaten vegetables yesterday.
④ I saw Kevin eats vegetables yesterday.
⑤ I saw Kevin eating vegetables yesterday.

3 다음 대화에서 어법상 어색한 문장은?

> A: Do you like going to a concert?
> B: Oh, I love it.
> A: ① Then, would you like to go to a rock
>   concert this weekend?
> B: ② I'd like to, but my dad never lets me
>   staying out late.
> A: ③ I'm sorry to hear that. ④ I want you
>   to come with me.
> B: ⑤ So do I.

4 다음 빈칸에 알맞은 말을 쓰시오.

> Please teach me how I should play tennis.
> = Please teach me _____ _____
> _____ _____.

5 다음 두 문장의 의미가 같도록 알맞게 바꿔 쓴 것은?

> Lisa was relieved as she had heard the
> news.
> = _____

① Lisa was relieved to have heard the
   news.
② Lisa was relieved to heard the news.
③ Lisa was relieved to hear the news.
④ Lisa is relieved to have heard the news.
⑤ Lisa is relieved to hear the news.

6 보기의 밑줄 친 부분과 쓰임이 같은 것을 고르시오.

> I have no money to lend you.

① I found it difficult to read this book.
② I am glad to see you.
③ He wants to travel to Europe.
④ I went to a department store to buy a gift.
⑤ She has no one to help her.

7 다음 중 빈칸에 들어갈 말이 다른 하나는?

① It's difficult _____ you to understand
   the book.
② The box is too heavy _____ her to
   carry.
③ It is stupid _____ you to believe every
   word she said.
④ It is important _____ me to make a
   lot of money.
⑤ It is impossible _____ them to start
   the car when it is out of gasoline.

8 다음 밑줄 친 부분과 바꿔 쓸 수 있는 말은?

> I <u>was to</u> go to school with my friend at 7 o'clock. But she didn't keep her promise.

① liked to   ② was able to

③ should   ④ was supposed to

⑤ was sure to

9 다음 중 어법상 틀린 문장은?

① We need to buy something cold to drink.

② They're looking for an apartment to live in.

③ I'm going to Australia so that I can take an English language course.

④ I was really shocked, so I didn't know what to say.

⑤ Sally doesn't smoke anymore. Eric got her give up that habit last year.

10 다음 중 어법상 올바른 문장은?

① We watched the full moon to rise yesterday.

② The police officers forced the crowd leave the building immediately.

③ They must be crazy to let him to drive their car.

④ Nancy studied enough hard to enter the university.

⑤ They seem to have worked together in the past.

11 다음 빈칸에 알맞지 <u>않은</u> 말은?

> A: Do you think the girl is pretty?
> B: Yeah, she is very beautiful but, _____, she isn't kind.

① needless to say   ② to be frank with you

③ to be sure   ④ so to speak

⑤ to be honest

12 다음 중 밑줄 친 부정사의 쓰임이 <u>다른</u> 하나를 고르시오.

① My dream is <u>to be</u> a famous movie star.

② Her hobby is <u>to watch</u> horror movies.

③ The function of the heart is <u>to pump</u> blood through the body.

④ His plan for the next vacation is <u>to go</u> to Egypt.

⑤ The conference is <u>to be</u> held in Seoul next Monday.

서술형 대비 문제

1 다음 문장의 밑줄 친 부분을 어법에 맞게 고쳐 쓰시오.

> A magical sunrise made me <u>to understand</u> why Korea is often called 'the Land of the Morning Calm.'

_____

2 다음 주어진 그림의 상황에 맞게 괄호 안의 단어들을 바르게 배열하시오.

(the problems, me, helped, solve, my mother, to)

➡ _____

3 괄호 안의 단어를 이용하여 그림과 일치하는 문장을 쓰시오.

(break into)

➡ We saw _____ .

4 두 문장의 뜻이 같도록 빈칸에 알맞은 말을 쓰시오.

(1) Kelly hoped that she had had a daughter.

= Kelly hoped _____ _____ _____ a daughter.

(2) The wind was strong enough, so it can break windows.

= The wind was strong _____ _____ _____ windows.

사랑은 포스트잇을 타고~

Will you marry me?

In 1980, 3M ⓐ <u>began to sell</u> the first Post-it notes all over the United States. Today, Post-it notes are one of the best selling office supply ⓑ <u>products in the world</u>. People use them for many different purposes. One man wrote, "Will you marry me?" on a Post-it note and put it on his girlfriend's computer monitor. She wrote "Yes!" and put it on his monitor again. One woman put a note on the back of her nephew's car before he left on a long journey. After 4,500 kilometers, he found ⓒ <u>it on his car</u>. He could still read the note! One university student was traveling by bus. She was waiting at a bus stop and felt very ⓓ <u>exhausted</u>. She was afraid to fall asleep and miss her bus, so she decided to put <u>Post-it notes</u> all over herself. The notes asked people ⓔ <u>wake</u> her up in time for her bus. She did fall asleep, but no one saw the notes and she missed her bus.

1　윗글은 무엇에 관한 글인가?

　① 포스트잇의 특징　　　　　② 포스트잇의 성공배경　　　　　③ 포스트잇을 만들게 된 배경

　④ 포스트잇의 다양한 쓰임　　⑤ 포스트잇의 다양한 종류

2　밑줄 친 Post-it notes에 적어 놓았을 내용을 추측하여 빈칸을 영어로 쓰시오.

　➡ Please _____ _____ _____ when the bus comes.

3　윗글의 밑줄 친 ⓐ~ⓔ 중 어법상 어색한 것은?

　① ⓐ　　　　　② ⓑ　　　　　③ ⓒ　　　　　④ ⓓ　　　　　⑤ ⓔ

A 보기와 같이 부정사를 이용하여 묻고 답하는 형식으로 말하기 연습을 하세요. 연습이 한 번 끝난 후 서로 역할을 바꿔 다시 말하기 연습을 하세요.

a figure skater
/ Yu-na Kim

 What do you want to be in the future?

 I'd like to be a figure skater like Yuna Kim.

1

a soccer player
/ Ji-sung Park

2

a rhythmic gymnast
/ Yeon-jae Son

 B 보기와 같이 enough to를 이용하여 묻고 답하는 형식으로 말하기 연습을 하세요. 연습이 한 번 끝난 후 서로 역할을 바꿔 다시 말하기 연습을 하세요.

you / reach the top
shelf / ?

No ➡ tall

 Can you reach the top shelf?

 No, I can't. I'm not tall enough to reach the top shelf.

1

Jane / carry the heavy
suitcase / ?

No ➡ strong

2

you / make people
laugh / ?

No ➡ funny

실전 서술형 평가 문제

출제의도 | 동작의 목적을 나타내는 문장 서술하기
평가내용 | to부정사의 목적을 나타내는 부사적 용법

서술형 유형	8점
난이도	중상

 보기와 같이 두 사람의 대화 상황을 목적을 나타내는 부정사를 이용하여 아래와 같이 서술하시오.

보기 Q: Why did Tiffany go to the fast-food restaurant?

A: Because she likes eating hamburgers.

➡ Tiffany(She) went to the fast-food restaurant to eat hamburgers.

1

Q: Why does Jessica go to the beach every weekend?
A: Because she likes swimming.

➡ _____

2

Q: Why did they go to Egypt?
A: They wanted to see the ancient pyramids.

➡ _____

3

Q: Why did Steve buy a new suit?
A: He wanted to wear it at the office party.

➡ _____

4

Q: Why do they recycle old plastic bottles?
A: They want to protect the environment.

➡ _____

평가영역	채점기준	배점
유창성(Fluency) & 정확성(Accuracy)	4개의 문장을 모두 올바른 표현과 함께 정확하게 완성한 경우 (문법, 철자가 모두 정확한 경우)	4×2 = 8점
	부정사를 만들지 못하였거나 문법, 철자가 1개씩 틀린 경우	문항당 1점씩 감점
	내용과 전혀 일치하지 않거나 답을 기재하지 못한 경우	0점

출제의도 | 지각동사를 이용하여 사진 묘사하기

평가내용 | 지각동사 + 목적어 + 동사원형/현재분사

서술형 유형	9점
난이도	중상

B 아래 사진은 강민이와 서윤이가 길을 가다가 보거나 들은 광경이다. 사진의 내용과 일치하는 문장을 지각동사를 이용하여 완전한 문장으로 완성하시오.

보기 "Look! Rebecca is playing tennis with her friend."

➡ We saw Rebecca playing tennis with her friend.

(see)

1

(see)

"Look! Sandra is waiting for a bus at the bus stop."

➡ _____

2

(hear)

"Listen! They are singing and dancing to their latest hit songs."

➡ _____

3

(feel)

"Be careful! The ground is shaking like an earthquake."

➡ _____

평가영역	채점기준	배점
유창성(Fluency) & 정확성(Accuracy)	3개의 문장을 모두 올바른 표현과 함께 정확하게 완성한 경우 (문법, 철자가 모두 정확한 경우)	3×3 = 9점
	지각동사를 사용하지 못하였거나 문법, 철자가 1개씩 틀린 경우	문항당 1점씩 감점
	내용과 전혀 일치하지 않거나 답을 기재하지 못한 경우	0점

실전 서술형 평가 문제

출제의도 | 의미상 주어를 활용하여 자신의 생각 표현하기

평가내용 | 의미상 주어 + to부정사

서술형 유형	8점
난이도	중

 C 보기와 같이 아래 주어진 표현을 이용하여 여러분에게 중요한 것과 중요하지 않은 일을 의미상 주어를 넣어 완전한 문장으로 쓰시오.

> **보기** learn English
>
> ➡ It's (not) important for me to learn English. _____

1	speak English well	**2**	read and write English well
3	get a college degree	**4**	have a smartphone
5	find an interesting job	**6**	own a personal computer
7	make a lot of money	**8**	study Korean history

1 _____

2 _____

3 _____

4 _____

5 _____

6 _____

7 _____

8 _____

평가영역	채점기준	배점
유창성(Fluency) & 정확성(Accuracy)	8개의 문장을 모두 올바른 표현과 함께 정확하게 완성한 경우 (문법, 철자가 모두 정확한 경우)	8×1 = 8점
	의미상 주어를 사용하지 못하였거나 문법, 철자가 1개씩 틀린 경우	문항당 1점씩 감점
	내용과 전혀 일치하지 않거나 답을 기재하지 못한 경우	0점

Chapter 2
동명사

Unit 1 • 주어와 보어로 쓰이는 동명사

Preview

Speaking in English is a must in our school.
영어로 말하는 것은 우리학교에서 필수이다.
My hobby is **jogging** in the morning.
내 취미는 아침에 조깅하는 것이다.

1 주어 자리에 명사나 대명사를 쓰지만 주어의 행위나 동작이 필요한 경우에는 동명사를 쓴다. 동명사는 문장에서 명사 역할만을 한다.

English is very important. 영어는 매우 중요하다. ➡ 명사 English는 동작을 표현하지 못함.
Learning English is very important. 영어를 배우는 것은 매우 중요하다. ➡ 동명사 주어가 행위를 표현하고 있음.
Dancing salsa was interesting. 살사 춤을 추는 것은 재미있었다. ➡ 동명사 주어가 행위를 표현하고 있음.

2 be동사 뒤, 보어 자리에는 명사나 형용사를 쓰지만, 동작의 내용을 보어로 나타낼 때에는 동명사를 쓴다.

My favorite activity is **doing** yoga. 내가 가장 좋아하는 활동은 요가를 하는 것이다.
One of her hobbies is **catching** and **collecting** butterflies. 그녀의 취미 중 하나는 나비를 잡고 수집하는 것이다.

기본기 탄탄 다지기

1 밑줄 친 부분이 문장에서 하는 역할을 고르시오.

(1) Riding a bike without a helmet is dangerous. _____

(2) Having good friends is very important. _____

(3) My favorite hobby is surfing the Internet. _____

(4) Her dream is becoming a news anchorwoman. _____

(5) Learning about other cultures is really fun. _____

helmet n. 헬멧, 안전모
anchorwoman n. 여성 앵커
main a. 주요한
goal n. 목표, 목적

2 다음 괄호 안의 단어를 이용하여 빈칸에 알맞은 동명사를 쓰시오.

(1) _____ new languages is very important. (learn)

(2) _____ TV for too long is bad for your eyes. (watch)

(3) My dream is _____ around the world. (travel)

(4) _____ too much ice cream is bad for your health. (eat)

(5) My main goal in life is _____ the poor. (help)

▶동명사 주어는 가주어 it을 쓰고 진주어인 동명사를 뒤로 잘 보내지 않는다. 주어로 동명사를 그대로 쓰거나 가주어를 쓸 경우 진주어는 to부정사로 바꿔 쓴다.
Finding a good job takes time.
= It takes time to find a good job.

▶현재 거의 모든 교과서와 학습지에 부정사와 동명사를 서로 바꿔 쓸 수 있다고 하는데 이는 틀린 설명이다. 부정사와 동명사의 속성이 서로 달라 구별해서 써야 하는 경우가 더 많다.

Preview

Seo-yoon *enjoys* **jogging** with her father. 서윤이는 그녀의 아빠와 조깅하는 것을 즐긴다.
My father *gave up* **smoking**. 아빠는 담배를 끊으셨다.

1 목적어로 명사나 대명사를 쓰지만, 동작의 내용을 나타낼 때에는 동명사를 쓴다. 동명사는 과거에 경험했거나 기억하고 있는 일, 또는 그 전에 한 일이나 이미 하고 있는 일이라는 과거의 의미를 내포하고 있기 때문에 다음 동사들은 동명사를 목적어로 쓴다.

enjoy	finish	give up	avoid	quit
deny	put off	mind	stop	dislike
consider	admit	suggest	practice	keep

Would you *mind* **closing** the door? 그 문 좀 닫아 주시겠어요?

I *finished* **cleaning** my room a few hours ago. 난 몇 시간 전에 내 방 청소를 끝냈다.

I think you should *avoid* **eating** high-fat food. 너는 기름진 음식을 먹는 걸 피해야겠어.

Have you ever *considered* **studying** abroad? 외국에서 공부하는 것을 생각해 본 적 있니?

기본기 탄탄 다지기

1 다음 괄호 안의 말을 알맞게 고쳐 빈칸을 완성하시오.

(1) We enjoy _____ tennis in the morning. (play)

(2) She suggested _____ to the restaurant. (go)

(3) My mother avoids _____ at a busy store. (shop)

(4) We'll have to practice _____ the ball into the basket. (throw)

(5) John's given up _____ sweets. (eat)

(6) I'm going to quit _____ to the institute. (go)

(7) Suddenly everybody stopped _____. (talk)

(8) The man admitted _____ the money. (steal)

▶동명사의 부정은 동명사 바로 앞에 not 또는 never를 쓴다.
I regret **not** having seen the movie yesterday.
She insisted on **never** meeting him again.

▶'having + V-ed'는 완료형 동명사로 본동사가 말하는 시점 그 이전에 끝난 일이나 행위를 나타낸다. 하지만 동명사는 부정사와 달리 이미 과거의 의미를 담고 있기 때문에 완료동사 'having + V-ed(과거분사)'를 쓰지 않아도 된다.
They now regret **having said** it.
= They now regret **saying** it.

They finished **having built** the tallest hotel in the world last year.
= They finished **building** the tallest hotel in the world last year.

Unit 3 • 목적어로 부정사만 쓰는 동사

He *decided* **to tell** the secret to his family. 그는 그의 가족에게 그 비밀을 말하기로 결심했다.
She *enjoys* **traveling** by train. 그녀는 기차로 여행하는 것을 즐긴다.

1 목적어로 동명사와 부정사를 쓸 때에는 동사의 특성에 따라서 구별해서 사용해야 한다. 부정사는 기본적으로 미래의 의미를 담고 있어서 앞으로 할 일이나 의무 또는 책무라는 의미를 내포하고 있다. 따라서, 아래 동사들은 부정사를 목적어로 쓸 수밖에 없다.

expect	want	hope	decide	plan	offer
promise	refuse	wish	agree	afford	choose

What types of customers do you *expect* **to attract**? 어떤 유형의 고객들을 끌어들일 것으로 예상하나요?

He was very angry when she *refused* **to marry** him. 그녀가 결혼 신청을 거절했을 때 그는 몹시 화가 났다.

2 아래 동사들은 의미에 큰 차이가 없기 때문에 동명사와 부정사를 구별 없이 모두 쓸 수 있다.

like	hate	love	start	begin	intend	continue	can't stand	prefer

It *began* **raining** (= **to rain**). 비가 내리기 시작했다.

I *dislike* **getting up** (= **to get up**) at six o'clock every morning. 난 매일 아침 6시에 일어나는 것을 싫어한다.

기본기 탄탄 다지기

1 괄호 안의 동사를 동명사와 부정사로 구분하여 쓰고, 둘 다 가능한 경우 모두 쓰시오.

can't stand ~을 참지 못하다
in front of ~앞에

(1) My children hope _____ to McDonald's for lunch. (go)

(2) I don't mind _____ with five roommates. (live)

(3) Could you please stop _____ so much noise? (make)

(4) He can't stand _____ in a long line. (wait)

(5) She likes _____ in front of the television. (sit)

(6) I practice _____ my guitar every night. (play)

(7) My dad promised _____ an iPad on my birthday. (buy)

서술형 기초 다지기 ❶

1 다음 보기와 같이 주어진 문장을 동명사가 주어인 문장으로 바꿔 쓰시오.

> It is hard at first to speak in English.
> ➡ Speaking in English is hard at first.

(1) It is essential to reduce the number of crimes.

➡ _____

(2) It is foolish not to admit the problem.

➡ _____

(3) It is wrong to cheat during a test.

➡ _____

(4) It takes three minutes to cook a soft-boiled egg.

➡ _____

2 다음 보기의 표현을 이용하여 문장을 완성하시오.

> visit the zoo   swim there   take the subway
> play soccer for a while   turn on the air-conditioner

(1) _____ is much faster than driving.

(2) It's very hot. Would you mind _____?

(3) Kelly is going to Haeundae during this vacation. She can enjoy

_____ .

(4) Tom had a car accident. His leg was broken. He should give up

_____ .

(5) It was cold and rainy yesterday, so we postponed _____ .

3 다음 괄호 안의 동사를 알맞은 형태로 바꾸어 쓰시오.

(1) My boss refused _____ me a raise, so I quit. (give)

(2) She denied _____ the purse. (steal)

(3) Would you consider _____ the food to the party? (bring)

(4) Ava was in a difficult situation, so I agreed _____ her. (help)

(5) They have decided _____ next year. (get married)

4 주어진 문장을 읽고 보기와 같이 빈칸을 완성하시오.

> She is sorry that she didn't realize how important education is.
> ➡ She now regrets <u>not realizing how important education is</u>   .

(1) Are you sorry you didn't find your passion earlier?

   ➡ Are you regret _____ ?

(2) It wasn't a good idea to do it again.

   ➡ It's better to avoid _____ .

(3) You shouldn't watch TV if you want to go to college.

   ➡ You should give up _____ .

5 다음 빈칸에 동명사와 부정사를 구별하여 쓰고, 둘 다 가능한 경우는 모두 쓰시오.

(1) Jane would like _____ (be) an artist because she loves _____ (draw). She has decided _____ (go) to an art school next year. A famous art school in New York agreed _____ (give) her a scholarship. Without it, she could not afford _____ (go).

(2) Scott doesn't like _____ (study). He loves _____ (repair) all kinds of things, but he prefers _____ (repair) cars. He wants _____ (be) a mechanic. He hopes _____ (have) his own garage one day.

Oral Test

Challenge 1 동명사가 어떻게 명사처럼 쓰이는가?

(1) 동명사는 '동사'와 '[   ]'가 합쳐진 말로 동사의 성질을 가지면서 명사의 역할을 하기 때문에 붙여진 이름이다. 부정사처럼 '~(는)것, ~하기'의 표현을 늘린 것으로 주어, 보어, 목적어가 동작을 나타낼 때 (대)명사 대신 동명사를 쓴다.

[   ] 역할 : **Doing** yoga is her hobby. 요가를 하는 것이 그녀의 취미이다.

[   ] 역할 : One of her hobbies is **doing** yoga. 그녀의 취미 중 하나는 요가를 하는 것이다.

[   ] 역할 : Cindy enjoys **doing** yoga. Cindy는 요가하는 것을 즐긴다.

(2) 동명사를 부정할 때는 동명사 바로 [   ]에 [   ] 또는 [   ]를 쓴다.

Not eating breakfast is not good for your health. 아침식사를 하지 않는 것은 건강에 좋지 않다.

Challenge 2 목적어로 쓰이는 동명사와 부정사를 구별할 수 있는가?

(1) [   ]는 '예전에 했던 일 또는 이미 하고 있는 일'이라는 과거의 의미가 내포되어 있다. 따라서 다음과 같은 동사의 목적어로 반드시 [   ]를 쓴다.

enjoy	finish	mind	postpone	avoid	consider
deny	practice	quit	stop	give up	put off

I'll *finish* **writing** the report on the accident by six. 나는 6시까지 사건 보고서 쓰는 것을 끝낼 것이다.

She *put off* **doing** the dishes because of the soccer game. 그녀는 축구 경기 때문에 설거지하는 것을 미뤘다.

(2) [   ]는 '현재나 앞으로 할 일'이라는 미래의 의미가 담겨 있다. 따라서 다음과 같은 동사의 목적어로 반드시 [   ]를 쓴다.

agree	decide	expect	hope	learn	afford	plan
wish	want	refuse	promise	offer	choose

I *planned* **to be** a farmer in my hometown, but I couldn't. 나는 고향에서 농부가 되려는 계획이었으나 그럴 수 없었다.

(3) 아래의 동사들은 [   ]와 [   ]를 모두 목적어로 가질 수 있으며 의미에 큰 차이가 없다.

like	hate	love	start	begin	intend	continue	can't stand	prefer

My son *hates* **doing** his homework. = My son *hates* **to do** his homework.
내 아들은 숙제하는 것을 싫어한다.

Preview

My idea *about* **working** is different from yours.
일에 대한 내 생각은 네 생각과 다르다.

I don't *approve of* **allowing** people to carry guns.
나는 사람들에게 총기 휴대를 허가하는 것에 찬성하지 않는다.

1 전치사 뒤에는 목적어로 (대)명사를 쓰지만 동작의 내용을 목적어로 할 때는 동명사를 쓴다. 전치사 뒤에는 반드시 명사만 써야 하므로 to부정사를 쓸 수 없고 명사 역할만 하는 동명사를 쓴다.

동사 + 전치사	apologize for, insist on, succeed in, believe in, think about, care about, worry about, approve of, thank for, plan on, feel like 등

They *apologized for* **being** late. 그들은 늦은 것에 대해 사과를 했다.

She is going to *succeed in* **finding** a new job. 그녀는 새 직업을 구하는 데 성공할 것이다.

형용사 + 전치사	interested in, excited about, fond of, tired of, good at, sad about, pleased about, capable of, afraid of, nervous about, responsible for, ashamed of, satisfied with 등

Are you *interested in* **volunteering** for my project? 내 일에 지원해 볼 마음이 있습니까?

They're *excited about* **going** to Jeju island. 그들은 제주도 가는 것에 신이 나 있다.

기본기 탄탄 다지기

1 다음 우리말과 같도록 괄호 안의 단어를 바르게 고쳐 쓰시오.

(1) 늦어서 죄송합니다. (be)

➡ I'm sorry for _____ late.

(2) 오늘 밤은 무슨 일이 있어도 제가 계산을 하겠습니다. (get)

➡ I insist on _____ the check tonight.

(3) 그녀는 가게에서 일하는 것을 지루해한다. (work)

➡ She is bored with _____ in a store.

(4) 나는 테니스를 잘 하지 못한다. (play)

➡ I'm not very good at _____ tennis.

(5) 그녀는 아무에게도 작별인사를 하지 않고 외국으로 갔다. (say)

➡ She went abroad without _____ good-bye to anybody.

▶ 'feel like + V-ing'는 '~하고 싶다'의 뜻이고, like는 동사가 아닌 전치사이다.
I don't *feel like* **working** anymore.

▶ look forward to (~하기를 고대하다), be used to (~에 익숙하다), object to (~에 반대하다)의 to도 모두 전치사이므로 동작의 내용을 나타낼 때는 동명사를 쓴다.
I'm *looking forward to* **seeing** you.
I'm *used to* **taking** the train.
We *objected to* **changing** our plans.

Unit 5 • go + ~ing

Preview

We **went camping** last week. 우리는 지난주에 캠핑하러 갔었다.
My father likes to **go fishing**. 우리 아빠는 낚시하러 가는 것을 좋아하신다.

1 'go + 동명사'는 '~하러 가다'의 의미로 주로 운동이나 레저 활동에만 쓴다. go 뒤에 to부정사를 쓰면 안 된다.
다음은 'go + 동명사'의 형태로 자주 쓰는 표현들이다.

go dancing	go jogging	go fishing	go shopping
go sightseeing	go skiing	go swimming	go (ice)skating
go hiking	go camping	go (water) skiing	go bowling

In the winter we **go snowboarding**. 겨울에 우리는 스노우보드를 타러 간다.

Kathy **went shopping** with her mother. Kathy는 그녀의 엄마와 함께 쇼핑하러 갔다.

Steve hasn't **gone bowling** in years. Steve는 몇 년간 볼링 치러 가지 않았다.

Chapter 2

기본기 탄탄 다지기

1 다음 괄호 안의 단어를 'go + –ing' 형태로 쓰시오.

(1) In the winter we _____. (ski)

(2) Kathy often _____. (rollerblade)

(3) Last night, my boyfriend and I _____. (bowl)

(4) Did you _____ yesterday? (shop)

(5) They like to _____. (hike)

(6) When I'm free, I like to _____. (jog)

(7) We _____ in the summer. (swim)

▶동사의 목적을 나타내어 '~하기 위
하여'를 뜻할 때는 to부정사를 쓴다.
'go + V–ing'는 운동이나 레저에 국한
되어 있다.

I can't *forget* **meeting** her at the beach. 해변에서 그녀를 만났던 일을 잊을 수 없어.
Please don't *forget* **to meet** Jason. Jason을 만나는 것을 잊지 마.

1 목적어로 동명사와 부정사를 모두 쓰지만 뜻이 달라지는 경우가 있다. 동명사는 과거의 의미, to부정사는 현재나 미래에 있을 일을 나타낸다.

과거(이전)에 했던 경험이나 행동		앞으로 해야 할 일, 의무, 책임
remember + **v-ing** : ~했던 것을 기억하다		remember + **to v** : ~할 것을 기억하다
try + **v-ing** : 한번 ~해보다	**VS.**	try + **to v** : ~하려고 노력하다
forget + **v-ing** : ~했던 것을 잊다		forget + **to v** : ~할 것을 잊어버리다
stop + **v-ing** : ~하는 것을 멈추다		stop + **to v** : ~하기 위하여 멈추다
regret + **v-ing** : ~했던 것을 후회하다		regret + **to v** : ~하게 되어 유감이다

She *forgot* **to make** a phone call to her mother. 그녀는 엄마한테 전화하는 것을 잊었다.

The baby *stopped* **crying** when she saw the puppy. 그 아기는 강아지를 보고 울음을 그쳤다.

기본기 탄탄 다지기

1 다음 괄호 안의 동사를 알맞은 형태로 바꾸어 쓰시오.

(1) She was very tired. She tried _____ her eyes open, but she couldn't. (keep)

(2) I tried _____ the shark, and its skin was rough. (touch)

(3) Please remember _____ the window when you go out. (lock)

(4) I can remember _____ in the hospital when I was four. (be)

2 다음 밑줄 친 부분에 유의하여 주어진 문장을 해석하시오.

(1) He stopped to smoke. ➡ _____

(2) He stopped smoking. ➡ _____

(3) I regret telling a lie. ➡ _____

(4) Do you remember to meet Susan tomorrow morning?

  ➡ _____

▶regret은 목적어로 동명사를 쓰면 과거 행동에 대한 후회를 나타내고, 부정사를 쓰면 나쁜 소식을 전하게 되어 유감이라는 의미가 된다.
We *regret* **to inform** our clients that Flight KE703 to Athens has been cancelled.

▶need + 동명사: ~돼야 할 필요가 있다 (수동의 의미)
need + 부정사: ~할 필요가 있다
My phone *needs* **repairing**.
= My phone *needs* **to be repaired**.
I *need* **to repair** my phone.

▶help + 부정사: ~하는 것을 돕다
can't help + 동명사: ~하지 않을 수 없다
Sports *help* **to mix** all sorts of people.
I *can't help* **laughing** when I see her strange hairstyle. (= I can't stop myself from laughing.)

서술형 기초 다지기 ②

1 보기와 같이 괄호 안의 전치사를 이용하여 문장을 완성하시오.

> Thank you + invite me to the party (for)
> ➡ Thank you for inviting me to the party. _____

(1) Are you interested + go to Vienna with us next weekend? (in)

➡ _____

(2) You can improve your English + do a lot of reading (by)

➡ _____

(3) He apologized + be so rude to me (for)

➡ _____

(4) I've been thinking + look for a new job (of)

➡ _____

2 보기와 같이 주어진 문장과 같은 뜻이 되도록 빈칸을 완성하시오.

> Lisa has already received a phone call.
> ➡ Lisa remembered receiving a phone call _____.

(1) Richard doesn't smoke anymore.

➡ Richard stopped _____.

(2) She didn't buy a cake for the party.

➡ She didn't remember _____.

(3) Eric didn't invite his boss to the party.

➡ Eric forgot _____.

(4) She used to eat desserts.

➡ She stopped _____.

(5) I met Brad Pitt at the airport.

➡ I'll never forget _____.

3 주어진 문장을 읽고 빈칸을 'go + 동명사'의 형태로 바꿔 쓰시오.

> I love to swim. Yesterday my father and I swam for hours.
> ➡ Yesterday my father and I _____went swimming_____.

(1) Once a month, I camp with my family in the summer and enjoy an exciting weekend.

➡ Once a month, I _____ with my family in the summer.

(2) Yesterday, we visited many stores and bought some clothes and makeup.

➡ Yesterday, we _____.

(3) My father takes his fishing pole to a farm pond every Saturday.

➡ My father _____ every Saturday.

4 괄호 안의 말을 알맞은 형태로 고쳐 쓰시오.

(1) Cindy stopped _____ (run) and walked the rest of the way home.

(2) My mom continued _____ (talk) about my misbehavior.

(3) I now regret _____ (say) what I said. I shouldn't have said it.

(4) We regret _____ (inform) you that we are unable to offer you the job.

(5) One of the boys admitted _____ (break) the window.

5 보기와 같이 괄호 안의 단어를 이용하여 두 문장의 뜻이 같아지도록 빈칸을 영작하시오.

> "Let's go to the beach!" said Kevin.
> ➡ Kevin suggested going to the beach _____. (suggested)

(1) Can you turn the music down, please?

➡ Would you _____? (mind)

(2) Jessica didn't forget that she met a ghost in the haunted house.

➡ Jessica didn't _____. (forget)

(3) Did you take the rubbish out before you left the house?

➡ Did you _____? (remember)

Oral Test

Challenge 1 전치사의 목적어로 쓰이는 동명사를 알고 있는가?

(1) 전치사 뒤에는 주로 명사나 대명사를 쓰지만 동작의 내용을 나타낼 때에는 반드시 [   ]를 써야 한다. 이때의 동명사가 전치사의 [   ]가 된다.

   I'm *afraid of* **being** scolded by my teacher. 선생님에게 꾸지람을 들을까봐 걱정이다.

   Thanks very much *for* **inviting** me to the party. 파티에 초대해 주셔서 정말 감사합니다.

(2) 'feel like + 동명사'는 '~하고 싶다'의 뜻으로 like가 [   ]이므로 like 뒤에 동명사를 쓴다.

(3) be used to(~에 익숙하다), look forward to(~하기를 고대하다), object to(~에 반대하다)에서 to가 모두 전치사이므로 동작을 나타낼 때에는 to 뒤에 동사원형이 아닌 [   ]를 쓴다.

Challenge 2 'go + V-ing'는 언제 사용하는가?

우리말 '~하러 가다'의 뜻으로 주로 운동이나 레저 활동에 자주 쓴다. go 뒤에 부정사를 쓰지 않고 [   ]를 쓴다.

   She loves to **go skydiving**. 그녀는 스카이다이빙 하러 가는 것을 좋아한다.

   I **go swimming** in the summer and **go snowboarding** every winter.
   나는 여름에 수영하러 가고 매년 겨울에는 스노우보드를 타러 간다.

Challenge 3 목적어로 동명사와 부정사의 의미 차이를 구별할 수 있는가?

remember, try, forget, stop, regret의 동사는 목적어로 동명사와 부정사를 모두 취하지만 뜻이 서로 달라진다. 과거(이전)에 했던 경험이나 행동은 [   ]를 쓰고, 앞으로 해야 할 일이나 의무, 책임은 [   ]를 목적어로 쓴다.

   He *remembered* **to send** the gift to his girlfriend. 그는 여자 친구에게 그 선물을 보내야 하는 걸 기억했다.

   The girl will never *forget* **being** punished by the teacher. 그 소녀는 선생님에게 벌 받은 것을 결코 잊지 못할 것이다.

   Jeremy *tried* **to unlock** the door. Jeremy는 그 문을 열려고 애를 썼다.

   She *tried* **writing** a letter in English. 그녀는 영어로 편지를 한 번 써봤다.

Unit 7 • 동명사의 의미상 주어

Would you mind *closing* the window?
창문 좀 닫아 주시겠어요?

Would you mind **my** *closing* the window?
내가 창문을 닫아도 될까요?

① 모든 동작에는 그 행위를 하는 주인인 주어가 있어야 한다. 문장의 주어와 동명사의 의미상 주어가 같은 경우, 그리고 일반인이 주어인 경우에는 의미상 주어를 따로 쓰지 않는다.

Do you mind *turning* on the TV? TV 좀 켜주겠니? ➡ turning의 의미상 주어는 문장 전체의 주어인 you

Reducing the number of crimes is essential. 범죄의 수를 줄이는 것이 중요하다. ➡ Reducing의 의미상 주어는 일반인

Smoking is not permitted anywhere in the museum. 미술관 내에서는 어디든지 금연이다.
➡ Smoking의 의미상 주어는 일반인

② 문장의 주어가 의미상 주어가 아닌 경우에는 동명사 바로 앞에 소유격 또는 목적격으로 동명사를 행하는 사람을 의미상 주어로 나타낸다.

We insisted on **his(= him)** *going* abroad with us. 우리는 그에게 우리와 함께 해외에 가자고 했다.
➡ his가 going의 의미상 주어

Do you mind **my** *sitting* next to you? 제가 옆에 앉아도 될까요? ➡ my가 sitting의 의미상 주어

기본기 탄탄 다지기

1 각 문장에서 동명사의 의미상 주어에 밑줄 치시오.

(1) The boss hates me doing the work slowly.

(2) She likes my playing the violin.

(3) I am sure of grandmother's living to ninety.

2 괄호 안의 단어를 이용하여 빈칸에 알맞은 의미상 주어를 쓰시오.

(1) She insisted on _____ going there at once. (I)

(2) I don't like _____ speaking ill of others. (she)

(3) She is looking forward to _____ returning home. (he)

(4) I remember _____ saying so. (Jane)

(5) The bad weather prevented _____ from going fishing. (we)

> ▶의미상 주어로 소유격은 다소 딱딱한 표현이어서 일상 영어에서는 목적격을 많이 쓴다. 사람의 이름은 소유격(Tom's)보다 그냥 이름(Tom)을 동명사 앞에 쓰는 경우가 많다. 영어권 사람들이 타동사나 전치사 뒤에 목적어를 취하는 것을 자연스럽게 생각하기 때문이다.
> He is aware of Susan going to the party.　　(= Susan's going)
> They insisted on me coming to the meeting.　　(= my coming)
>
> ▶전체 문장의 목적어가 동명사의 의미상 주어가 될 때가 있는데 '동사 + 목적어 + (전치사) + 동명사'의 형태를 갖는다.
> Please forgive me for being late.

Unit 8 • 동명사 없이는 못 사는 표현들

I'm **looking forward to** meet**ing** her again.
나는 그녀를 다시 만날 것을 기대한다.

I **have trouble** teach**ing** that student.
나는 저 학생을 가르치는 데에 어려움이 있다.

1 반드시 동명사를 쓰는 여러 가지 관용 표현들이 있다.

on(upon) + V-ing	~ 하자마자	cannot help + V-ing	~하지 않을 수 없다
be busy + V-ing	~하느라 바쁘다	It's no use + V-ing	~해도 소용없다
look forward to + V-ing	~하기를 고대하다	be worth + V-ing	~할 가치가 있다
be accustomed(used) to + V-ing	~하는데 익숙하다	keep(prevent) ~ from + V-ing	~가 ...하지 못하게 하다
There's no use + V-ing	~하는 것은 불가능하다	feel like + V-ing	~하고 싶다
be good at + V-ing	~하는 것을 잘하다	have difficulty (in) + V-ing	~하는 데 어려움을 겪다
object to + V-ing	~에 반대하다	not/never ~ without + V-ing	~하면 반드시 ...하다
far from + V-ing	전혀 ~아닌	above + V-ing	결코 ~하지 않는

Did you **have** any **difficulty** getting a visa? 비자를 얻는데 어려움을 겪었니?

She **is used to** liv**ing** alone. 그녀는 혼자 사는 데에 익숙하다.

My wife **objected to** mov**ing** to another place. 내 아내는 또 다른 곳으로 이사하는 것에 반대했다.

Bad weather **prevented** us **from** starting. 악천후 때문에 우리는 출발하지 못했다.

She **never** goes out **without** los**ing** her cell phone. 그녀는 외출만 하면 휴대전화를 잃어버린다.

He is **far from** sav**ing** money. 그는 돈을 전혀 저축하지 않는다.

기본기 탄탄 다지기

1 다음 빈칸에 알맞은 말을 보기에서 골라 올바른 형태로 쓰시오.

laugh at ~에 웃다
sight n. 광경, 시야

laugh	get	read	wear	go

(1) We're looking forward to _____ on a picnic this weekend.

(2) My mother was busy _____ dinner ready.

(3) The lady never goes out without _____ a scarf.

(4) I'd read this book if I were you. This book is worth _____.

(5) We could not help _____ at this sight.

Unit 9 • 동명사 vs. 현재분사

We *are* **living** in Seoul. (현재분사)
우리는 서울에 살고 있다.

Her dream *is* **living** in a big house with a garden. (동명사)
그녀의 꿈은 정원이 있는 큰 집에서 사는 것이다.

① V-ing가 be동사 뒤에 위치할 경우 진행형으로 쓰인 현재분사와 보어로 쓰인 동명사의 위치와 형태가 똑같다. 주어가 생물체(사람/ 동물)인 경우 'be + V-ing'가 '~하고 있다'의 뜻인 진행형으로 쓰인 현재분사이고, 주어가 행위를 할 수 없는 어떤 대상이나 개념이 오는 경우에 V-ing는 '~(는)것'의 뜻인 동명사가 된다.

Newly-married couples *are* **traveling** by railroad. 신혼부부가 기차로 여행하고 있다.

Our dream *is* **traveling** around the world in the future. 우리의 꿈은 미래에 전 세계를 여행하는 것이다.

② V-ing가 명사 앞에서 명사를 꾸며줄 경우(V-ing + 명사)에 위치가 같아서 구별하기 힘들 수 있으나 명사가 동작을 할 수 있는 생물체(사람/ 동물)인 경우 V-ing는 '~하는'의 뜻인 현재분사이고, 명사가 행위를 할 수 없는 사물인 경우 동명사가 된다.

현재분사	동명사
명사의 '동작, 행동'을 표현하기 위해 사용한다. (~하고 있는, ~하게 하는)	명사의 용도나 목적을 위해 명사화된 것이다. (~하기 위한, ~하는 것)
a **running** girl = a girl who is running (춤추고 있는) a **sleeping** tiger = a tiger which is sleeping (잠자는)	a **waiting** room (용도: 대기실) = a room for waiting ≠ a room which is waiting

기본기 탄탄 다지기

1 밑줄 친 부분이 현재분사로 쓰였으면 '현', 동명사로 쓰였으면 '동'을 쓰시오.

kill time 시간을 죽이다

(1) She is <u>listening</u> to music. _____

(2) He is <u>cooking</u> for our customers. _____

(3) What I like best is <u>listening</u> to K-pop music. _____

(4) All of the members of KARA killed time in the <u>waiting</u> room. _____

(5) <u>Camping</u> cars are very expensive. _____

(6) Do you know the <u>smiling</u> girl over there? _____

서술형 기초 다지기 ③

1 보기와 같이 동명사를 이용한 문장으로 바꾸어 빈칸을 완성하시오.

> I want to smoke here. Is it okay?
> ➡ Would you mind ___my(me)___ ___smoking___ here?

(1) She insisted that I start at once.

   ➡ She insisted on _____ _____ at once.

(2) Her parents didn't want Jessica to buy a new smartphone.

   ➡ Her parents didn't approve of _____ _____ a new smartphone.

(3) I remember that she danced with a ghost last night.

   ➡ I remember _____ _____ with a ghost last night.

(4) We were surprised. They came to the party.

   ➡ We were surprised at _____ _____ to the party.

(5) Susan fall in love with him. I'm sorry about it.

   ➡ I'm sorry about _____ _____ in love with him.

2 다음 우리말과 의미가 같도록 괄호 안의 말을 이용하여 빈칸을 완성하시오.

(1) 그녀는 다른 프로젝트를 하느라고 바빴다. (work)

   ➡ She _____ _____ _____ on the other project.

(2) 그 영화는 볼 가치가 있다. (watch)

   ➡ The movie is _____ _____ .

(3) 그런 기술을 배워봐야 소용없다. (learn)

   ➡ _____ _____ _____ _____ _____ such a skill.

(4) 그녀는 잘 모르는 사람들과 이야기하는 데에 어려움을 겪는다. (talk)

   ➡ She _____ _____ _____ to people she doesn't know well.

(5) 그는 바닥에서 자는 데에 익숙하다. (sleep)

   ➡ He _____ _____ _____ _____ on the floor.

3 다음 밑줄 친 부분만 우리말로 해석하고, 현재분사인지 동명사인지 구분하시오.

(1) My father's job is <u>working in a zoo</u>. ➡ _____

(2) She is <u>watching TV</u> in the living room. ➡ _____

(3) You should bring <u>a sleeping bag</u>. ➡ _____

(4) <u>Racing cars</u> speed at the maximum speed. ➡ _____

(5) They bought a new <u>washing machine</u>. ➡ _____

(6) <u>A smiling girl</u> walked into the room. ➡ _____

4 'worth –ing' 또는 'not worth –ing'를 이용하여 빈칸을 완성하시오.

> I'd read that book if I were you. That book <u>is worth reading</u>_____.

(1) I wouldn't read that book if I were you. That book _____.

(2) I'd visit the museum if I were you. The museum _____.

(3) I wouldn't repair this radio if I were you. This radio _____.

(4) I'd discuss the subject if I were you. The subject _____.

5 다음 주어진 문장을 'have difficulty –ing'를 이용하여 빈칸을 완성하시오.

> I found a place to set up my camera, but it was difficult.
> ➡ I had <u>difficulty finding a place to set up my camera</u>_____.

(1) They found a place to live in, but it was difficult.

➡ They had _____.

(2) Steve finds it difficult to make good friends.

➡ Steve has _____.

(3) It won't be difficult to get a ticket for the movie.

➡ You won't have any _____.

Oral Test

Challenge 1 동명사의 의미상 주어는 어떻게 나타내는가?

(1) 문장의 주어나 목적어가 동명사의 의미상 주어가 되는 경우와 의미상 주어가 일반인(we, they, people)일 때는 의미상 주어를 따로 밝히지 않는다.

I'm sorry for **asking** you this again. 이것을 다시 물어봐서 죄송합니다.

Finding a good job is not easy. 좋은 직업을 찾는 것은 쉽지 않다.

(2) 동명사의 의미상 주어가 문장의 주어와 일치하지 않는 경우에 동명사 바로 앞에 [＿＿＿＿＿] 으로 나타낸다. 일상영어에서는 목적격을 많이 쓴다. 특히, 사람의 이름은 소유격 대신 그냥 이름을 그대로 쓰는 경우가 많다.

We can't understand **his(him) being** lazy. 우리는 그가 게으른 것을 이해할 수 없다.

My father worried about **our(us) coming** home late. 아빠는 우리가 집에 늦게 온 것에 대해 걱정하셨다.

Challenge 2 동명사의 관용표현들을 암기하고 있는가?

on(upon) + V-ing		cannot help + V-ing	
be busy + V-ing		It's no use + V-ing	
look forward to + V-ing		be worth + V-ing	
be accustomed(used) to + V-ing		keep(prevent) ~ from + V-ing	
There's no use + V-ing		feel like + V-ing	
be good at + V-ing		have difficulty (in) + V-ing	
object to + V-ing		not/never ~ without + V-ing	
far from + V-ing		above + V-ing	

Challenge 3 동명사와 현재분사는 어떻게 구별하는가?

(1) be동사 뒤에 V-ing가 올 경우 주어가 행동을 할 수 있는 사람이나 생물인 경우 [＿＿＿＿＿], 주어가 동작을 할 수 없는 대상인 경우 [＿＿＿＿＿] 가 된다.

[＿＿＿＿＿] : She is **teaching** English. 그녀는 영어를 가르치고 있다.

[＿＿＿＿＿] : Her job is **teaching** English. 그녀의 직업은 영어를 가르치는 것이다.

(2) V-ing가 명사 앞에서 명사를 꾸며줄 경우, 명사가 동작을 할 수 있는 생물체(사람 / 동물)인 경우 V-ing는 '~하는'의 뜻인 [＿＿＿＿＿] 이고, 명사가 행위를 할 수 없는 사물인 경우 [＿＿＿＿＿] 가 된다.

[＿＿＿＿＿] : Look at the **dancing** girl on the stage. 무대 위에서 춤을 추고 있는 소녀를 봐라.

[＿＿＿＿＿] : She is wearing **dancing** shoes. 그녀는 무용화를 신고 있다.

1 다음 빈칸에 들어갈 말이 차례대로 나열된 것은?

> · The woman denied _____ the money.
> · Her family hopes _____ to Egypt this summer.

① to steal - to travel   ② stealing - traveling
③ to steal - traveling   ④ stealing - to travel
⑤ to be stolen - being traveled

2 다음 대화의 빈칸에 들어갈 가장 알맞은 것은?

> A: All the fish and even the plants are dying in the river.
> B: If people don't stop _____, we won't see them any more.

① throw trash there
② throwing trash there
③ to throw trash there
④ throw not trash there
⑤ not throwing trash there

3 빈칸에 들어갈 말이 순서대로 바르게 짝지어진 것은?

> · She was busy _____ about her beauty.
> · It is so noisy. Please stop _____ noise.
> · We go _____ every Saturday.
> · It is no use _____ about it.

① to talk - to make - hiking - to worry
② talking - making - to hike - worrying
③ talking - making - to hiking - to worry
④ to talk - to make - to hike - worrying
⑤ talking - making - hiking - worrying

4 다음 대화의 밑줄 친 부분과 쓰임이 다른 하나는?

> A: I don't like writing a diary in English. It's so boring and useless.
> B: Oh! I don't think so. It's a good way to practice English.

① He began learning French.
② Would you mind opening the door for me?
③ I am looking forward to seeing her again.
④ Do you know the girl smiling at me?
⑤ Kevin is interested in making movies.

[5–6] 다음 글을 읽고 물음에 답하시오.

> Dear Andy,
>   I'd like to listen to Vivaldi's "The Four Seasons." I learned about it in my music class, and I really liked it. I especially enjoyed ⓐ_____ to the Spring part. I could hear birds singing and the sound of spring rain. I'd like ⓑ_____ to the music again. And I'd like you to say hello to Jaemin in Class 8. Thank you.

5 윗글에서 ⓐ, ⓑ에 들어갈 listen의 형태가 바르게 짝지어진 것은?

① listening - to listen   ② listening - listen
③ to listen - listening   ④ to listen - to listen
⑤ listening - listening

6 윗글을 쓴 목적으로 알맞은 것은?

① To request music
② To advertise a new CD
③ To complain about a radio program
④ To introduce Vivaldi's music to a student
⑤ To inform the students of a music test

7 다음 문장에서 밑줄 친 곳에 들어갈 동사의 알맞은 형태를 쓰시오.

> Forks and knives are mostly used in Europe and the Americas because people there cook meat without _____ it into small pieces.

① cut   ② cutting   ③ having cut
④ being cut   ⑤ to cut

8 다음 밑줄 친 부분이 바르게 쓰인 것을 고르시오.

① I remember to meet a ghost in the haunted house.
② I'll never forget to see the Queen last year.
③ Michael is used to eat spicy food.
④ I object to his go there without my permission.
⑤ She stopped exercising because she got weak.

[9–10] 다음 두 문장을 한 문장으로 쓸 때 빈칸에 알맞은 말을 쓰시오.

9
> Yesterday she screamed in the parking lot. I couldn't understand it.

➡ I couldn't understand _____ _____ in the parking lot.

10
> His daughter leaves for Singapore. He will call you before it.

➡ He will call you before _____ _____ _____ for Singapore.

11 다음 보기의 밑줄 친 부분과 쓰임이 같은 것은?

> Will you show me another swimming suit?

① There is no smoking area in this building.
② Look at the sleeping tiger.
③ Eric is practicing the violin.
④ Be careful of the boiling water.
⑤ My dog is running in the park.

12 다음 빈칸에 알맞은 말을 쓰시오.

> As it was snowing heavily, we couldn't go up the mountain.
> = The heavy snow _____ us _____ _____ up the mountain.

서술형 대비 문제

1 다음 두 문장이 같은 의미가 되도록 괄호 안의 말을 이용하여 빈칸을 완성하시오.

Whenever I see her face, I always laugh. (never ~ without)

➡ _____

2 다음 우리말과 일치하도록 괄호 안에 주어진 단어를 올바른 순서대로 배열하시오.

> • 그들은 적절한 조치를 취하지 않고 있는 경찰을 비난하고 있다. (taking, blame, not, for, the police)

➡ They _____ proper measures.

3 괄호 안의 단어들을 배열하여 문장을 완성하시오.

I (in, volunteering, for your project, interested, am)

➡ I _____ .

4 괄호 안의 어구를 사용하여 사진과 일치하는 문장을 쓰시오.

(feel like, spaghetti)

➡ Steve _____ .

5 주어진 문장을 읽고 be good at을 이용한 한 문장으로 요약해서 쓰시오.

I'm not a good art student. I try to draw paintings, but I'm not good at it.

➡ _____

나한테 바라는 게 왜 이렇게 많아?

You are a member of your family, a player on the community baseball team, ⓐ <u>and</u> a student in your school. You are also a citizen of your country. In short, you occupy several different positions in the complex structure of society. This means you should play many roles in different situations. Generally, you have little difficulty ⓑ <u>to perform</u> each of your roles because you know what is expected of you. This knowledge guides you through your daily interactions. But sometimes you will get caught in a conflict. Each of your roles ⓒ <u>makes</u> demands on you, and you may be asked to play two or more roles at the same time. When many roles make ⓓ <u>conflicting</u> demands on you, you may feel quite uncomfortable and at times frustrated. For example, your family is going on a picnic this coming Sunday. But your best friend wants you ⓔ <u>to join</u> his or her birthday party on the same day. When such role conflicts occur, you need to do more important things first. Thus, the ability to decide what to do in what order is an essential skill and can help you fulfill multiple social roles.

1 Choose the best main idea of this paragraph.

① 다양한 역할 수행에는 갈등이 있을 수 있다.
② 학교 교육은 풍부한 교육을 제공한다.
③ 지역사회 발전을 위한 많은 노력이 요구된다.
④ 시민정신은 국가발전의 원동력이다.
⑤ 화목한 가정은 건강한 사회의 기초이다.

2 밑줄 친 ⓐ~ⓔ 중 어법상 <u>어색한</u> 부분을 찾아 바르게 고쳐 쓰시오.

_____

보기와 같이 'be interested in + V–ing'를 이용하여 묻고 답하는 형식으로 말하기 연습을 하세요. 연습이 한번 끝난 후 서로 역할을 바꿔 다시 말하기 연습을 하세요.

play soccer / ?

No ➡ watch movies

Are you interested in playing soccer?

No, I'm not. I prefer watching movies. What about you?

 I'm not interested in watching movies.

1

cook / ?

No ➡ wash dishes

2

read novels / ?

No ➡ take pictures

 보기와 같이 동명사를 이용하여 묻고 답하는 형식으로 말하기 연습을 하세요. 연습이 한 번 끝난 후 서로 역할을 바꿔 다시 말하기 연습을 하세요.

watch TV at home

➡ listen to K-pop music

What do you enjoy when you have free time?

I enjoy watching TV at home. How about you?

 I like listening to K-pop music.

1

travel around the country

➡ go fishing with my dad

2

make Korean food

➡ eat fast food

실전 서술형 평가 문제

출제의도 | 전치사의 목적어로 쓰이는 동명사를 이용한 문장 완성
평가내용 | '전치사 + V–ing'

서술형 유형	10점
난이도	중하

A 보기와 같이 알맞은 전치사와 동명사를 이용하여 완전한 문장을 쓰시오.

보기

go to the party with us

1

be late for the movie

2

find a good job

3
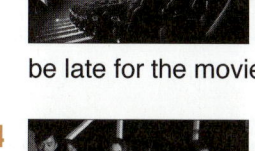
make so much noise

4

see the famous actress

5

go to Disneyland

보기 Are you interested in <u>going to the party with us</u> ?

1 We're worried _____.

2 Wilson has succeeded _____.

3 She apologized _____.

4 I'm looking forward _____.

5 My children are excited _____.

평가영역	채점기준	배점
유창성(Fluency) & 정확성(Accuracy)	5개의 문장을 모두 올바른 표현과 함께 정확하게 완성한 경우 (문법, 철자가 모두 정확한 경우)	5×2 = 10점
	전치사를 바르게 쓰지 못하였거나 동명사를 쓰지 못한 경우	문항당 1점씩 감점
	내용과 전혀 일치하지 않거나 답을 기재하지 못한 경우	0점

출제의도 | 동사에 따른 부정사와 동명사 구별하여 사진 묘사하기

평가내용 | 목적어로 쓰이는 동명사와 부정사

서술형 유형	14점
난이도	중상

B 주어진 표현을 이용하여 보기와 같이 동명사 또는 부정사를 이용한 완전한 문장을 서술하시오.

보기

Eric / enjoy

1

the thief / deny

2

Tom / put off

3

Jane / stop

4

his family / hope

5

Kelly / want

6

my mother / finish

7

Peter / forget

보기 Eric enjoys playing soccer.

1 _____

2 _____

3 _____

4 _____

5 _____

6 _____

7 _____

평가영역	채점기준	배점
유창성(Fluency) & 정확성(Accuracy)	7개의 문장을 모두 올바른 표현과 함께 정확하게 완성한 경우 (문법, 철자가 모두 정확한 경우)	7×2 = 14점
	동명사, 부정사를 만들지 못하였거나 문법, 철자가 1개씩 틀린 경우	문항당 1점씩 감점
	내용과 전혀 일치하지 않거나 답을 기재하지 못한 경우	0점

출제의도 | 동명사를 이용하여 과거의 경험 나타내기

평가내용 | 동사 + 동명사

서술형 유형	10점
난이도	중

C 보기와 같이 'can remember, can't remember'를 이용하여 Sarah가 기억하는 일과 기억하지 못하는 일을 쓰시오.

보기 She was in the hospital when she was seven. (can't remember)

1 She cried on her first day at school. (remember)
2 She went to Korea when she was eight. (remember)
3 She said she wanted to be a math teacher. (can't remember)
4 Once she was bitten by a rattlesnake. (can't remember)
5 Once she fell into a deep well. (remember)

보기 Sarah can't remember being in the hospital when she was seven.

---

1 _____

2 _____

3 _____

4 _____

5 _____

평가영역	채점기준	배점
유창성(Fluency) & 정확성(Accuracy)	5개의 문장을 모두 올바른 표현과 함께 정확하게 완성한 경우 (문법, 철자가 모두 정확한 경우)	5×2 = 10점
	동명사를 만들지 못하였거나 문법, 철자가 1개씩 틀린 경우	문항당 1점씩 감점
	내용과 전혀 일치하지 않거나 답을 기재하지 못한 경우	0점

Chapter **2**

Chapter 3
분사

Unit 1 • 분사의 종류와 역할

Her **smiling** *face* made everyone happy.
그녀의 웃는 얼굴은 모든 사람들을 행복하게 했다.

I fixed *the lamp* **broken** by my son.
나는 내 아들이 망가뜨린 그 램프를 고쳤다.

① 형용사는 명사의 상태만을 설명할 뿐 동작을 표현해 주지 못한다. 분사가 단독으로 명사 바로 앞에서 명사의 동작을 표현할 때 '~하는'의 뜻으로 현재분사 V-ing를 쓰고, 명사가 동작을 직접 하지 않고 어떤 동작을 받거나 당하는 경우에는 과거분사 V-ed를 쓴다. '~된, ~되어진'의 뜻이다.

That **sleeping** *tiger* is very dangerous. 저 잠자고 있는 호랑이는 매우 위험하다.

I visited the **destroyed** *city* soon after the war. 나는 전쟁이 끝난 직후에 파괴된 도시를 방문했다.

② 분사가 한 단어가 아닌 몇 개의 단어로 길어져 명사를 꾸며주는 경우 반드시 명사 뒤에서 명사의 동작을 나타낸다. 마찬가지로 현재분사(V-ing)는 '~하는, 하고 있는'의 뜻이고, 과거분사는 '~해진, ~된'의 뜻으로 명사가 직접 동작을 하지 않고 동작을 받거나 당하는 경우에 쓴다.

The girl (**playing** the guitar) is a ghost. 기타를 치고 있는 그 소녀는 귀신이다.

This is *a smartphone* (**made** in Korea). 이것은 한국에서 만들어진 스마트폰이다.

기본기 탄탄 다지기

1 주어진 글을 읽고 괄호 안에 알맞은 분사를 고르시오.

(1) She looked at a (floating / floated) cloud.

(2) The garden was covered with (falling / fallen) leaves.

(3) Do you know the girl (sat / sitting) on the sofa?

(4) The man (slept / sleeping) under the tree is my teacher.

(5) Who were those people (waiting / waited) outside?

(6) George showed me some pictures (painting / painted) by his father.

(7) Most of the goods (made / making) in this factory are exported.

(8) She threw a stone at a (running / run) bus.

▶보통 현재분사는 '진행, 능동'의 의미를 가지고 과거분사는 '완료, 수동'의 뜻으로 쓴다고 하지만 명사의 행동 유무에 따라 정확한 해석과 쓰임을 익히는 게 더 중요하다.

▶분사가 목적어, 보어 부사(구) 등을 동반하여 길어지는 경우에 명사 바로 뒤에서 명사를 수식한다.

▶흔히 분사가 명사 뒤에서 수식할 때 '관계대명사 + be동사'가 생략되었다고 이를 시험에 출제하기도 하는데, 이는 현대영어에서 거의 쓰지 않는 문법이다. The girl (who is) playing the guitar ~에서 The girl playing the guitar~이나 The girl is playing ~이나 모두 전달하는 시제와 정보가 같기 때문에 굳이 관계대명사와 be동사 (who is)를 쓸 필요가 없이 간결하게 표현한다.

Unit 2 ● 보어 자리에서 명사의 동작을 설명하는 분사

Patricia *was* **jogging** in the park.
Patricia는 공원에서 조깅을 하고 있었다.

We *saw* Patricia **jogging** in the park.
우리는 Patricia가 공원에서 조깅하고 있는 것을 봤다.

1 주어가 행동이 가능한 사람이나 동물인 경우 현재분사가 주격보어 자리에 쓴다. '~한 채로, ~ 하고 있는'으로 해석한다. 주어가 동작을 당하는 경우에는 과거분사를 주격보어 자리에 쓴다. 우리말 '~된 채로, ~해진'으로 해석한다.

The girl *sat* **reading** a weekly magazine. 그 소녀는 주간지를 읽는 채로 앉아 있었다.
= The girl *was* **reading** a weekly magazine.

The bank *remained* **closed** for two months. 그 은행은 2달 동안 계속 닫혀 있었다.
= The bank *was* **closed** for two months.

2 5형식 문장(주로 지각동사, 사역동사)에서 목적어의 동작을 나타내기 위해 목적격 보어 자리에 분사를 쓴다. 목적어가 행동을 하는 생물체인 경우 현재분사를 쓰고 목적어가 동작을 당하거나 받는 경우 과거분사를 쓴다.

She *kept* me **waiting** for two hours. 그녀는 나를 2시간이나 기다리게 했다.

I *saw* him **scolded** by his mother. 나는 그가 엄마에게 혼나는 것을 봤다.

I *heard* my name **called** in the crowd. 나는 많은 사람들 속에서 내 이름이 불리는 것을 들었다.

She *had* her suitcase **carried** by the porter. 그녀는 짐꾼에게 그녀의 여행 가방을 옮기게 했다.

Chapter 3

기본기 탄탄 다지기

1 주어진 글을 읽고 괄호 안에 알맞은 분사를 고르시오.

(1) The dog kept (barked / barking) all night.

(2) I must have my car (fixing / fixed) in a couple of days.

(3) She stood (looking / looked) at the picture.

(4) I saw my first love (stood / standing) at the bus stop.

(5) This article was (writing / written) by the distinguished journalist.

(6) She came (run / running) toward me.

(7) When she came to her senses, she found herself (lying / lain) on the floor.

> **bark** v. 짖다
> **a couple of days** 이틀 정도
> **article** n. 기사
> **distinguished** a. 유명한
> **toward** ~을 향해서
> **lying** lie(눕다)의 현재분사형

My parents looked very **shocked** at my grades.
우리 부모님은 내 성적에 큰 충격을 받으신 것처럼 보였다.

My grades were **shocking**.
내 성적은 충격적이었다.

① 사람의 감정을 나타내는 분사가 명사를 꾸며주거나 설명할 때 그 명사와 주어가 남에게 감정을 주는 주체인 경우 현재분사(V-ing)를 쓰고, 감정을 느끼거나 받는 대상이 되는 경우에는 과거분사(V-ed)를 쓴다.

exciting 흥분시키는	– excited 흥분된	surprising 깜짝 놀랄만한	– surprised 깜짝 놀란
amazing 놀라운(주로 칭찬)	– amazed 놀란(감탄한)	boring 지루하게 하는	– bored 지겨워하는
confusing 혼란스럽게 하는	– confused 혼동된, 혼란스러운	disappointing 실망하게 하는(시키는)	– disappointed 실망한(받은)
interesting 흥미로운, 재미있는	– interested 관심이(흥미가) 있는	satisfying 만족스럽게 하는	– satisfied 만족스러운
embarrassing 난처하게 하는	– embarrassed 난처한	disgusting 구역질 나는	– disgusted 정떨어진, 넌더리 난

It was an **amazing** *performance*. 그것은 기가 막힌 공연이었다.

The *K-pop concert* was pretty **exciting**. 그 K-pop 콘서트는 꽤 흥미진진했다.

We were really **excited** by the musical. 우리는 그 뮤지컬 때문에 정말로 흥분되었다.

기본기 탄탄 다지기

1 우리말에 맞도록 괄호 안의 단어를 이용하여 빈칸에 쓰시오.

(1) 그는 그의 딸이 도둑을 잡았다는 소리를 듣고 놀란 듯 보였다. (surprise)

➡ He looked _____ to hear his daughter caught the thief.

(2) 그녀는 충격을 받은 표정으로 그 공포영화를 보았다. (shock)

➡ She watched the horror movie with a _____ face.

(3) 우리는 그 공연에 실망했다. (disappoint)

➡ We were _____ in the performance.

(4) 그 아기는 시끄러운 소리 때문에 두려움을 느꼈다. (frighten)

➡ The baby was _____ by the loud noise.

(5) 그 소녀들은 흥미진진한 축구 경기를 보고 있었다. (excite)

➡ The girls were watching an _____ soccer game.

▶보통 영문법 책에서는 사람일 때는 과거분사를 쓰고, 사물에는 현재분사를 쓴다고 하는데 이는 틀린 설명이다. 사람은 남에게 감정을 줄 수도 있고 감정을 받을 수도 있다. 따라서 감정을 일으키는 주체이면 현재분사를, 감정을 느끼는 대상이 되면 과거분사를 쓴다.
The teacher is a very **boring** person.
그 선생님은 매우 지루한 사람이다.

▶어떤 사물이나 대상, 그리고 상황은 감정을 받을 수 있는 생물체가 아니므로 과거분사를 쓰지 못하고 남에게 감정을 주는 현재분사만 사용된다.
The movie was **disappointing**.
그 영화는 실망스러웠다.

1 주어진 문장을 명사를 수식하는 분사를 활용하여 보기와 같이 쓰시오.

> Do you know the boy? + He is playing basketball.
> ➡ Do you know the boy playing basketball? _____

(1) Who is the girl? + She is wearing a blue cap.

➡ _____

(2) The cars are nice. + They were made in Korea.

➡ _____

(3) The woman was injured in the accident. + She was taken to the hospital.

➡ _____

(4) The story was written by T. J. Johnson. + It is very weird.

➡ _____

(5) The man is a very famous actor. + He is surrounded by many female fans.

➡ _____

(6) The student is my cousin. + He is sitting in the front row.

➡ _____

2 다음 괄호 안의 단어를 이용하여 문장을 완성하시오.

(1) 그의 이야기는 매우 재미있는 것처럼 들린다. (interest, very, sound)

➡ His story _____.

(2) 나는 도둑이 어떤 아이들에게 맞는 것을 보았다. (children, by, beat, some)

➡ I saw a thief _____.

(3) 그녀는 소파에서 신문을 읽는 채로 앉아 있었다. (the newspaper, read, sat)

➡ She _____ on the sofa.

(4) 나는 집 밖에서 내 이름이 불리는 것을 들었다. (call, heard, my name)

➡ I _____ outside the house.

(5) 나는 그녀가 설거지하고 있는 것을 발견했다. (wash, found, her)

➡ I _____ the dishes.

3 보기와 같이 분사를 이용하여 빈칸을 완성하시오.

> The concert disappointed them.　➡ The concert was ___disappointing___.
> ➡ They were ___disappointed___ in the concert.

(1) Physics interests Michelle.

➡ Michelle thinks physics is very _____.

➡ Michelle is very _____ in physics.

(2) Ann is going to Indonesia next week. She has never been there before. The idea of going on this trip excites her.

➡ Ann is _____ about going on this trip.

➡ Ann thinks it is going to be an _____ trip.

4 보기와 같이 생략할 수 있는 부분에 밑줄을 긋고 문장을 다시 써 보시오.

> The woman who is sitting over there is a famous pianist.
> ➡ The woman sitting over there is a famous pianist.

(1) The girl who is waiting at the bus stop is my sister.

➡ _____

(2) The information that was found on that Website was incorrect.

➡ _____

(3) Do you know the man who is standing by the window?

➡ _____

5 주어진 동사를 알맞은 분사형태로 고쳐 빈칸을 완성하시오.

(1) My teacher made the report _____ by me. (write)

(2) Anthony had a short story _____ by us. (translate)

(3) She remained _____ with her salary. (satisfy)

(4) She is taking care of _____ children. (cry)

Oral Test

Challenge 1 분사가 문장에서 어떤 역할을 하는가?

형용사는 명사의 상태만을 표현할 뿐 명사의 동작을 나타내주지 못한다. 분사가 바로 명사의 앞이나 뒤에서 명사의 [   ]을 나타내 준다.

Challenge 2 명사의 동작을 설명하는 분사를 알고 있는가?

분사가 명사를 단독으로 꾸밀 경우 명사 바로 앞에 쓴다. 분사가 수식어구를 동반하여 길어지는 경우에는 반드시 명사 [   ]에서 동작을 표현해 준다. 명사가 행동을 하는 주체가 되면 [   ]를 쓰고, 명사가 행동을 받거나 당하는 경우 [   ]를 쓴다.

They were watching the **shocking** *news*. 그들은 충격적인 뉴스를 보고 있었다.
We have to sweep the **fallen** *leaves*. 우리는 떨어진 잎들을 쓸어야 한다.

Challenge 3 보어 자리에 쓰이는 분사를 알고 있는가?

(1) 주격 보어 자리에 분사를 쓸 경우 주어가 동작을 하는 주체인 경우 [   ]를 쓰고, 동작을 당하는 경우에는 [   ]를 쓴다.

He *came* **singing** with his brother. 그는 그의 형과 노래를 하면서 왔다.
She *seems* **surprised** by the news. 그녀는 그 소식에 놀란 것처럼 보인다.

(2) 목적격 보어 자리에 분사를 쓸 경우 목적어가 동작을 하는 주체인 경우 [   ]를 쓰고, 동작을 당하는 경우에는 [   ]를 쓴다.

We heard *the doorbell* **ringing**. 우리는 초인종이 울리는 소리를 들었다.
Helen had *her watch* **stolen** in the bus. Helen은 버스에서 시계를 도난당했다.

Challenge 4 감정을 나타내는 분사는 어떻게 쓰는가?

사람의 감정과 관련된 동사가 명사를 수식하거나 설명할 때, 그 명사와 주어가 다른 사람의 감정을 일으키는 주체인 경우에는 [   ]를 쓰고, 감정을 느끼거나 받는 대상이 되는 경우에는 [   ]를 쓴다.

Sunny is **bored** because her job is **boring**. Sunny는 그녀의 직업이 지루하기 때문에 지루해한다.
We were **amused** by the children's behavior. 우리는 아이들의 행동 때문에 즐거웠다.
This was a very **fascinating** book. 이것은 정말 흥미로운 책이었다.

Unit 4 ● 분사구문 만들기

Preview

When she **heard** the news, she turned pale.
= **Hearing** the news, she turned pale.
그 소식을 들은 그녀는 얼굴이 창백해 졌다.

1 분사구문은 '접속사 + 주어 + 동사'로 되어 있는 부사절을 V-ing가 이끄는 부사구로 짧게 줄여 쓴 구문이다.

분사구문 만드는 방법	① 부사절의 접속사를 생략한다.
	② 부사절의 주어를 생략한다. (단, 부사절의 주어와 주절의 주어가 같아야 함)
	③ 동사를 분사형인 V-ing로 바꾼다. (단, 부사절의 시제와 주절의 시제가 같아야 함)

After you **finish** your homework, you can go shopping.
➡ **Finishing** your homework, you can go shopping. 숙제를 마친 후에 너는 쇼핑을 하러 갈 수 있다.

When we **opened** the door, we smelled something strange.
➡ **Opening** the door, we smelled something strange. 그 문을 열었을 때 우리는 이상한 냄새를 맡았다.

2 분사구문의 부정형은 분사 바로 앞에 not / never를 쓴다.

As we **don't use** the car often, we've decided to sell it.
➡ **Not using** the car often, we've decided to sell it. 그 차를 자주 사용하지 않기 때문에 우리는 팔기로 결정했다.

기본기 탄탄 다지기

1 다음 문장과 뜻이 같도록 빈칸에 알맞은 말을 쓰시오.

take a rest 휴식을 취하다
next to ～옆에
deserve to ～을 받을 만하다
get a raise 월급이 오르다

(1) While I walked in the street, I happened to meet her.
➡ _____ in the street, I happened to meet her.

(2) As I was sick, I stayed at home and took a rest.
➡ _____ sick, I stayed at home and took a rest.

(3) If you turn to the left, you will see the post office.
➡ _____ to the left, you will see the post office.

(4) Although I live next to his house, I don't know him.
➡ _____ next to his house, I don't know him.

(5) Because she works very hard, she deserves to get a raise.
➡ _____ very hard, she deserves to get a raise.

Preview

When she **saw** me, she ran away. 나를 보았을 때 그녀는 도망을 갔다.
= **Seeing** me, she ran away.

① 시간을 나타내는 분사구문은 접속사 when(~할 때), after(~이후에), while(~동안에) 등을 생략하고 동사를 분사형인 V-ing로 바꿔 짧고 빠르게 의미를 전달하는 부사구로 만든 것이다. 분사구문으로 고칠 때는 반드시 부사절의 주어와 주절의 주어가 같아야 한다. 주어가 다를 경우 분사구문으로 만들지 않는다.

While **I** was traveling across Europe, **I** noticed the differences in architecture.
➡ **Traveling** across Europe, I noticed the differences in architecture.
유럽 전역을 걸쳐 여행하는 동안 나는 건축양식의 차이점들을 알게 됐다.

While **I** was traveling across Europe, **the differences** in architecture became very clear.
내가 유럽 전역을 걸쳐 여행하는 동안 건축 양식의 차이점들은 분명해졌다.
➡ 부사절의 주어와 주절의 주어가 다르므로 분사구문으로 줄여 쓰지 않는다.

Chapter 3

기본기 탄탄 다지기

1 다음 문장과 뜻이 같도록 빈칸에 알맞은 말을 쓰시오.

(1) Before I came to the United States, I took some English classes.
➡ Before _____ to the United States, I took some English classes.

(2) While I walked in the park, I happened to meet my old friend.
➡ _____ in the park, I happened to meet my old friend.

(3) After we finished the work, we watched the game on TV.
➡ After _____ the work, we watched the game on TV.

2 다음 우리말과 뜻이 같도록 괄호 안의 말을 알맞은 형태로 쓰시오.

(1) 그 역에 도착한 나는 그에게 전화를 걸었다. (arrive)
➡ _____ at the station, I called him up.

(2) 출근하기 전에 그녀는 아침식사를 했다. (leave)
➡ Before _____ for work, she had breakfast.

▶부사절의 시제가 'be + V-ing'인 경우 be동사는 뜻에 큰 영향을 주지 않으므로 생략하고 V-ing로 시작하는 분사구문을 만든다.

▶시간을 나타내는 분사구문은 시간의 전후가 혼동이 될 수 있어 가급적 시간의 접속사는 생략하지 않는 것이 좋다. 현대영어에서는 거의 시간의 접속사를 쓴다.

▶접속사 when은 '~하자마자'의 뜻인 upon + -ing 또는 on + -ing로 바꿔 써도 의미에 큰 차이가 없다.
When we entered the house, we took off our shoes.
= **Upon** entering the house, we took off our shoes.
= **On** entering the house, we took off our shoes.
= **When** entering the house, we took off our shoes.

Unit 6 • 분사구문의 쓰임 2 (이유, 조건)

Preview

Because Gregory **didn't feel** too well, he left work early.
= **Not feeling** too well, Gregory left work early.
몸이 좋지 않은 Gregory는 일찍 회사를 떠났다.

① 이유를 나타내는 분사구문은 접속사 because, as, since(~ 때문에) 등을 생략하고 동사를 분사형인 V−ing로 바꿔 짧고 빠르게 의미를 전달하는 부사구로 만든 것이다.

As he **was** poor, he could not afford to buy the car.
➡ **Being** poor, he could not afford to buy the car. 가난했기 때문에 그는 그 차를 살 여력이 없었다.

② 조건을 나타내는 분사구문은 접속사 if(~라면)를 생략하고 동사를 분사형인 V−ing로 바꿔 짧고 빠르게 의미를 전달하는 부사구로 만든 것이다.

If you **meet** her once, you'll like her.
➡ **Meeting** her once, you'll like her. 그녀를 한 번 만나보면 너는 그녀를 좋아하게 될 것이다.

기본기 탄탄 다지기

1 다음 분사구문의 의미를 밑줄 친 부분에 유의하여 이유나 조건을 구분하여 쓰시오.

(1) <u>Being</u> angry with me, she shouted at me. _____

(2) <u>Turning</u> to the left, you'll see the white building. _____

(3) <u>Losing</u> weight a lot, she had to buy new clothes. _____

▶이유(원인), 조건을 나타내는 부사절 접속사는 주절만으로 인과관계 및 조건을 파악할 수 있으므로 접속사는 거의 생략해서 쓸 수 있다. 하지만 주절의 시제를 통해 분사구문의 시제를 예측해야 하는 단점이 있다.

▶조건을 나타내는 분사구문은 주절에 특정 조동사 will이 함께 사용된다.

2 다음 두 문장의 의미가 같도록 빈칸에 접속사 Because 또는 If를 쓰시오.

(1) Being sick and tired, she went to bed early.
➡ _____ she was sick and tired, she went to bed early.

(2) Not having a passport, you can't travel abroad.
➡ _____ you don't have a passport, you can't travel abroad.

(3) Turning to the right, you will find the building.
➡ _____ you turn to the right, you will find the building.

(4) Not arriving on time, he couldn't take the exam.
➡ _____ he didn't arrive on time, he couldn't take the exam.

1 다음 밑줄 친 부사절을 분사구문으로 바꿔 쓰시오.

(1) <u>If you turn around</u>, you will find a frozen lake.

➡ _____, you will find a frozen lake.

(2) <u>While I was watching TV</u>, I fell asleep.

➡ _____, I fell asleep.

(3) <u>When she played tennis</u>, she hurt her right ankle.

➡ _____, she hurt her right ankle.

(4) <u>Because she felt confident</u>, she asked for a raise.

➡ _____, she asked for a raise.

(5) <u>While I was taking a shower</u>, I heard the telephone ring.

➡ _____, I heard the telephone ring.

(6) <u>If I find her address</u>, I'll send Jane a wedding invitation.

➡ _____, I'll send Jane a wedding invitation.

(7) <u>When I arrived at the station</u>, I found him waiting for me.

➡ _____, I found him waiting for me.

(8) <u>Since Alice had a slight cold</u>, she went to bed early.

➡ _____, Alice went to bed early.

(9) <u>Because I didn't know her address</u>, I wasn't able to contact her.

➡ _____, I wasn't able to contact her.

(10) <u>Since Kevin has two jobs</u>, he has little free time.

➡ _____, Kevin has little free time.

(11) <u>When I opened the door</u>, I saw a man on his knees.

➡ _____, I saw a man on his knees.

(12) <u>Because he is a foreigner</u>, he needs a visa to stay in this country.

➡ _____, he needs a visa to stay in this country.

2 다음 보기에서 알맞은 접속사를 골라 분사구문을 부사절로 바꿔 쓰시오.

when	if	because

(1) Being poor, she didn't go to college.

➡ _____, she didn't go to college.

(2) Taking this bus, you will get to the City Hall.

➡ _____, you will get to the City Hall.

(3) Walking along the street, I met an old friend of mine.

➡ _____, I met an old friend of mine.

3 자연스러운 문장이 되도록 바르게 연결하고 분사구문으로 고쳐 다시 써 보시오.

(1) When she heard the news, •	• (a) she always watches TV.
(2) If you get up early, •	• (b) he got a bad grade at the mid-term test.
(3) As Tom studied very little, •	• (c) she has to use public transportation.
(4) After she finishes her homework, •	• (d) you will not be late for school.
(5) Since she doesn't have a car any more, •	• (e) she jumped for joy.

(1) _____

(2) _____

(3) _____

(4) _____

(5) _____

Oral Test

Challenge 1 분사구문을 만들 수 있는가?

분사구문은 '접속사 + 주어 + 동사'로 되어 있는 부사절을 [   ]가 이끄는 부사구로 간략하게 만든 구문이다.

(1) 부사절의 [   ]를 생략한다.

(2) 부사절의 [   ]와 주절의 [   ]가 같은 경우 부사절의 [   ]를 생략한다.

(3) 부사절의 [   ]와 주절의 [   ]가 같은 경우 부사절 내의 동사를 [   ]로 바꾼다.

When she **saw** me, she got so embarrassed.

➡ ~~she~~ **saw** me, she got so embarrassed.

➡ **saw** me, she got so embarrassed.

➡ **Seeing** me, she got so embarrassed. 그녀는 나를 보자 매우 난처해했다.

Challenge 2 분사구문이 나타내는 의미를 파악할 수 있는가?

(1) [   ]을 나타내는 접속사 : when, after, before, while

When she got to the bus stop, she found the bus had left.

= [   ] to the bus stop, she found the bus had left. 버스 정류장에 도착한 그녀는 버스가 떠난 것을 알았다.

= [   ] [   ] to the bus stop, she found the bus had left.

= [   ] [   ] to the bus stop, she found the bus had left.

(2) [   ]을 나타내는 접속사 : because, as, since

As she is kind, she is loved by everybody.

= [   ] kind, she is loved by everybody. 친절한 그녀는 모든 사람에게 사랑을 받는다.

(3) [   ]을 나타내는 접속사 : if

If you turn to the left, you'll find the drugstore.

= [   ] to the left, you'll find the drugstore. 왼쪽으로 돌면 약국을 찾을 수 있을 것이다.

Preview

Although they **work** for the same bank, they don't know each other.
= **Working** for the same bank, they don't know each other.
같은 은행에서 일하지만, 그들은 서로를 모른다.

① 양보를 나타내는 분사구문은 접속사 although, though(~임에 불구하고) 등을 생략하고 동사를 분사형인 V-ing로 바꿔 짧고 빠르게 의미를 전달하는 부사구로 만든 것이다.

Although ostriches **have** wings, they can't fly.
➡ **Having** wings, ostriches can't fly. 날개가 있는데도 타조는 하늘을 날지 못한다.

Though Harry **is** American, he can speak Korean well.
➡ **Being** American, Harry can speak Korean well. 미국인인데도 Harry는 한국어를 잘한다.

기본기 탄탄 다지기

1 다음 우리말과 뜻이 같도록 괄호 안의 단어를 적절히 활용하여 빈칸에 알맞은 말을 쓰시오.

(1) 비록 그녀는 아팠지만 병원에 가지 않았다. (be)

➡ _____ ill, she didn't go to the hospital.

(2) 나는 열심히 공부했는데도 시험에 떨어졌다. (study)

➡ _____ hard, I failed in the exam.

(3) 두 배로 열심히 일했지만 그녀는 충분한 대가를 받지 못했다. (work)

➡ _____ double tides, she didn't get paid enough.

> **work double tides** 두 배로 일하다
> **get paid** 봉급을 받다
> **above V-ing** 결코 ~이 아니다
> **tell a lie** 거짓말을 하다
> **a fear of heights** 고소공포증

2 다음 문장과 뜻이 같도록 빈칸에 알맞은 말을 쓰시오.

(1) Though he is poor, he is above telling a lie.

➡ _____ poor, he is above telling a lie.

(2) Although she has a fear of heights, she wants to try bungee jumping.

➡ _____ a fear of heights, she wants to try bungee jumping.

> ▶양보를 나타내는 부사절 접속사는 주절만으로 양보의 의미를 파악할 수 있으므로 접속사는 생략해서 쓸 수 있다. 하지만 주절의 시제를 통해 분사구문의 시제를 예측해야 하는 단점이 있다.

Unit 8 • 분사구문의 쓰임 4 (동시동작, 연속동작)

Reading a newspaper, he watched TV.
그는 신문을 보면서 TV를 봤다.
We started in the morning **arriving** in Seoul at noon.
우리는 아침에 출발해서 정오에 서울에 도착했다.

① 분사구문의 동시동작은 '~하면서(as)'의 뜻으로 분사구문의 동작이 주절의 동작과 동시에 일어날 때 쓴다. 동시동작을 나타낼 때는 보통 콤마(,)를 쓴다.

She extended her hand, **smiling** brightly. 그녀는 밝게 웃으면서 손을 내밀었다.
= She extended her hand while she smiled brightly.

Looking at me, he stood by the window. 나를 쳐다보면서 그는 창문 옆에 서 있었다.
= As he looked at me, he stood by the window.

② 분사구문의 연속동작은 2개의 동사가 시간적 차이를 갖는 경우이다. 이런 경우 분사나 본동사 둘 중에 앞에 있는 쪽이 먼저 발생한 동작을 나타낸다. '~하고 나서, 그리고 ~하다'로 해석한다.

Opening the box, she **took out** a handgun. 그녀는 상자를 열고 나서 권총 한 자루를 꺼냈다.
= She opened the box and then took out a handgun.

The crowd **stood up**, **clapping** and **cheering**. 관중들이 일어섰고 박수를 치며 환호했다.
= The crowd stood up and then clapped and cheered.

Chapter 3

기본기 탄탄 다지기

1 다음 우리말과 뜻이 같도록 괄호 안의 단어를 알맞은 분사로 쓰시오.

(1) 그녀는 의자에 앉고 나서 잡지를 읽었다.
➡ She sat on the chair, _____ a magazine. (read)

(2) 그녀는 부드럽게 노래를 부르면서 방에 들어왔다.
➡ She walked in the room, _____ softly. (sing)

(3) 나는 내 여동생이 집에 오기를 기다리면서 늦게 잠들었다.
➡ I got to sleep late _____ for my sister to get home. (wait)

(4) 천천히 걸으면서 우리는 대화를 시작했다.
➡ _____ slowly, we started talking. (walk)

(5) 그 열차는 6시에 부산을 떠나고 나서 9시에 서울에 도착했다.
➡ The train left Busan at 6, _____ in Seoul at 9. (arrive)

▶동시동작을 나타내는 분사구문은 동시에 이루어지고 있는 일이므로 순서가 바뀌어도 무관하다.

She watched TV, **talking** on the phone.
= She talked on the phone, **watching** TV.

Preview

Having graduated from college, she became a pilot.
대학을 졸업한 후에 그녀는 비행사가 되었다.
Having read the newspaper, I know about the accident.
신문을 읽었기 때문에 나는 그 사고를 알고 있다.

1 V−ing로 시작하는 분사구문은 주절의 시제가 현재면 현재, 과거면 과거로 같은 시제임을 내포하고 있다. 하지만 주절보다 더 앞서 행해진 일이나 동작은 'having + V−ed'의 형태로 더 이전에 행해진 일임을 알린다.

Knowing little of the city, I **hired** a guide. ➡ Knowing은 주절의 과거시제 hired를 보고 과거임을 알 수 있다.
➡ As I <u>knew</u> little of the city, I <u>hired</u> a guide. 나는 그 도시에 대해 잘 몰랐기 때문에, 안내인을 고용했다.

Having bought a book, she **went** to school. ➡ having bought가 went보다 더 이전의 과거
➡ After she <u>had bought</u> a book, she <u>went</u> to school. 책 한 권을 산 그녀는 학교에 갔다.

Having finished the course, I **can look for** a job. ➡ having finished가 can look for보다 더 이전의 과거
➡ As I <u>finished</u> the course, I <u>can look for</u> a job. 교육 과정을 끝마친 나는 직장을 구할 수 있다.

기본기 탄탄 다지기

1 두 문장의 뜻이 같도록 괄호 안에서 알맞은 것을 고르시오.

(1) When I traveled across Europe, I went to the Eiffel Tower.
➡ (Having traveled / Traveling) across Europe, I went to the Eiffel Tower.

(2) As she worked all day long, she looks tired.
➡ (Having worked / Working) all day long, she looks tired.

(3) As he studied hard, he can get good grades.
➡ (Studying / Having studied) hard, he can get good grades.

(4) As I had no money with me, I walked home.
➡ (Having / Having had) no money with me, I walked home.

(5) After Tiffany had found the smartphone, she brought it to the police.
➡ (Having found / Finding) the samrtphone, Tiffany brought it to the police.

서술형 기초 다지기 ❸

1 다음 밑줄 친 부분을 분사구문으로 바꾸어 쓰시오.

(1) The old lady got on the bus, <u>and then she looked for an empty seat.</u>

➡ The old lady got on the bus, _____.

(2) <u>As we had dinner together,</u> we talked about our next project.

➡ _____, we talked about our next project.

(3) Jason left the office at 9 <u>and arrived in New York at 11.</u>

➡ Jason left the office at 9, _____.

(4) The beautiful girl handed me a broom, <u>and then she smiled charmingly.</u>

➡ The beautiful girl handed me a broom, _____.

(5) <u>While I ate the cherry pie,</u> I struck several pits and nearly broke a tooth.

➡ _____, I struck several pits and nearly broke a tooth.

2 보기와 같이 우리말에 맞도록 괄호 안의 말을 이용하여 빈칸을 완성하시오.

> 열이 났음에도 불구하고 Cindy는 대중들 앞에서 연설을 했다. (a fever, have)
> ➡ _____Having a fever_____, Cindy delivered a speech in public.

(1) 비록 네가 말한 것을 인정하지만 나는 아직 그것을 믿지 않는다. (what, admit, say, you)

➡ _____, I still don't believe it.

(2) 해변에 살고 있지만 그는 수영을 못한다. (the seashore, on, live)

➡ _____, he can't swim.

(3) 매우 아픈데도 Kevin은 5시간 동안 영어를 가르쳤다. (sick, be, very)

➡ _____, Kevin taught English for five hours.

(4) 비록 답을 알았지만 나는 손을 들지 않았다. (the answers, know)

➡ _____, I didn't raise my hand.

(5) 비록 우리는 경기를 매우 열심히 했지만 졌다. (play, very hard, the game)

➡ _____, we lost it.

3 두 문장의 뜻이 같도록 빈칸에 알맞은 분사구문을 쓰시오.

(1) Although we ate 8 slices of pizza, we are still hungry.

➡ _____ , we are still hungry.

(2) If you drive carefully, you'll be able to avoid accidents.

➡ _____ , you'll be able to avoid accidents.

(3) Because she could watch the city through the window, she enjoyed taking the bus.

➡ _____ , she enjoyed taking the bus.

(4) Because she had failed in the exam, she didn't come back.

➡ _____ , she didn't come back.

(5) Although he slept all day long, he actually feels more tired.

➡ _____ , he actually feels more tired.

4 보기와 같이 주어진 접속사를 이용하여 부사절이 있는 문장으로 다시 쓰시오.

> Not having come to school yesterday, he has to come today. (because)
> ➡ Because he didn't come to school yesterday, he has to come today.

(1) Being tired, I didn't go to the party. (as)

➡ _____

(2) Having read the book, I threw it away. (after)

➡ _____

(3) Having failed several times, Olivia succeeded at last. (after)

➡ _____

(4) Not being sick, she couldn't be absent from school. (because)

➡ _____

(5) Having lost my cell phone, I have to buy a new one now. (as)

➡ _____

Oral Test

Chapter 3

Challenge 1 양보를 나타내는 분사구문은 무엇인가?

양보를 나타내는 접속사 although, though가 이끄는 부사절을 분사구문으로 간략하게 고쳐 의미 전달을 빠르게 한다.

Though she lives next door, she doesn't even say hello to us.

➡ ☐☐☐☐☐☐☐ next door, she doesn't even say hello to us. 옆집에 사는데도 그녀는 우리한테 인사조차 하지 않는다.

Challenge 2 동시동작과 연속동작을 정확히 구별할 수 있는가?

(1) 분사구문의 ☐☐☐☐☐은 분사구문의 동작과 주절의 동작이 동시에 일어날 때 쓴다.

She came home, **reading** a letter. 그녀는 편지를 읽으면서 집에 왔다.
= She came home as she read a letter.

(2) 분사구문의 ☐☐☐☐☐은 어느 한 동작이 발생한 후에 다소 시간적 차이를 두고 다음 동작이 연이어 발생할 때 쓴다.

They finished dinner, **going** out for a movie. 그들은 저녁 식사를 마치고 나서 영화를 보러 나갔다.
= They finished dinner and then went out for a movie.

Challenge 3 분사구문의 시제는 어떻게 표현하는가?

분사구문도 시제를 나타낼 수 있다. V-ing로 시작하는 분사구문은 주절의 시제가 현재면 현재, 과거면 분사구문도 과거로 시제가 서로 같다. 주절의 시제보다 그 이전에 먼저 행해진 행위를 표현할 때는 ☐☐☐☐☐를 쓴다. 다시 말해서 주절의 시제가 현재면 분사구문은 과거(또는 현재완료), 주절의 시제가 과거이면 분사구문의 시제는 대과거(had + V-ed)로 항상 주절의 시제보다 더 과거 이전에 먼저 동작이 발생했음을 내포하고 있다.

☐☐☐☐☐ her before, I recognized her at once. 전에 그녀를 만났기 때문에 나는 그녀를 즉시 알아보았다.
= As I **had met** her before, I **recognized** her at once.

Unit 10 ● being, having been의 생략

Frightened by her voice, he turned pale.
그녀의 목소리에 겁이 나서, 그는 창백해 졌다.
Raised in London, she speaks English fluently.
런던에서 자란 그녀는 영어를 유창하게 한다.

① 부사절 내의 동사가 수동태 (be + V-ed)일 때 be동사 다음에 있는 과거분사(V-ed)는 그대로 두고 be동사만 Being으로 쓰고 주절의 시제보다 더 이전의 과거를 나타내는 경우에는 Having been으로 고쳐서 분사구문을 만든다. be동사를 분사구문으로 만들기 위해 분사형으로 고친 being, having been은 의미상 중요한 역할을 하지 않으므로 둘 다 생략해서 쓴다. 따라서 과거분사 V-ed로 시작하는 분사구문이 탄생하게 된다.

When she was **left** alone, she felt sorrow.

　(Being) **Left** alone, she felt sorrow. 홀로 남겨진 그녀는 슬퍼했다.

　➡ 부사절의 was(과거)와 주절의 felt(과거)의 시제가 같으므로 V-ing형인 Being으로 고침.

As the cake was **made** in a hurry, it is not so good.

　(Having been) **Made** in a hurry, the cake is not so good. 급하게 만들어진 이 케이크는 맛이 없다.

　➡ 부사절의 was(과거)가 주절의 is(현재)보다 더 과거이므로 Having been으로 고침.

기본기 탄탄 다지기

1 주어진 동사를 V-ing 또는 V-ed 중 알맞은 형태로 바꾸어 빈칸을 채우시오.

(1) ＿＿＿＿＿＿＿ the street, you should look both ways. (cross)

(2) ＿＿＿＿＿＿＿ brightly, she shook hands with me. (smile)

(3) ＿＿＿＿＿＿＿ in easy English, the book will be read by many people. (write)

(4) ＿＿＿＿＿＿＿ from the sky, the island looks like a human face. (see)

(5) ＿＿＿＿＿＿＿ with her sister, she sings much better. (compare)

(6) ＿＿＿＿＿＿＿ what to do, he remained silent. (not, know)

(7) ＿＿＿＿＿＿＿ three years ago, the building looks new. (build)

▶부사절 내의 동사가 'be동사 + 형용사'인 경우 마찬가지로 be동사는 의미상 큰 역할을 차지하지 않으므로 being과 having been을 생략한다. Though he was **famous** for his works, he wasn't personally well known.
➡ (Being) **Famous** for his works, he wasn't personally well known.

Preview

If *it* **snows** a lot tomorrow, *we*'ll go skiing.
= **It snowing** a lot tomorrow, **we**'ll go skiing.
내일 눈이 많이 오면 우리는 스키를 타러 갈 거야.

① 분사구문을 만들 때 반드시 주어가 같은 경우에만 주어를 생략하고 V-ing가 이끄는 부사구로 만드는데 부사절의 주어와 주절의 주어가 서로 다른 경우 각각의 주어를 따로 모두 표기해 주는 것을 독립 분사구문이라고 한다. 분사 바로 앞에 주어를 쓴다.

As *it* **was** fine, *we* went on a picnic.
➡ **It being** fine, **we** went on a picnic. 날씨가 좋아서 우리는 소풍을 갔다.

When *I* **got** to Ken's house, *he* was having dinner.
➡ **I getting** to Ken's house, **he** was having dinner. 내가 Ken의 집에 도착했을 때 그는 저녁을 먹고 있었다.

② 주어가 서로 다르더라도, 부사절의 주어가 일반인일 경우에는 분사구문의 주어를 생략해서 하나의 숙어처럼 사용하는데 이를 비인칭 독립 분사구문이라 한다.

Frankly speaking, I was not interested in Susan. 솔직히 말하면 나는 Susan에게 관심이 없었다.

Considering your age, you did a good job. 네 나이를 감안하면 정말 잘했다.

Chapter 3

기본기 탄탄 다지기

1 두 문장의 의미가 같도록 빈칸에 알맞은 말을 쓰시오.

(1) As it snowed last night, the game was postponed.
➡ _____ last night, the game was postponed.

(2) As it was fine, we went fishing.
➡ _____ fine, we went fishing.

2 우리말에 맞도록 괄호 안의 말을 이용하여 빈칸에 알맞은 말을 쓰시오.

(1) 엄밀히 말하자면, 그건 정확하지 않다. (strictly)
➡ _____ _____, that is not correct.

(2) 그의 억양으로 판단하건대, 그는 외국인임에 틀림없다. (judging)
➡ _____ his accent, he must be a foreigner.

▶독립 분사구문에서 유도부사 there는 생략하지 않는다.
As **there** was no vacant seat, we kept standing all the way.
= **There** being no vacant seat, we kept standing all the way.
빈자리가 없어서 우리는 줄곧 서 있었다.

▶비인칭 독립 분사구문
strictly speaking 엄밀히 말하면
judging from ~로 판단하건대
frankly speaking 솔직히 말하면
generally speaking 일반적으로 말해
talking/speaking of ~에 대해 말하자면
considering (that) ~을 감안하면, 고려하면
admitting that ~은 인정하지만
granted that ~이 사실이라 해도
roughly speaking 대체로/대강 말하면

Unit 12 • with + 명사 + 분사

She listened to me **with** *her eyes* **shining**.
그녀는 눈이 반짝인 채로 내 말을 들었다.
She sat on a chair **with** *her legs* **crossed**.
그녀는 다리를 꼰 채로 의자에 앉아 있었다.

1 'with + 명사 + 분사'는 '어떤 동작이 벌어지는 상태를 가지고(with) 있다'라는 의미로 '명사가(를) ~한 채로'의 뜻이다. 현재분사와 과거분사를 결정짓는 것은 바로 명사의 행동 유무이다. 명사가 행동을 할 수 있는 주체인 경우 현재분사(V-ing)를 쓰고, 행위를 당하거나 받는 대상이 되는 경우 과거분사(V-ed)를 쓴다.

Cathy always explains things **with** *her arms* **folded**. Cathy는 항상 팔짱을 낀 채로 설명한다.

We saw our dad crying **with** *tears* **running** down his cheeks. 우리는 아빠가 뺨에 눈물을 흘리며 우는 것을 봤다.

She stood there **with** *her eyes* **closed**. 그녀는 눈을 감은 채로 거기에 서 있었다.

기본기 탄탄 다지기

1 다음 괄호 안의 단어 중에서 알맞은 것을 고르시오.

(1) I fell asleep with my TV (turned / turning) on.

(2) She spoke with tears (falling / fallen) down her cheeks.

(3) I am sure I went out with the door (locked / locking).

(4) She came in with her boots (covering / covered) in mud.

(5) I can't write with you (stood / standing) there.

(6) My mother kept sleeping with the alarm clock (rung / ringing).

> fall asleep 잠이 들다
> mud n. 진흙

서술형 기초 다지기 ④

1 다음 두 문장의 의미가 같도록 부사절을 분사구문으로 바꾼 후 생략할 수 있는 부분은 ( ) 치시오.

(1) As he was injured in his leg, the soccer player could no longer play.

➡ _____, the soccer player could no longer play.

(2) As I had been deceived by her sweet words, I couldn't believe what she said.

➡ _____, I couldn't believe what she said.

(3) After we finished the work, we watched the game on TV.

➡ _____, we watched the game on TV.

(4) Although the pyramids were built more than five thousand years ago, they still remain nearly perfect.

➡ _____,
the pyramids still remain nearly perfect.

(5) As she had not met him before, she didn't know him.

➡ _____, she didn't know him.

(6) As it was printed in haste, this book has many misprints.

➡ _____, this book has many misprints.

2 주어진 문장을 분사구문으로 고쳐 쓰시오.

(1) As it became darker, we turned the light on.

➡ _____

(2) As it was fine, they went shopping.

➡ _____

(3) As there are many umbrellas, you can have one.

➡ _____

(4) When the class was over, the children left quickly.

➡ _____

(5) After homework was done, the girls rushed out.

➡ _____

3 우리말과 뜻이 같도록 빈칸을 완성하시오.

(1) 점심 식사가 끝난 후에, 나는 도서관에 갔다.

➡ _____ finished lunch, I went to the library.

(2) 수영을 배운 적이 없어서, 그 여자는 걱정이 되었다.

➡ _____ _____ learned to swim, the woman was worried.

(3) 솔직히 말해서, 나는 너를 이해하지 못하겠다.

➡ _____ _____ , I don't understand you.

(4) 일반적으로 말하자면, 중남미인들은 낙천적이다.

➡ _____ _____ , Latin Americans are optimistic.

(5) 그 보고서로 판단하건대, 그녀는 정직한 게 분명하다.

➡ _____ _____ the report, she must be honest.

4 다음을 보기와 같이 'with + 명사 + 분사'를 이용한 문장으로 고쳐 쓰시오.

Jessica smiled and tears ran down her cheeks.
➡ Jessica smiled with tears running down her cheeks _____ .

(1) Ava worked all afternoon and the windows were locked.

➡ Ava worked all afternoon _____ .

(2) Cindy was sitting on the armchair and her legs were crossed.

➡ Cindy was sitting on the armchair _____ .

5 주어진 우리말과 같아지도록 문장을 완성하시오.

(1) 그녀는 그녀의 머리를 벽에 기댄 채로 거기에 서 있었다. (her head, lean, with)

➡ She stood there _____ against the wall.

(2) 그는 라디오를 켜 놓은 상태로 잠이 들었다. (turn on, with, the radio)

➡ He fell asleep _____ .

(3) Olivia는 눈을 감은 채로 운전을 할 수 있다. (close, her eyes, with)

➡ Olivia can drive the car _____ .

Oral Test

Challenge 1 과거분사로 시작하는 분사구문은 무엇인가?

부사절 내의 수동태 문장을 [＿＿＿＿＿＿] 또는 [＿＿＿＿＿＿＿＿] 으로 고칠 때 이 둘을 생략하여 과거분사로 시작하는 분사구문을 만든다.

As we **were excited** about the news, we **shouted** with joy.

➡ [＿＿＿＿＿＿＿] **excited** about the news, we shouted with joy.

➡ **Excited** about the news, we shouted with joy. 그 소식에 흥분한 우리는 기뻐서 소리를 질렀다.

As I **was run over** by a taxi yesterday, I'**m** black and blue all over my body.

➡ [＿＿＿＿＿＿＿] **run over** by a taxi yesterday, I'm black and blue all over my body.

➡ **Run over** by a taxi yesterday, I'm black and blue all over my body. 어제 택시에 치인 나는 온몸에 멍이 들었다.

Challenge 2 독립 분사구문이 무엇인가?

(1) 분사구문의 의미상 주어가 주절의 주어와 다를 때는 의미상 주어를 [＿＿＿＿＿＿＿] 앞에 써 주어야 한다. 주어가 서로 다른 경우 각각의 주어를 따로 모두 표기해 주는 것을 [＿＿＿＿＿＿＿] 이라고 한다.

As *it* **was** cold, *we* **stayed** at home.

➡ It **being** cold, we stayed at home. 날씨가 추워서 우리는 집에 있었다.

When *the sun* **had set**, *we* **started** for home.

➡ The sun **having set**, we started for home. 해가 지자 우리는 집으로 출발했다.

(2) 주어가 서로 다르더라도, 부사절의 주어가 'we, you, they' 등과 같은 일반인일 경우에는 분사구문의 주어를 생략해서 하나의 숙어처럼 사용하는데 이를 [＿＿＿＿＿＿＿] 이라 한다.

Generally speaking, women live longer than men. 일반적으로 여자가 남자보다 더 오래 산다.

Challenge 3 'with + 명사 + 분사'는 어떻게 해석하는가?

'with + 명사 + 분사'는 '명사(이)가 ~한 채로'라고 해석되는 분사구문이다. 여기서 분사는 명사의 동작이나 행위를 설명해 주는데, 명사가 행동이 가능한 주체인 경우 [＿＿＿＿＿] 를, 행동을 받거나 당하는 대상인 경우 [＿＿＿＿＿] 를 쓴다.

He listened to me **with** *his arms* [＿＿＿＿＿]. 그는 팔짱을 낀 채 내 말을 들었다.

She was cooking **with** *water* [＿＿＿＿＿]. 그녀는 물을 틀어놓은 채로 요리를 하고 있었다.

1 다음 문장을 분사구문으로 고칠 때 빈칸에 알맞은 말을 쓰시오.

(1) When I came into the house, I found a puppy.

➡ _____ into the house, I found a puppy.

(2) As I didn't have money, I could not buy the dress.

➡ _____ _____ money, I could not buy the dress.

2 다음 밑줄 친 부분을 고칠 때 가장 잘 고쳐진 것은?

> The poor boy couldn't play badminton with his arm breaking.

① with breaking his arm
② with broken his arm
③ with break his arm
④ with his arm to break
⑤ with his arm broken

[3–5] 다음 문장의 빈칸에 알맞은 접속사를 보기에서 골라 쓰시오.

While	Before	Though	Because

3 _____ knowing her e-mail address, I sent her an e-card.

4 _____ reading the novel, he fell asleep.

5 _____ studying very hard for six months, he failed in the exam.

6 다음 밑줄 친 부분의 쓰임이 나머지 넷과 다른 것은?

① The girl sat by the window, listening to music.
② Smiling brightly, she welcomed us.
③ Patricia was in the kitchen, making cookies.
④ Richard answered the phone, watching TV.
⑤ She is busy cooking in the kitchen.

[7–9] 다음 밑줄 친 ①~⑤ 중 생략할 수 있는 것을 모두 고르시오.

7 ① Being surrounded ② by ③ the sea, ④ Japan has a mild ⑤ climate.

8 ① Having ② been bored ③ with her job, Karen ④ is searching for ⑤ another job again.

9 ① The man ② who ③ is talking ④ to John is from ⑤ Korea.

10 다음 빈칸에 들어갈 말로 알맞은 것은?

> Driving along the lane, you'll see the farmhouse.
> = _____ you drive along the lane, you'll see the farmhouse.

① If
② While
③ Though
④ Since
⑤ When

98

11 다음 밑줄 친 부분을 바꿔 쓸 때 알맞은 것은?

> As I had spent all my money, I came home on foot.

① Spent all my money
② Having spent all my money
③ Spending all my money
④ Being spent all my money
⑤ I spent all my money

[12–13] 괄호 안의 단어를 알맞은 분사형으로 고쳐 쓰시오.

12

> Donna teaches young children. She enjoys her job, but it's often _____ (exhaust). At the end of a day's work, she is often _____ (exhaust).

13

> She's one of the most _____ (bore) people I've ever met. She never stops talking and she never says anything _____ (interest).

14 다음 중 어법상 어색한 것을 고르시오.

① Judging from the sky, it may be fine tomorrow.
② The movie made all the people bored.
③ The airplane leaves at 3 arriving there at 7.
④ He must be crazy to drive with his eyes closed.
⑤ Writing in simple English, this book is good for beginners.

15 다음 두 문장을 한 문장으로 쓸 때 빈칸을 완성하시오.

> Eric visited Ms. White in the hospital. And then he gave her a bouquet with words of comfort.
> ➡ Eric visited Ms. White in the hospital, _____ her a bouquet with words of comfort.

16 다음 두 문장의 뜻이 틀린 것은?

① Although she came with her boyfriend, she didn't tell anybody.
  ➡ Coming with her boyfriend, she didn't tell anybody.
② Because she missed her family, she sent an e-mail to her sister.
  ➡ Missing her family, she sent an e-mail to her sister.
③ They sat under the tree and they sang happily.
  ➡ Sitting under the tree, they sang happily.
④ While Tom is watching TV, we are singing.
  ➡ Watching TV, we are singing.
⑤ As it was fine yesterday, I went on a picnic.
  ➡ It being fine yesterday, I went on a picnic.

서술형 대비 문제

1 **다음 빈칸에 알맞은 말을 쓰시오.**

(1) 솔직히 말해서 그녀의 강의는 지루했다.

➡ _____, her lecture was boring.

(2) 일반적으로 말해 영어는 말하기 쉽지 않다.

➡ _____, English is not easy to speak.

2 **주어진 문장과 의미가 같도록 분사구문을 이용하여 문장을 완성하시오.**

Education has destroyed creativity and produced ordinary people.

➡ Education has destroyed creativity, _____.

3 **다음 문장에서 어법상 어색한 부분을 찾아 바르게 고쳐 쓰시오.**

It was a night when there was a full moon with a few ragged clouds drifting over it. She was found dead at the bottom of the stairs with her neck breaking. She must have tried to come down without turning on the lights.

_____ ➡ _____

4 **사진을 보고 주어진 두 문장을 분사를 이용하여 한 문장으로 완성하시오.**

The people are waiting for the bus in the rain.
They are getting wet.

➡ _____

Grammar in Reading

나 미국 보내 주고 우리 아빠 라면만 드셔!

If you want to go abroad to study a foreign language, there are a number of things you should consider before making a decision. First, you should decide which country you want to go to. For instance, in recent years, many Asian students have been going to the United States to learn English. <u>If you study in the United States, you will be able to practice English both in and out of the classroom.</u> In addition, you can meet people from all around the world, so you are in an English-speaking setting 24 hours a day. You may also have an opportunity to learn about different cultures. On the other hand, you should know there is also a disadvantage of going to the United States - the high cost.

Chapter 3

1 윗글의 밑줄 친 문장을 분사구문을 이용하여 다시 쓰시오.

➡ _____

2 What will be the next topic of this paragraph?

① various advantages of learning English in America
② outstanding learning ability of Asian students
③ inexpensive tuition for American universities
④ expenses for learning English in America
⑤ reasons why the U.S.A. is good for learning English

3 Choose the main idea of this paragraph.

① Learning foreign languages is a difficult job.
② At the moment, there are many Asian students studying English.
③ Studying abroad provides many opportunities for students.
④ There are advantages and disadvantages of studying abroad.
⑤ Learning other cultures is important.

Super Speaking

 Pair work A 보기와 같이 분사를 이용하여 묻고 답하는 형식으로 말하기 연습을 하세요. 연습이 한 번 끝난 후 서로 역할을 바꿔 다시 말하기 연습을 하세요.

the woman / hold / flowers / ?

➡ she / TV star

A: Do you know the woman holding flowers?

B: Yeah, she is a TV star. She is famous enough to be known by every teenager in Korea.

1

the girl / stand / over there / ?

➡ she / figure skater

2

the man / wear / sunglasses / ?

➡ he / superstar

Pair work B 보기와 같이 분사구문을 이용하여 묻고 답하는 형식으로 말하기 연습을 하세요. 연습이 한 번 끝난 후 서로 역할을 바꿔 다시 말하기 연습을 하세요.

the nearest subway station / ?

➡ the left

A: Could you tell me how to get to the nearest subway station?

B: Go straight ahead for one block. Turning to the left, you can find it.

1

the nearest bank / ?

➡ the right

2

the nearest convenience store

➡ the left

실전 서술형 평가 문제

출제의도 | 부사절을 분사구문으로 만들기
평가내용 | 분사구문을 이용한 상황 묘사

서술형 유형	6점
난이도	중하

 보기와 같이 주어진 사진과 일치하도록 분사구문을 이용한 문장으로 빈칸을 완성하시오.

보기 Walking along the path _____, I saw many kinds of wild flowers.

(the path, along, walk)

1

_____, she seems to be very rich.

(her appearance, judge, from)

2

_____, this book is suitable for beginners.

(English, easy, write, in)

3

_____, she always comes late.

(the school, live, near)

평가영역	채점기준	배점
유창성(Fluency) & 정확성(Accuracy)	3개의 문장을 모두 올바른 표현과 함께 정확하게 완성한 경우 (문법, 철자가 모두 정확한 경우)	3×2 = 6점
	분사구문을 만들지 못하였거나 문법, 철자가 1개씩 틀린 경우	문항당 1점씩 감점
	내용과 전혀 일치하지 않거나 답을 기재하지 못한 경우	0점

Chapter 3

출제의도 | 접속사를 생략하여 분사구문으로 있었던 일 나타내기

평가내용 | 분사구문 만들기

서술형 유형	6점
난이도	중

B 다음은 하루 동안 Alice가 한 일들이다. 주어진 표현을 이용하여 Alice가 한 일들을 보기와 같이 묘사하시오.

보기

AM 8:00
➡ go jogging in the morning

listen to music

1

PM 12:00
➡ meet my boyfriend at lunch time

eat spaghetti

2

PM 2:00
➡ watch a scary movie with my friends in the afternoon

eat popcorn

3

PM 6:00
➡ clean the floor in the evening

listen to the radio

보기 Listening to music, Alice went (was going) jogging in the morning.

1 _____

2 _____

3 _____

평가영역	채점기준	배점
유창성(Fluency) & 정확성(Accuracy)	3개의 문장을 모두 올바른 표현과 함께 정확하게 완성한 경우 (문법, 철자가 모두 정확한 경우)	3×2 = 6점
	분사구문을 만들지 못하였거나 문법, 철자가 1개씩 틀린 경우	문항당 1점씩 감점
	내용과 전혀 일치하지 않거나 답을 기재하지 못한 경우	0점

출제의도 | 분사를 이용하여 감정 나타내기
평가내용 | 감정을 나타내는 분사

서술형 유형	8점
난이도	중

 C 괄호 안의 말을 이용하여 알맞은 현재분사와 과거분사를 써서 문장을 완성하시오.

Jessica is reading a book. She really likes it. She can't put it down. She has to keep reading.

1 The book is really _____ . (interest)

2 Jessica is really _____ . (interest)

3 The story is _____ . (excite)

4 Jessica is _____ about the story. (excite)

5 The people in the story are _____ . (fascinate)

6 Jessica doesn't like to read books when she is _____ and _____ . (bore, confuse)

7 Jessica didn't finish the last book she started because it was _____ and _____ . (bore, confuse)

8 What is the most _____ book you've read lately? (interest)

평가영역	채점기준	배점
유창성(Fluency) & 정확성(Accuracy)	8개의 문장을 모두 올바른 표현과 함께 정확하게 완성한 경우 (문법, 철자가 모두 정확한 경우)	8×1 = 8점
	분사를 만들지 못하였거나 문법, 철자가 1개씩 틀린 경우	문항당 1점씩 감점
	내용과 전혀 일치하지 않거나 답을 기재하지 못한 경우	0점

Chapter 4
시제

That T-shirt is very cheap. I **will** buy it.
저 티셔츠는 매우 싸다. 그것을 살 거야.

The restaurant **opens** at ten tomorrow morning.
그 레스토랑은 내일 아침 10시에 연다.

1 미래의 일을 예측 또는 추측(prediction)하거나 앞으로 일어날 객관적인 사실을 표현할 때 will과 be going to 를 구별 없이 쓴다.

The population of older people **will** increase. 노인 인구가 증가할 것이다.
= The population of older people **is going to** increase.

2 be going to는 말하기 전부터 이미 마음의 결정을 해 놓은 계획(prior plans)을 나타낼 때 쓴다. 이미 예정되어 있는 일에는 will을 쓰지 않는다.

We**'re going to** visit the zoo on Sunday. 우리는 일요일에 그 동물원에 방문할 거야.
When **are** you **going to** go on holiday? 언제 휴가를 갈 예정이니?

3 이미 정해진 일정 또는 기차, 영화, 비행기 시간표와 같이 확실히 정해진 일정에는 현재시제가 미래를 나타낸 다. leave, arrive, start, come, begin, end, close, open 등이 자주 쓰이는 동사들이다.

The Olympic Games **takes place** every four years. 올림픽은 4년마다 개최된다.
The concert **begins** at nine tonight. 그 콘서트는 오늘 밤 9시에 시작한다.

기본기 탄탄 다지기

1 다음 괄호 안에서 알맞은 표현을 고르시오.

(1) We've just heard that Julie needs some help. We (will / are going to) help her.

(2) My grandfather (will / is going to) move to Florida next week.

(3) The movie (is going to begin / begins) at 10:00 tomorrow morning.

(4) A: What are you going to do this evening?
B: I (will / am going to) watch a movie with Kevin.

(5) People (will / are going to) find life on other planets.

(6) My plane (arrives / is going to arrive) at 5:00 tomorrow afternoon.

▶말하는 순간에 결정한 일이나 '~하 겠다'라는 의지(willingness)를 나타낼 때는 will을 쓴다.
Maybe we **will** stay in and watch television tonight.

▶말하는 사람의 마음과 관계없이 눈 앞에 뻔히 일어날 상황을 말할 때는 현재의 상황이나 증거를 바탕으로 '~ 할 것이다'라고 예측하는 경우에는 be going to를 쓴다.
Look at those clouds! It's **going to** rain soon.
The woman is walking toward the hole now, so she **is going to** fall into it.

Unit 2 • 미래시제 2

He **is meeting** his first love this Saturday.
그는 이번 토요일에 그의 첫사랑을 만날 예정이다.
If she **gets** a job, she will buy a car.
직업을 갖게 되면 그녀는 차를 살 것이다.

1 개인의 정해진 일정에는 현재진행 시제로 미래를 나타낼 수 있다. be going to와 같은 의미로 쓰인다. 단, 기차, 비행기 시간표나 영화 상영 시간표는 현재시제를 써서 정해진 일정을 나타낸다.

We**'re having** a party next Saturday. 우리는 다음 주 토요일에 파티를 할 예정이다.

= We**'re going to** have a party next Saturday.

Sally **is flying** to Tokyo in two hours. Sally는 2시간 후에 비행기로 도쿄에 갈 예정이다.

2 조건의 부사절(if, unless)과 시간의 부사절(when, before, after, until) 안의 시제는 반드시 현재시제를 써서 미래를 나타낸다. 미래를 뜻한다 하더라도 will을 쓰지 않는다.

I will give you a call **when** she **arrives** here. 그녀가 도착하면 네게 전화해 줄게.

If you **visit** the zoo, you will be amazed. 그 동물원에 방문하면 너는 놀라게 될 거다.

He will miss the bus **unless** he **walks** more quickly. 더 빨리 걷지 않으면 그는 버스를 놓칠 거다.

기본기 탄탄 다지기

1 주어진 괄호 안의 시제를 알맞은 형태로 고쳐 빈칸을 완성하시오.

(1) I _____ _____ Jane at 8 o'clock on Saturday. (meet)

(2) The game _____ at 3 o'clock tomorrow afternoon. (start)

(3) If you _____ me now, I won't see you again. (leave)

(4) I'll stay home until I _____ over my cold. (get)

(5) The soccer game _____ at 7 and _____ at 10. (start / end)

(6) What time do you _____ college tonight? (finish)

(7) When _____ you _____ your holiday this summer? (take)

(8) If I don't do my homework tonight, I _____ _____ in trouble tomorrow. (be)

▶개인의 정해진 일정에 현재진행 시제로 미래를 나타내는데 특히 움직임을 나타내는 동사 또는 교통을 나타내는 come, go, fly, travel, leave 등과 자주 쓰인다.
Tomorrow I'm **going** to a concert.

▶명사절과 형용사절 안의 시제가 미래를 나타낼 때는 미래시제를 쓴다.
I don't know **when** they **will come** back home.
I wonder **if** Peter **will win** the race tomorrow.
She thinks about the day **when** she **will be** a mother.

▶몇 분 이내에 일어날 아주 가까운 미래를 표현할 때는 be about to를 쓴다. '막 ~하려고 한다'의 뜻이다.
The movie **is about to** begin.

Unit 3 ● 현재완료 시제

Have you ever **eaten** Korean food?
한국음식 먹어본 적 있니?

I **have forgotten** my umbrella.
나는 내 우산을 놓고 왔다.

① 현재완료 시제는 'have(has) + V−ed(과거분사)'로 만들고 <mark>과거에 시작한 일</mark>과 '지금은 ～하다'라는 의미를 둘 다 포함하고 있는 시제이다. 과거에 일어난 일이 현재까지 영향을 미치어 '현재까지 ～했다'의 뜻이 된다.

용법	예문	의미
경험	**Have** you *ever* **seen** a koala? 코알라를 본적 있니?	과거부터 현재까지의 반복된 일이나 경험을 나타내고 주로 ever, never, before, once, often과 함께 쓴다.
완료	She **has** *just* **arrived** at the restaurant. 그녀는 막 그 레스토랑에 도착했다.	과거에 시작하여 조금 전 또는 최근에 완료된 일. '지금 막 ～했다'로 해석하고 주로 just, already, yet, now, recently와 함께 쓴다.
계속	I **have studied** Spanish *for* eight months. 나는 8개월 동안 스페인어를 공부하고 있다.	과거에 시작된 동작이나 상태가 현재까지 계속되고 있는 일을 나타내고 주로 for, since와 함께 쓴다.
결과	She **has broken** her leg. 그녀는 다리가 부러졌다.	과거의 일이 현재 어떤 결과를 낳아 영향을 미칠 때 사용하고 주로 lost, has gone to와 함께 쓴다.

기본기 탄탄 다지기

1 다음 문장의 현재완료 시제의 용법을 구분하시오.

(1) Have you ever seen a UFO? _____

(2) Jane's looking for her key. She has lost it. _____

(3) I've already arrived here. _____

(4) She has taught English at her school for 5 years. _____

2 다음 괄호 안의 말을 현재완료 시제로 고쳐 빈칸에 쓰시오.

(1) She _____ _____ Chinese since she was 10 years old. (learn)

(2) The man _____ _____ _____ the broken roof yet. (not / fix)

(3) I _____ _____ in Seoul for 5 years. (live)

(4) My child _____ _____ Harry Potter over three times. (read)

▶have gone to와 have been to는 형태가 비슷하나 그 뜻이 전혀 다르므로 주의한다.
1. have gone to + 장소 : ～에 가버렸다 (그래서 지금 여기 없다) (결과, 완료)
She **has** gone to Toronto.
2. have been to + 장소 : ～에 가본 적이 있다(경험), ～에 갔다 왔다(완료)
She **has** never **been** to Toronto.

▶현재완료는 명확한 과거를 나타내는 부사(구)(yesterday, last～, then, ～ago, just now)와 의문사 when과 함께 쓸 수 없다.
They have arrived in Busan yesterday. (X)
→ They **arrived** in Busan **yesterday**. (O)
She has studied English literature when she was at college. (X)
→ She **studied** English literature **when** she was at college. (O)

서술형 기초 다지기 ❶

1 보기와 같이 be going to를 이용하여 문장을 완성하시오.

airplane

Q: Is Nancy going to travel by train?

A: No, she isn't. She is going to travel by airplane.

(1)

Q: Are they going to make a special dessert this evening?

A: _____

watch a movie

(2)

Q: Is Jessica going to have a party next week?

A: _____

go to Seoul

2 주어진 문장을 읽고 문장이 뜻하는 바가 현재이면 present, 미래이면 future를 쓰시오.

(1) Where is Jack? Is he working?　　　　　　　　　　　　　　　_____

(2) Are you going out tonight?　　　　　　　　　　　　　　　　_____

(3) That tree's growing very fast.　　　　　　　　　　　　　　_____

(4) My parents are coming to stay with me this weekend.　　　_____

3 다음 괄호 안의 말을 현재완료 시제로 빈칸을 완성하고 용법을 구별하시오.

(1) _____ you ever _____ a TV star? (meet)　　　　_____

(2) I _____ already _____ the Internet but found nothing. (search)　_____

(3) She _____ _____ to Brazil. (go)　　　　　　　_____

(4) Steve _____ _____ for this company for 5 years. (work)　_____

4 다음 단어들을 이용하여 미래의 의미를 지닌 현재시제 문장을 만드시오.

(1) the meeting / begin / at 9 tomorrow morning

➡ _____

(2) there / be / a conference / at 10:00 tonight

➡ _____

5 괄호 안의 말을 이용하여 빈칸에 알맞은 시제를 써 넣으시오.

(1) Before Kathy _____ home today, she _____ her homework. (go / do)

(2) If I _____ some time off this winter, I _____ to Brazil for my vacation. (get / go)

(3) When I _____ back to Sao Paulo, I _____ to the beach. (get / go)

(4) As soon as I _____, I _____ on light clothes and _____ in the sun. (arrive / put / walk)

6 다음 괄호 안의 동사를 이용하여 현재완료 문장을 만드시오.

(1) Peter can't play soccer and his leg is in a cast.

➡ He _____. (break)

(2) The light was off, Now it is on.

➡ Somebody _____. (turn)

(3) This morning I was expecting a letter. Now I have it.

➡ The letter _____. (arrive)

7 보기와 같이 주어진 표현과 be going to를 이용하여 상황에 맞는 문장을 쓰시오.

Alice has a camera.

➡ She is going to take a picture. _____

take a picture

(1)

Bob is in a restaurant.

➡ _____

order a meal

(2)

Sue is in the supermarket.

➡ _____

buy some fruit

Oral Test

Chapter 4

Challenge 1 will과 be going to의 쓰임을 정확히 알고 있는가?

(1) 미래의 일을 단순히 예측하거나 앞으로 일어날 일에는 will과 be going to 둘 다 쓸 수 있지만 말하기 전부터 이미 마음의 결정을 해 놓은 예정된 계획에는 반드시 [   ]를 쓴다.

It **will** snow tomorrow. = It **is going to** snow tomorrow. 내일 눈이 올 것 같다.
I**'m going to** wear my black dress tonight. 나는 오늘 밤에 검은색 드레스를 입을 거야.

(2) 기차, 영화, 비행기 시간표와 같이 이미 확실히 정해져 있는 일정에는 [   ]를 써서 미래를 나타낸다.

There **is** a conference next Friday. 다음 주 금요일에 회담이 열린다.
What time does the movie **begin** tomorrow? 내일 그 영화가 몇 시에 시작하니?

Challenge 2 미래를 나타내는 중요 표현들은 어떤 것들이 있을까?

(1) 어떤 일을 하기로 이미 정한 개인의 일정에는 [   ] 시제로 미래를 나타낼 수 있다.

We**'re taking** a trip to Brazil next month. 우리는 다음 달에 브라질로 여행을 갈 예정이다.

(2) 조건의 부사절과 시간의 부사절이 미래의 뜻을 내포하더라도 미래시제를 쓰지 않고 반드시 [   ]를 써서 미래를 나타낸다. 몇 분 이내에 일어날 아주 가까운 미래로 '막 ~하려고 한다'는 [   ]로 나타낸다.

She will look for a job **after** she **graduates**. 그녀는 졸업한 후에 직업을 찾을 것이다.
Tom **is about to** open the window. Tom은 막 창문을 열려고 한다.

Challenge 3 현재완료의 대표적인 4가지 용법을 알고 있는가?

현재완료 시제는 과거에 시작한 일이 현재 시점에 완료된 행동 및 상황을 말한다. 형태는 [   ]로 쓴다. 과거에 시작한 일과 지금은 어떠한지를 모두 포함하고 있으므로 '현재까지 ~했다'의 뜻으로 해석한다.

[   ] : 과거부터 현재까지의 반복된 일이나 경험을 나타낸다.

Have you *ever* **seen** the sunrise? 해돋이를 본 적이 있니?

[   ] : 과거에 시작하여 방금 전 또는 최근에 완료된 일을 나타낸다.

Have you **finished** your homework *yet*? 숙제를 벌써 끝냈니?

[   ] : 과거에 시작된 동작이나 상태가 현재까지 계속되고 있는 일을 나타낸다.

They **have been** at the hotel *for* a week. 그들은 일주일째 그 호텔에 머물고 있다.

[   ] : 과거의 일이 현재 어떤 결과를 낳아 영향을 미칠 때 사용한다.

Someone **has broken** the window. 누군가 창문을 깼다.

Unit 4 ● 현재완료 계속적 용법

Preview

Lisa started to study Korean in 2010. She still studies it. It is 2013.
Lisa는 2010년에 한국어 공부를 시작했다. 그녀는 아직도 한국어를 공부하고 있다. 2013년이다.

→ She **has studied** Korean **for** 3 years. Lisa는 3년 동안 한국어를 공부하고 있다.
→ She **has studied** Korean **since** 2010. Lisa는 2010년부터 한국어를 공부하고 있다.

1 현재완료 계속은 과거에 시작하여 현재까지 계속 이어지는 동작이나 상태를 나타낸다. '과거부터 지금까지 쭉 ~해왔다'의 뜻으로 for/ since가 이끄는 부사구와 함께 쓴다. for(~동안에)는 시간의 길이(a length of time)를 나타내고 since(~이래로)는 과거에 시작된 특정한 시점(starting point)을 나타낸다.

I **have known** Jennifer **for** ten years. 나는 Jennifer를 10년 동안 알고 지내고 있다.
We **have been** here **since** eight o'clock. 우리는 8시부터 여기에 있었다.
My sister **has lived** in New York **for** ten years. 내 언니는 뉴욕에서 10년 동안 살고 있다.

2 since 뒤에는 '주어 + 동사'가 올 수 있는데, 이때 동사는 과거에 시작한 특정한 시점을 나타내므로 반드시 '과거시제'를 써야 한다.

I**'ve studied** English *since* I **was** a middle school student. 나는 중학생 때부터 영어를 공부해 오고 있다.
Rebecca **has worked** here *since* she **finished** university. Rebecca는 대학을 졸업한 이후로 이곳에서 일하고 있다.

기본기 탄탄 다지기

1 다음 글을 읽고 빈칸에 for 또는 since를 알맞게 쓰시오.

(1) He has worked here _____ two years.

(2) I have not visited the art museum _____ 2004.

(3) I've had a bad cold _____ almost a week.

(4) Sunny hasn't eaten anything _____ yesterday.

2 주어진 단어를 활용하여 현재완료 시제를 만들고, 괄호 안의 표현 중 알맞은 것을 고르시오.

(1) I _____ (not, be) to Europe since I (return / returned)
in 1999.

(2) Jane _____ (study) Japanese since she (was / is)
a student.

(3) Not you but I _____ (know) the news since I first
(met / meet) her.

▶ when은 과거의 한 시점을 나타내기 때문에 현재완료와 함께 쓰지 않는다.
She **has loved** chocolate **since** she was a little girl.
She **loved** chocolate **when** she was a little girl.

▶ 현재완료 시제와 함께 How long~? 으로 물어보는 의문문은 과거에 시작하여 현재까지 계속되고 있는 행동이나 상태를 물어보므로 for 또는 since가 있는 현재완료의 계속적 용법으로 대답한다.
A: How long have they been married?
B: They've been married **for** 10 years.

Unit 5 ● 과거시제 VS. 현재완료 시제

Scott **was** a teacher for 7 years. Scott은 7년 동안 선생님이었다.
(과거에 시작해서 과거에 끝나 지금은 선생님이 아님.)

Eric **has been** a teacher for 7 years. Eric은 7년 동안 선생님을 하고 있다.
(과거에 시작해서 지금도 선생님임.)

1 과거시제는 과거에 있었던 사실을 전달하는 것이 주요 목적이므로 현재와는 전혀 무관하며, 현재완료는 과거의 특정 시간이 중요하지 않은 현재 시점에 완료된 동작이나 현재까지 지속되고 있는 동작이나 상태를 나타낸다.

과거시제	현재완료 시제
과거에 시작한 일이 과거에 끝나 현재와는 아무런 관련 없이 과거 사실만 전달한다. We **lived** in California for ten years. 우리는 캘리포니아에서 10년 동안 살았다.	현재까지 영향을 미치는 동작이나 상태이며, 과거의 특정한 시간이 중요하지 않고 언급하지도 않는다. We **have lived** in California for ten years. 우리는 캘리포니아에서 10년 동안 살고 있다.
정확한 과거 시점을 언급하고 싶을 때는 과거시제를 쓰고 주로 특정 과거를 나타내는 부사(구)와 함께 쓴다. (ago, yesterday, last night(year, month, week), in + 과거 연대) She **finished** her homework two hours **ago**. 그녀는 2시간 전에 숙제를 끝마쳤다.	과거의 동작을 나타내지만 과거의 특정한 때를 알 수 없고 과거의 특정한 때를 나타내는 부사(구)와 함께 쓰지 않는다. **Have** you ever **seen** a ghost? 귀신을 본 적이 있니?

기본기 탄탄 다지기

1 괄호 안의 시제 중 알맞은 것을 고르시오.

explode v. 폭발하다
geography n. 지리학

(1) They (learned / have learned) Chinese since 2012.

(2) The car (exploded / has exploded) at 9:30 a.m. yesterday.

(3) They (haven't visited / didn't visit) the city yet.

(4) Kevin (visited / has visited) Thailand when he was a child.

(5) She (was / has been) in China since June.

(6) I (read / have read) the book two hours ago.

(7) William (has studied / studied) geography since he went to college.

Unit 6 · 현재완료 진행시제

Ava began to watch TV three hours ago, and she is still watching TV.
Ava는 3시간 전에 TV를 보기 시작했고 지금도 여전히 보고 있다.
→ How long **has** she **been watching** TV? 그녀는 얼마나 오랫동안 TV를 보고 있니?
→ She **has been watching** TV for three hours. 그녀는 3시간 동안 TV를 보고 있다.

1 현재완료 진행은 과거에 시작해서 현재까지 진행 중인 동작을 강조할 때 쓴다. 형태는 'have(has) been + V-ing'이고 '계속 ~하고 있다'의 뜻으로 해석한다.

It started to snow last night. It's still snowing.

→ It **has been snowing** since last night. 어젯밤부터 눈이 내리고 있다.

I started to use the Internet two hours ago. I'm still using it.

→ I **have been using** the Internet for two hours. 나는 2시간 동안 인터넷을 쓰고 있다.

2 현재완료 진행형은 과거에 시작하여 현재도 진행 중임을 강조하고, 현재진행 시제(be + V-ing)는 과거에 시작하여 얼마나 오랫동안 계속되고 있는지는 중요하지 않고 지금 현재 눈으로 보고 말하는 진행 중인 동작을 나타낸다.

They **have been talking** for two hours. 그들은 2시간 동안 얘기하고 있다.

Look at that woman! She **is running** toward us. 저 여자를 봐! 그녀는 우리에게 달려오고 있어.

기본기 탄탄 다지기

1 다음 우리말과 뜻이 같도록 괄호 안의 동사를 현재완료 진행시제로 만드시오.

(1) 그녀는 3시간 동안 공부를 하고 있다.

  → She _____ for 3 hours. (study)

(2) 그는 2시간 동안 월드컵을 보고 있는 중이다.

  → He _____ the World Cup for 2 hours.

(3) 5시간째 비가 내리고 있다.

  → It _____ for 5 hours. (rain)

(4) 얼마나 오랫동안 영어를 배우고 있니?

  → How long _____ you _____ English?
  (learn)

> ▶How long은 완료시제와 함께 쓰고 When은 과거시제와 함께 쓴다.
>
> A: When did it start raining?
> B: It began raining an hour ago.
>
> A: How long has it been raining?
> B: It has been raining for an hour.

서술형 기초 다지기 ②

1 주어진 두 문장을 보기와 같이 for과 since를 이용한 현재완료 진행시제의 문장을 만드시오.

> The rain started two hours ago. It's still raining now.
> ➡ It has been raining for two hours.

(1) Gina started to collect stamps since high school. She's still collecting them.

➡ _____

(2) Lisa is sitting in the sun. She began to sit at 2:00. It's now 4:00.

➡ _____

(3) John started to travel around the world in 2011. He's still traveling.

➡ _____

(4) They started to play basketball four hours ago. They're still playing basketball.

➡ _____

2 주어진 동사를 과거 또는 현재완료를 이용하여 빈칸을 완성하시오.

(1) A: I _____ (see) Nancy yesterday.

B: Oh, really? I _____ (not / see) her for weeks.

(2) A: _____ you ever _____ (eat) at Outback Steak House?

B: Yes, I have. I _____ (eat) there many times. In fact, my daughter and I _____ (eat) there last night.

(3) A: What _____ you _____ (do) last Saturday?

B: I _____ (stay) at home.

(4) A: _____ you _____ (be) to the United States?

B: Yes, I _____ (go) to Miami last winter.

(5) A: I _____ (known) Bob for two years.

B: Really? When _____ you _____ (meet) him?

3 보기와 같이 for과 since를 이용하여 현재완료 계속적 용법의 문장을 완성하시오.

> I / work / here / six years
> ➡ I have worked here for six years.

(1) My dad / study / Korean / 1999.

➡ _____

(2) I / not see / Karen / she left for Singapore

➡ _____

(3) We / be / in Paris / we were married

➡ _____

(4) My wife and I / known / each other / we were in high school

➡ _____

(5) Alice / read / three science books / Tuesday

➡ _____

4 다음 문장을 보기와 같이 how long과 when을 이용한 의문문을 만드시오.

> She's waiting for a bus.　➡ How long has she been waiting for a bus?
> 　　　　　　　　　　　　➡ When did she start waiting for a bus?

(1) He is speaking on the phone.　➡ _____
　　　　　　　　　　　　　　　➡ _____

(2) It's raining.　➡ _____
　　　　　　　➡ _____

(3) Peter is using this book.　➡ _____
　　　　　　　　　　　　　➡ _____

(4) Jessica is learning the Present Perfect.
　　　　　　　　　　　　　➡ _____
　　　　　　　　　　　　　➡ _____

Oral Test

Challenge 1 현재완료 계속적 용법은 언제 사용하는가?

'과거부터 지금까지 쭉 ~해왔다'의 뜻으로 현재완료 계속은 for나 since와 함께 쓴다. [   ]는 과거에 시작된 특정한 시작점을 나타내고 [   ]는 시간의 길이를 나타낸다.

I haven't eaten anything *since* breakfast. 나는 아침식사 이후로 아무것도 먹지 않았다.

The weather **has been** quite hot *since* last week. 지난주부터 날씨가 꽤 덥다.

Challenge 2 과거시제와 현재완료 시제의 차이를 정확히 알고 있는가?

과거에 이미 끝나 현재와는 아무런 관련이 없는 경우 [   ] 시제를 쓰고, 과거에 시작하여 현재까지 지속되고 있는 동작이나 상태 또는 과거에 대한 얘기를 하지만 결국 말하고자 하는 것은 현재의 상황일 때 [   ] 시제를 쓴다.

Kimberly **left** the office an hour ago. Why don't you call her at home?
Kimberly는 한 시간 전에 사무실을 나갔어요. 집으로 한번 전화해 보세요.

They **have built** a big house next to the building. 그들은 그 건물 옆에 큰 집을 지었다.

Challenge 3 현재완료 진행시제는 언제 쓰는가?

(1) 과거에 시작해서 현재까지 [   ] 중인 동작을 강조하고자 할 때는 현재완료 진행형을 쓰며 형태는 [   ]로 쓴다. 현재완료 계속적 용법을 쓸 수도 있는데 진행 중인 동작을 강조하거나, 특히 상태가 아닌 동작이 계속됨을 나타낼 때는 현재완료보다는 현재완료 진행시제를 더 많이 쓴다.

She **has been making** her own homepage all day. 그녀는 온종일 자기 홈페이지를 만들고 있는 중이다.

Steve **has met** many people **since** he came here. Steve는 여기에 온 이후로 많은 사람들을 만났다.

(2) When은 [   ] 시제와 함께 쓰고 How long은 [   ] 시제와 함께 쓴다.

When did she **start** eating breakfast? 그녀가 언제 아침식사를 하기 시작했니?

How long has she **been eating** breakfast? 그녀는 얼마나 오랫동안 아침식사를 하고 있니?

Unit 7 • 과거완료 시제

Preview

The train left at 9 o'clock. We arrived at 9:15.
그 열차는 9시에 떠났다. 우리는 9시 15분에 도착했다.
➡ When we arrived, the train **had** already **left**.
우리가 도착했을 때 그 열차는 이미 떠났다.

1 과거에 발생한 일은 과거시제(the simple past)를 쓴다. 과거보다 더 이전에 일어난 일, 즉 과거보다 더 과거는 어떻게 표현할까? 바로 과거완료(had + V−ed)를 쓴다. 두 개의 동작 중 어느 것이 먼저 일어났는지를 시간적으로 명확히 구분하고자 할 때 과거완료를 쓴다. 과거보다 더 먼저 발생한 일은 과거완료를 쓰고 나중에 일어난 일은 과거시제로 쓴다.

I **had written** the letter before you **came** home. 나는 네가 집에 오기 전에 그 편지를 썼다.
  1st Action   2nd Action

She **bought** a car when she **had saved** enough money. 그녀는 충분한 돈을 모았을 때 차를 구입했다.
  2nd Action   1st Action

2 현재완료(have + V−ed)는 현재와 관련이 있지만, 과거완료(had + V−ed)는 과거에 시작한 일이 과거의 어느 시점까지 영향을 미친 경우이므로 현재와 아무런 관련이 없다.

We aren't tired. We **have walked** in Central Park. 우리는 피곤하지 않다. 우리는 센트럴 파크를 걸었다.

We weren't tired. We **had walked** in Central Park. 우리는 피곤하지 않았다. 우리는 센트럴 파크를 걸었었다.

기본기 탄탄 다지기

1 다음 글을 읽고 괄호 안에서 알맞은 시제를 고르시오.

(1) When we arrived at the airport, the plane (took / had taken) off.

(2) She had studied Korean for two years when she (had gone / went) to Seoul.

(3) The lawyer (went / had gone) somewhere, so the client had to wait.

(4) They (had done / did) their project last week.

(5) I (have had / had had) four tests so far this semester.

(6) We aren't hungry. We (had eaten / have eaten) lunch.

(7) Mom (have / had) fixed dinner before Dad got home from work.

▶ 과거완료도 현재완료와 마찬가지로 완료, 경험, 계속, 결과의 뜻을 나타낼 수 있다. 하지만 과거완료는 과거에 이미 끝난 동작이나 상태이므로 현재와는 아무 관련이 없다.

▶ 일상영어에서는 과거완료는 자주 쓰는 시제가 아니다. 특히 원어민들은 before와 after 같이 어떤 일이 먼저 일어났는지를 정확히 알 수 있는 경우에는 과거완료를 쓰지 않고 과거시제를 쓴다.

After I **had finished** my homework, I watched TV.
After I **finished** my homework, I watched TV. (more natural)

Unit 8 ● 현재완료 VS. 현재완료 진행

Preview

Kevin **has fixed** the radio. Kevin은 그 라디오를 고쳤다.
(수리가 모두 끝남)

James **has been fixing** the radio. James는 그 라디오를 고치고 있다.
(수리가 끝나지 않고 진행 중임)

① 현재완료는 이미 불특정한 과거에 끝난 동작이나 상태를 나타내는 반면, 현재완료 진행은 곧 끝나거나 아직 끝나지 않고 지금도 계속 진행되고 있는 동작을 의미한다.

She **has done** her homework. (She isn't doing it right now.) 그녀는 숙제를 했다.
She **has been doing** her homework. (She is doing it now.) 그녀는 숙제를 하고 있다.

② 현재완료 계속과 현재완료 진행은 둘 다 과거부터 지금까지 계속 진행되고 있는 동작을 나타내어 큰 의미 차이가 없어 보이나 차이가 있다면 현재완료 진행이 현재진행 중임을 더 강조한다는 것이다.

Carl **has read** the papers so far. Carl은 지금까지 그 서류를 읽었다.
Carl **has read** the papers for two hours. Carl은 2시간 동안 그 서류를 읽고 있다.
Carl **has been reading** the papers for two hours. Carl은 2시간 동안 그 서류를 읽고 있는 중이다.

기본기 탄탄 다지기

1 다음 괄호 안의 동사를 현재완료 또는 현재완료 진행으로 만들어 빈칸을 완성하시오.
(둘 다 가능한 경우 현재완료 진행시제를 쓰시오.)

(1) Judy _____ (jog) in the park for an hour.

(2) I _____ (study) French since I was in primary
school.

(3) She _____ (wash) her car. Now it is clean.

(4) He _____ (lose) his wallet. He can't find it.

(5) Julia _____ (talk) with her friend for an hour.

(6) My parents _____ (go) fishing. They'll be back in
five hours.

(7) Sara _____ (just / eat) a healthy salad for lunch.

▶ live, work, teach, rain, snow, study, stay, wear 등과 같은 동사는 현재완료 계속과 현재완료 진행을 for와 since의 부사구와 함께 둘 다 큰 의미 차이 없이 쓴다.

I've lived in Egypt for 5 years.
= I've been living in Egypt for 5 years.

She has taught for nine years.
= She has been teaching for nine years.

Preview

Frank started waiting at 9:00. I arrived at 11:00.
Frank는 9시부터 기다리기 시작했다. 나는 11시에 도착했다.

When I **arrived**, Frank **had been waiting** for two hours.
내가 도착했을 때 Frank는 2시간 동안 기다리고 있었다.

1 과거완료 진행시제는 'had been + V-ing'로 쓰며, 두 개의 동작 중 어느 것이 먼저 일어났는지를 시간적으로 구별함과 동시에 진행 중인 동작을 강조하기 위해 사용한다. 과거보다 더 먼저 발생하여 계속된 동작을 강조할 때는 과거완료 진행을 쓰고 나중에 일어난 일은 과거시제를 쓴다.

We **had been playing** soccer for an hour when it **started** to rain.
우리는 비가 내리기 시작했을 때 한 시간 동안 축구를 하고 있었다.

I **had been waiting** for 30 minutes before the bus **came**. 나는 버스가 오기 전까지 30분 동안 기다리고 있었다.

Ava **didn't** show up until 4 o'clock. We **had been waiting** for two hours.
Ava는 4시가 되어서야 나타났다. 우리는 2시간 동안 기다리고 있었다.

2 과거완료 진행시제는 과거에 발생한 어떤 일에 대한 원인을 나타내고 과거시제는 결과를 나타낸다.

Her eyes **were tired**. She **had been using** her smartphone for hours.
　　　　　결과　　　　　　　　　　　원인
그녀의 눈은 피곤했다. 그녀는 몇 시간 동안 스마트폰을 사용하고 있었다.

기본기 탄탄 다지기

1 괄호 안의 시제 중 알맞은 것을 고르시오.

(1) It had been snowing for a while before we (left / had been leaving).

(2) I realized I (had / have) been working too hard, so I decided to have a holiday.

(3) Jennifer's eyes were red because she (have / had) been crying.

(4) It had been raining for a week when I (am arriving / arrived) in Seoul.

(5) James (has / had) been teaching at the University since June.

(6) The students were confused. They (have / had) been trying to learn the Past Perfect Continuous.

▶다음 문장의 시제 차이를 구별해 보라.
· John **had cooked** breakfast when we got up.
· John **had been cooking** breakfast when we got up.
· John **cooked** breakfast when we got up.

첫 번째 문장은 우리가 일어나기 전에 아침식사 준비를 막 완료된 경우이고, 두 번째 문장은 우리가 일어나기 이전에 식사 준비를 하고 있던 진행 중인 동작을 강조하고 있다. 마지막 문장은 먼저 우리가 일어났고 그리고 나서 John이 아침을 만든 것이다.

서술형 기초 다지기 ❸

1 다음 우리말과 같도록 괄호 안의 단어를 알맞은 시제로 고쳐 문장을 완성하시오.

(1) Ava가 도착했을 때 Tom은 아파트를 떠났다.

➡ Tom _____(leave) his apartment when Ava _____(arrive).

(2) 우리가 파티에 도착했을 때 Lisa는 이미 집으로 갔다.

➡ When we _____(get) to the party, Lisa _____(already, go) home.

(3) Alex는 그의 여자 친구에게 편지를 보낸 후에 극장에 갔다.

➡ After Alex _____(send) a letter to his girlfriend, he _____(go) to the movie theater.

(4) Jason은 자러 가기 전에 현관문을 잠갔다.

➡ Jason _____(lock) the front door before he _____(go) to bed.

(5) 나는 카우아이로 가기 전에는 그렇게 아름다운 해변을 본 적이 없었다.

➡ Before I _____(go) to Kauai, I _____(never, see) such a beautiful beach.

(6) Susan은 태국으로 이사 가기 전에 태국어를 공부했다.

➡ Susan _____(study) Thai before she _____(move) to Thailand.

2 다음 괄호 안의 지시대로 문장을 완성하시오.

(1) How long have you jogged? (현재완료 진행시제로)

➡ _____

(2) It had rained for several hours. (과거완료 진행시제로)

➡ _____

(3) She had worked as a CEO for five years. (과거완료 진행시제로)

➡ _____

(4) Nancy has spoken on the phone since six o'clock. (현재완료 진행시제로)

➡ _____

(5) Jessica has visited her aunt and uncle for the last three days. (현재완료 진행시제로)

➡ _____

3 보기와 같이 주어진 단어를 이용하여 과거완료 진행시제 문장으로 만드시오.

> William was very tired when he got home.
> ➡ William had been working hard all day.   (William / work / hard / all day)

(1) When I got home, Mom was sitting in front of TV. She had just turned it off.

➡ _____ (she / watch / TV)

(2) The two girls came into the house. One had a black eye and the other had a cut lip.

➡ _____ (they / fight)

(3) The two boys came into the house. They had a soccer ball and they were both very tired.

➡ _____ (they / play / soccer)

(4) There was nobody in the room, but there was the smell of cigarette smoke.

➡ _____ (somebody / smoke / in the room)

(5) When Helen came back from the beach, she looked very red from the sun.

➡ _____ (she / lie / in the sun / too long)

4 보기와 같이 괄호 안의 단어들을 이용하여 과거완료 시제 문장으로 쓰시오.

> I wasn't hungry.
> ➡ I had just eaten two hamburgers.   (I / just / eat / two hamburgers)

(1) They arrived at the movie theater late.

➡ _____ (the movie / already / begin)

(2) I went to the party, but Sara wasn't there.

➡ _____ (she / go / out)

(3) They weren't eating when I saw them.

➡ _____ (they / just / finish / their lunch)

(4) We rushed to the station, but we were too late.

➡ _____ (the train / just / leave)

Challenge 1 과거완료 시제는 언제 사용하는가?

과거완료(had + V-ed)는 과거에 발생한 어떤 일보다 더 먼저 발생한 일을 나타낸다. 과거보다 더 먼저 발생한 일은 [   ] 시제를 쓰고 나중에 일어난 일은 [   ] 시제를 쓴다.

I had never **seen** such a pretty girl before **I met** Kelly. 나는 Kelly를 만나기 전에 그렇게 예쁜 소녀를 본 적이 없었다.

Challenge 2 현재완료와 현재완료 진행시제의 차이를 알고 있는가?

[   ]는 구체적인 때는 모르지만 과거에 시작하여 현재 시점에 완료된(Perfected, Completed) 행동 및 상황을 나타내고 [   ]은 과거에 시작하여 현재에도 진행 중임을 강조하고자 할 때 쓴다. 특히 상태가 아니라 동작이 계속됨을 나타낼 때는 현재완료보다 현재완료 진행형을 더 많이 쓴다.

She has already **eaten** sushi. 그녀는 이미 초밥을 먹었다. (She isn't eating it right now.)

She has been eating sushi. 그녀는 초밥을 먹고 있다. (Now she is eating it.)

Challenge 3 과거완료 진행시제의 쓰임을 알고 있는가?

(1) [   ] 시제는 'had been + V-ing'의 형태로 과거의 어떤 일이 발생하기 더 이전의 과거에 계속되어 왔던 동작을 강조할 때 쓴다. 나중에 일어난 일은 [   ] 시제를 쓴다.

We **had been playing** tennis for two hours before the accident **happened**.

우리는 그 사고가 발생하기 전에 2시간 동안 테니스를 치고 있던 중이었다.

(2) 과거완료 진행시제는 과거에 발생한 일에 대한 [   ]을 나타내고, 과거시제는 [   ]를 나타낼 때도 쓰인다.

The grass <u>was wet</u>. It **had been raining** all morning. 잔디가 젖었다. 아침 내내 비가 오고 있었다.
     결과   원인

Scott **went** to the doctor last Saturday. He **hadn't been feeling** well.
   결과   원인

Scott은 지난 토요일에 의사 진찰 받으러 갔다. 그는 몸이 좋지 않았다.

[1-2] 다음 문장과 뜻이 같도록 빈칸에 알맞은 말을 쓰시오.

1

Megan is in China. She arrived there a week ago.

➡ Megan _____ _____ _____ _____ for a week.

2

Tom started waiting at 2 p.m. and I arrived at 5 p.m.

➡ When I arrived, Tom _____ _____ _____ for three hours.

3 다음 밑줄 친 부분과 같은 용법으로 쓰인 것은?

I have known her for 30 years.

① How long have you been in Tokyo?
② She has painted the ceiling.
③ He has gone to Italy.
④ He has already written a letter.
⑤ I've been to England once.

4 다음 빈칸에 들어갈 말이 바르게 짝지어진 것은?

My father _____ me a new smartphone yesterday because I _____ my old one.

① bought - have lost
② bought - lost
③ has bought - lost
④ has bought - have lost
⑤ bought - had lost

5 다음 밑줄 친 동사를 알맞은 형태로 고친 것은?

I cancel my departure if it rains tomorrow.

① had canceled
② have canceled
③ canceled
④ was canceling
⑤ will cancel

6 다음 밑줄 친 부분이 일어나는 시점이 나머지와 다른 것은?

① Tom and Susan work in the same office.
② She usually does her homework after dinner.
③ My younger brother often skips breakfast.
④ After they visit the sites, they will go shopping.
⑤ Ann always starts the show at 7:00 in the morning.

7 다음 글을 읽고 빈칸에 들어갈 알맞은 것을 고르시오.

I decided to get up early before the ship entered the harbor. But my room was very hot so I couldn't sleep for hours. At last I fell asleep, but I woke up too late. Oh, no! I took my camera and rushed up. But everything was finished. The ship _____ the harbor.

① was entering
② has entered
③ had already entered
④ is going to enter
⑤ has already entered

8 다음 밑줄 친 부분이 어법상 어색한 것을 고르시오.

① <u>Had you ever been</u> to a family restaurant?
② She <u>has been reading</u> for two hours.
③ How long <u>has</u> your mother <u>been</u> in the hospital?
④ I <u>haven't taken</u> a vacation for five years.
⑤ John is in a hurry. He's <u>giving</u> a presentation to his boss in fifteen minutes.

9 다음 밑줄 친 현재진행형의 용법이 나머지와 다른 것을 고르시오.

① Tomorrow I'm <u>going</u> to a concert.
② They <u>are having</u> a surfing contest now.
③ The students <u>are arguing</u> greatly over the issue.
④ They <u>are discussing</u> the topic in depth later tonight.
⑤ Passengers <u>are boarding</u> the plane.

10 다음 빈칸에 들어갈 말로 가장 적절한 것은?

> By the time the concert began, many of the girls _____ in a line for two hours.

① have stood
② have been stood
③ has stood
④ have been standing
⑤ had been standing

11 다음 빈칸에 들어갈 말이 바르게 짝지어진 것은?

> • They had been talking _____ over an hour when I arrived.
> • The dog has swum in the river _____ 3 o'clock.

① for - for
② for - since
③ of - since
④ since - for
⑤ for - from

12 다음 빈칸에 들어갈 알맞은 시제를 고르시오.

> A: I _____ visit Mexico. Could you give me any tips?
> B: You'd better not ask for directions in Mexico.
> A: Thanks. I'll keep that in mind.

① used to
② was about to
③ will
④ am going to
⑤ was going to

13 다음 우리말을 영어로 바르게 옮긴 것은?

> 그들은 10살 때부터 서로 알고 지냈다.

① They know each other for 10 years old.
② They have known each other since they were 10 years old.
③ They have known each other for 10 years.
④ They have known each other since they have been 10 years old.
⑤ They knew each other since they were 10 years old.

서술형 대비 문제

1 다음 괄호 안에 주어진 말을 이용하여 질문을 완성하시오.

> A: _____ Portugal? (ever)
> B: No, I haven't. But my father has been there.

[2–3] 다음 두 문장을 한 문장으로 표현할 때 빈칸에 알맞은 말을 쓰시오.

2
> Harold and Laura are married. They got married six years ago.

➡ Harold and Laura _____ for six years.

3
> Walter began to learn Korean this morning. He is still learning it.

➡ Walter _____ Korean since this morning.

4 다음 우리말과 뜻이 같도록 괄호 안의 말을 알맞게 배열하시오.

> 그녀는 3년 동안 마술을 배워오고 있다.
> (she, for three years, magic, been, learning, has)

➡ _____

5 괄호 안의 어구를 이용하여 사진과 일치하는 문장을 쓰시오.

(wearing / her new shoes)

➡ Betty took off her shoe.
   She _____ all day.

Grammar in Reading

냄새가 난다, 냄새가 나! 누가 신발 벗은 거야?

Our sense of smell is nowadays being used for various purposes. (a) One area in which smells achieve particular results is marketing. (b) For some time manufacturers have taken advantage of our sense of smell to sell more household goods. (c) They spend millions of dollars hunting for the right aroma as they believe perfume influences the way consumers perceive a brand. (d) In addition, painting walls with a white color may be effective to help patients relax in the waiting room of a dental office. (e) In one survey, people were asked what they <u>consider</u> most when they bought a detergent. The scent of the detergent was found to be the most important factor.

1 Choose the sentence that does NOT belong in this paragraph.

① (a)   ② (b)   ③ (c)   ④ (d)   ⑤ (e)

2 According to the paragraph, why is the smell of a product so important?

① The smell of a product affects our health.
② Our clothes should always smell good.
③ Most consumers are persuaded by the scent of a product.
④ All newly made products should smell fresh.
⑤ The smell of a product is more important than the color.

3 윗글에서 밑줄 친 consider를 알맞은 시제로 고쳐 쓰시오.

_____

A 보기와 같이 완료 시제를 이용하여 묻고 답하는 형식으로 말하기 연습을 하세요. 연습이 한 번 끝난 후 서로 역할을 바꿔 다시 말하기 연습을 하세요.

you / ever / see / a shooting star / ?

Yes ➡ 10 years ago

A: Have you ever seen a shooting star?

B: Yes, I have. I saw it 10 years ago.

1

Carl / ever / try / waterskiing / ?

Yes ➡ last week

2

you / eat / pepperoni pizza / before / ?

Yes ➡ two years ago

B 보기와 같이 완료 시제를 이용하여 묻고 답하는 형식으로 말하기 연습을 하세요. 연습이 한 번 끝난 후 서로 역할을 바꿔 다시 말하기 연습을 하세요.

work with Christina

A: What are your plans for this evening?

B: I'm going to work with Christina.

1

go to the Korean Conversation Club

2

go to an ice hockey match

실전 서술형 평가 문제

출제의도 | 현재완료와 과거시제를 이용하여 경험 나타내기
평가내용 | 현재완료와 과거시제 구별

서술형 유형	14점
난이도	하

Chapter **4**

 다음은 Alex가 지난 몇 년간 사업차 다녀온 곳이다. 보기와 같이 현재완료와 과거시제를 이용하여 어떤 도시들을 방문했는지를 쓰시오.

2007		2008	
May	Seattle	February	New York
September	Bangkok	April	Istanbul
2009		**2010**	
March	Seoul	January	Cairo
July	Shanghai	December	Mexico City

보기 He has been to Seattle. He went there in May, 2007.

---

1 _____

2 _____

3 _____

4 _____

5 _____

6 _____

7 _____

평가영역	채점기준	배점
유창성(Fluency) & 정확성(Accuracy)	7개의 문장을 모두 올바른 표현과 함께 정확하게 완성한 경우 (문법, 철자가 모두 정확한 경우)	7×2 = 14점
	현재완료, 과거시제를 만들지 못하였거나 문법, 철자가 1개씩 틀린 경우	문항당 1점씩 감점
	내용과 전혀 일치하지 않거나 답을 기재하지 못한 경우	0점

출제의도 | 현재완료와 현재완료 진행시제를 이용하여 문장 서술하기		서술형 유형	16점
평가내용 | 현재완료와 현재완료 진행시제의 구별		난이도	중하

B 다음 표를 읽고 보기와 같이 현재완료 진행시제와 현재완료 시제를 이용하여 문장을 하나씩 만드시오.

Name	Job	Hour	Item
David	makes hamburgers	2 hours	90 hamburgers
Marco	fries potato chips	4 hours	5 kilos of potato chips
Dorothy	prepares salads	3 hours	20 salads
Paul	takes orders	5 hours	150 orders
Kimberly & Tom	clean tables	2 hours	40 tables

> 보기 David has been making hamburgers for 2 hours.
>
> He has made 90 hamburgers so far.

1 _____

_____

2 _____

_____

3 _____

_____

4 _____

_____

평가영역	채점기준	배점
유창성(Fluency) & 정확성(Accuracy)	8개의 문장을 모두 올바른 표현과 함께 정확하게 완성한 경우 (문법, 철자가 모두 정확한 경우)	8×2 = 16점
	현재완료와 현재완료 진행시제를 만들지 못하였거나 문법, 철자가 1개씩 틀린 경우	문항당 1점씩 감점
	내용과 전혀 일치하지 않거나 답을 기재하지 못한 경우	0점

실전 서술형 평가 문제

출제의도 | 조건의 부사절을 이용하여 미래를 나타내기
평가내용 | 미래를 나타내는 시제

서술형 유형	9점
난이도	중상

 보기와 같이 주어진 문장과 의미가 같도록 조건의 부사절을 이용하여 문장을 서술하시오.

보기 Edward must run very fast and he will win the race.

➡ If Edward runs very fast, he will win the race.

OR If Edward doesn't run very fast, he won't win the race.

1  The dress will be expensive, so Sarah won't buy it.

➡ _____

_____

2  Take the subway or you'll be late for work.

➡ _____

_____

3  Don't write on the desk! You'll be in trouble.

➡ _____

_____

평가영역	채점기준	배점
유창성(Fluency) & 정확성(Accuracy)	3개의 문장을 모두 올바른 표현과 함께 정확하게 완성한 경우 (문법, 철자가 모두 정확한 경우)	3×3 = 9점
	조건의 부사절을 만들지 못하였거나 문법, 철자, 시제가 1개씩 틀린 경우	문항당 1점씩 감점
	내용과 전혀 일치하지 않거나 답을 기재하지 못한 경우	0점

Chapter 5
조동사

Unit 1 • 능력 (expressing ability)

Richard fell down and broke his leg.
Richard는 넘어져서 다리가 부러졌다.
He could play soccer last week, but he can't play soccer now.
그는 지난주에 축구를 할 수 있었지만 지금은 할 수 없다.

1 조동사 can은 현재와 미래의 능력(ability)을 나타낸다. 과거의 능력은 could를 써서 과거에 할 수 있었던 능력(ability)을 나타낸다.

Olivia can speak Korean, but she can't speak Japanese. Olivia는 한국어를 할 줄 알지만 일본어는 할 줄 모른다.
I couldn't drive five years ago. 나는 5년 전에는 운전을 하지 못했다.

2 능력을 나타내는 can과 could는 조동사구인 be able to와 같은 의미로 사용할 수 있다. 하지만 일상 영어에서 be able to는 자주 쓰지 않고 can과 could를 더 자주 쓴다.

He can lift two people at the same time. 그는 동시에 두 명의 사람을 들 수 있다.
= He is able to lift two people at the same time.
She couldn't finish the exam yesterday. 그녀는 어제 시험을 끝낼 수 없었다.
= She wasn't able to finish the exam yesterday.

기본기 탄탄 다지기

1 다음 괄호 안에서 알맞은 것을 고르시오.

(1) A bear (can / cans) climb trees.

(2) I (can / could) swim when I was 7 years old.

(3) When he was three years old, he (can / was able to) play the piano.

(4) I (can / could) come and help you tomorrow if you want.

(5) It's summer now. Gina and I (are / were) able to play tennis outdoors.

(6) We (could / will be able to) go out tomorrow.

(7) (Can / Could) she play the guitar last year?

▶현재에는 갖고 있진 않지만 미래에 가지게 될 능력에는 can을 쓰지 않고, will be able to를 쓴다.
Next year, I'll be able to drive.

▶어려움이 있거나 불만스러운 일에는 주로 be able to를 쓴다.
After I spoke to my teacher, I was able to do it.
I tried very hard, but I wasn't able to do all of my math problems.

▶특별한 상황에서 주로 상태를 나타내는 동사 see, hear, smell, taste, feel, understand, remember는 주로 be able to를 쓰지 않고 can/could를 쓴다.
When I opened the door, I could smell gas.
When I opened the door, I was able to smell gas. (uncommon)

Unit 2 • 가능성 (expressing possibility)

Take an umbrella with you. It **may** rain today.
우산을 가져가라. 오늘 비가 올지 몰라.
We **might** go camping this summer.
우리는 이번 여름에 캠핑을 갈지도 모른다.

1 100% 현재의 사실이라고 확신할 때는 현재형을 쓰고, 현재나 미래에 발생할지 모르는 일에 대한 가능성(50% 이하 가능성)은 may, might, can, could를 써서 나타낸다. '~일지도 모른다'의 뜻이다.

Jessica **is** at home now. (100% 확신) Jessica는 지금 집에 있다.
Jessica **may** be at home now. (50% 이하 가능성) Jessica는 지금 집에 있을지도 모른다.

2 가능성을 나타낼 때 could와 might는 과거가 아닌 현재나 미래를 나타낸다. 가능성을 나타내는 may, might, can, could는 바람직하지 않은 일이 일어날 수 있음을 내포하기도 한다.

He **might** not come to the meeting tomorrow. 그는 내일 회의에 못 올지도 모른다.
The phone's ringing. It **could** be Jane. 전화벨이 울린다. Jane일 수도 있어.
Children **can** have cancer. 어린이들도 암에 걸릴 수 있다.
Look at those dark clouds. It **could** start raining. 저 시커먼 구름 좀 봐. 비가 내릴 거 같아.

기본기 탄탄 다지기

1 밑줄 친 조동사의 뜻이 가능(possibility)인지 능력(ability)인지를 구별하시오.

(1) Anybody can make a mistake. (possibility / ability)

(2) His flight could be late. (possibility / ability)

(3) Can you speak both English and Chinese well? (possibility / ability)

(4) Skiing on the hills can be quite dangerous. (possibility / ability)

2 주어진 문장을 우리말로 해석해 보시오.

(1) It may be true. ➡ _____

(2) She may be in her office. ➡ _____

(3) There might not be a meeting on Friday.

➡ _____

▶발생하지 않을 가능성을 말할 때 may not 또는 might not을 쓴다. can/could not을 쓰지 않는다.
She **may not**(might not) come tomorrow.
(may not과 might not은 축약해서 쓰지 않는다.)

▶의문문은 could를 쓰고 may를 쓰지 않는다. might를 쓰기도 하는데 거의 쓰지 않는다.
Could that answer be correct?
Might that answer be correct? (very formal)

▶maybe는 한 단어로 부사의 역할을 하며 항상 문장 맨 앞에 쓴다. may be는 두 단어로 '조동사 + 동사원형'이므로 문장에서 동사 역할을 한다. 둘 다 perhaps 또는 possibly와 같은 뜻이다.
Maybe Ted is in the library.
= Ted **may be** in the library.

Chapter **5**

You **must** do your homework.
너는 숙제를 해야 한다.

I **have to** write my essay by tomorrow.
나는 내일까지 에세이를 써야 한다.

1 must와 have to는 필요와 의무를 나타낸다. '~해야 한다'의 뜻으로 상대방에게 그 일을 꼭 하라는 강한 강조의 의미를 지니고 있다. 일상 영어에서는 must 보다 have to를 더 많이 쓴다. must의 부정 must not(= mustn't)은 '~해서는 안 된다'라는 강한 금지를 나타낸다.

Tom **has to** study for his test. Tom은 시험을 위해 공부를 해야 한다.

You **must** take an English course. You can't graduate without it.
너는 영어 수업을 들어야 한다. 그것 없이는 졸업을 할 수 없다.

Look at the sign! We **mustn't** swim here. 표지판을 봐! 우리는 여기서 수영을 해서는 안 된다.

2 have to의 부정인 don't have to는 '~할 필요가 없다'란 뜻으로 불필요(lack of necessity)를 나타낸다. don't have to와 같은 뜻으로 don't need to를 쓰고 영국식 영어에서는 need not을 쓴다.

She **doesn't have to** wear a suit to work. 그녀는 정장 차림으로 출근할 필요가 없다.
= She **doesn't need to** wear a suit to work.
= She **need not** wear a suit to work. (영국식 영어)

기본기 탄탄 다지기

1 다음 빈칸에 have to 또는 has to를 구별하여 쓰시오.

(1) You _____ eat more fresh vegetables.

(2) Richard _____ work late.

(3) They _____ get up early tomorrow.

(4) Does Sunny _____ work tomorrow?

2 주어진 글을 읽고 빈칸에 mustn't 또는 don't(doesn't) have to를 쓰시오.

(1) If you want to keep your job, you _____ be late for work.

(2) Lisa can sleep late tomorrow morning because she _____ work.

(3) We'll have a flying car. We _____ worry about traffic jam.

▶have got to는 have to와 같은 뜻으로 쓰이지만 주로 말하는 영어에서 긍정문으로만 쓴다. 부정문과 의문문으로는 보통 쓰지 않는다.
I **have got to** buy a new computer.

▶must와 have got to는 미래형과 과거형이 없어서 미래는 will have to, 과거는 had to로 쓴다.
Next week, I'll **have to** go to Seoul.
I **had to** get up early yesterday.

▶must not은 영국식 영어로 자주 쓰이고 미국식 영어에서는 주로 can't를 쓴다.
You **mustn't** tell a lie to your teacher.
You **can't** tell a lie to your teacher.

서술형 기초 다지기 ❶

1 can, could를 be able to를 이용하여 바꾸어 쓰시오.

(1) It's summer now. My friends and I can play beach volleyball.

➡ _____

(2) She can go hiking in the mountains.

➡ _____

(3) Can you speak any foreign languages?

➡ _____

(4) He could play the piano when he was five.

➡ _____

(5) She couldn't come to the party.

➡ _____

2 보기와 같이 may를 이용하여 같은 의미가 되도록 빈칸을 완성하시오.

Perhaps we'll go out.
➡ We <u>may go out</u>   .

(1) Perhaps she will come tomorrow.

➡ She _____ .

(2) I don't know if we'll get an invitation.

➡ We _____ .

(3) I'm not sure if my friends are visiting me.

➡ My friends _____ .

(4) Perhaps I'll go to the movie theater this weekend.

➡ I _____ .

(5) You don't know if Tiffany will come to the party.

➡ Tiffany _____ .

3 주어진 문장을 괄호 안의 지시대로 바꾸어 쓰시오.

(1) I've got to study English tonight. (must 사용)

➡ _____

(2) You've got to drive slowly through the school zone. (have to 사용)

➡ _____

(3) To get a cheap ticket, you've got to book in advance. (have to 사용)

➡ _____

(4) Jennifer has to walk to school. (have got to 사용)

➡ _____

(5) She can't go to the movie tonight because she has to study for final exams. (must 사용)

➡ _____

4 보기와 같이 mustn't 또는 don't have to를 이용하여 같은 의미의 문장을 다시 쓰시오.

> • It isn't necessary for you to wear a suit to the office.
>   ➡ You don't have to wear a suit to the office.
> • It is forbidden to smoke on the train.
>   ➡ You mustn't smoke on the train.

(1) It is forbidden to touch pictures in the museum.

➡ _____

(2) It isn't necessary for you to go to school today.

➡ _____

(3) It isn't necessary for you to stay in your seat throughout the flight.

➡ _____

(4) It is forbidden to spend your time playing video games.

➡ _____

(5) It isn't necessary for you to finish your homework by tomorrow.

➡ _____

Oral Test

Challenge 1 능력을 나타내는 조동사를 알고 있는가?

(1) 조동사 can은 [   ]와 [   ]의 능력을 나타낸다. 과거에 할 수 있었던 능력은 [   ]를 쓴다.

Can Steve write with his left hand? Steve는 왼손으로 글을 쓸 줄 아니?

When I was a child, I **could** ride a bicycle with no hands. 내가 어렸을 때 손을 놓고 자전거를 탈 수 있었다.

(2) 능력을 나타내는 can과 could는 [   ]와 같은 의미로 쓰지만 일상 영어에서는 can과 could를 더 자주 쓴다.

These cells **are able to** reduplicate themselves. 이들 세포는 자기 복제를 할 수 있다.

Challenge 2 가능성을 나타내는 조동사를 알고 있는가?

100% 현재의 사실을 나타낼 때는 [   ]을 쓰고 현재나 미래에 발생할 가능성이 50% 이하지만 발생 가능한 일을 나타낼 경우에는 [   ], [   ], [   ], [   ]로 표현할 수 있다. 가능성을 나타내는 might와 could는 과거형이 아닌 [   ]나 [   ]를 나타낸다.

Tom and Jane **are** in the library. Tom과 Jane은 도서관에 있다. (100% 확신)

Tom and Jane **may(might, could)** be in the library. Tom과 Jane은 도서관에 있을지도 모른다. (50% 이하의 가능성)

Customers' needs **can** change daily. 고객들의 요구는 날마다 바뀔 수 있다.

Ava **might** not come to the concert tonight. She isn't feeling well.
Ava는 오늘 밤 그 콘서트에 오지 않을 수도 있다. 그녀는 몸이 좋지 않다.

Challenge 3 필요와 의무를 나타내는 조동사를 알고 있는가?

(1) must와 have to, have got to는 필요(necessity)나 의무(obligation)를 나타낸다. 일상 영어에서는 [   ] 보다 [   ]를 더 많이 쓴다. have to와 have got to는 주어가 3인칭 단수인 경우에 [   ]와 [   ]를 쓴다.

It's Sunday, but I **have to** work. 일요일이지만 나는 일해야 한다.

She **must** see the dentist tomorrow. 그녀는 내일 치과에 가야 한다.

(2) '~해서는 안 된다'의 뜻인 must의 부정은 [   ]를 쓰고 have(has) to의 부정은 [   ]로 우리말 '~할 필요가 없다'의 뜻으로 의미가 완전히 다르다. 불필요함을 나타내는 같은 뜻으로 [   ]를 쓰고 영국식 영어에서는 주로 [   ]을 쓴다.

Unit 4 ● 충고하기 (giving advice)

Preview

You **shouldn't** eat so much.
너는 그렇게 많이 먹지 않는 게 좋겠다.

It's cold outside. You'**d better** wear a coat.
밖이 춥다. 너는 코트를 입는 게 좋을 거야.

① should와 ought to는 '~해야 한다, ~하는 게 좋겠다'라는 뜻으로 충고나 제안할 때 사용한다. 부정은 각각 should not(= shouldn't)와 ought not to(= oughtn't to)로 쓴다. 일상 영어에서는 should를 더 많이 쓴다.

You **should** stop smoking. 너는 담배 피우는 것을 끊어야 한다.

We **oughtn't to** use cell phones when we drive cars. 우리는 차를 운전할 때 휴대전화를 사용해서는 안 된다.

You **ought to** eat lots of fruit and vegetables. 너는 과일과 야채를 많이 먹어야 한다.

② 'had better + 동사원형'은 '~하는 게 좋겠다/ 낫겠다'의 의미로 should보다 더 강한 어감이나 경고의 메시지 (strong advice or warning)를 담고 있어 충고를 따르지 않을 때는 어떤 문제가 발생할 수 있다는 뜻을 내포하고 있다. 부정은 'had better not + 동사원형'을 쓴다.

It's raining. You **had better** cancel your date. 비가 온다. 너는 데이트를 취소하는 게 좋겠다.

I'**d better not** go to school today. I'm feeling sick. 난 오늘 학교에 가지 않는 게 낫겠어. 몸이 아파.

기본기 탄탄 다지기

1 다음 괄호 안에서 알맞은 것을 고르시오.

(1) You (should / ought) be more careful.

(2) It's your fault. You (should / ought) to apologize to her.

(3) When you're in a library, you (should not / ought not) to speak loudly.

(4) You (shouldn't / oughtn't) stay up late. You have an exam tomorrow.

2 다음 빈칸을 had better를 이용하여 완성하시오.

(1) Kathy _____ him the truth. (tell)

(2) We _____ late or we'll miss the plane. (not, be)

(3) You _____ your car in a safe area. (park)

> ▶ 'would rather + 동사원형'은 '~하는 것이 더 좋다, ~하고 싶다'의 뜻으로 어떤 것을 더 선호한다는 의미로 had better와는 전혀 다르다. 'would prefer to + 동사원형'으로 바꿔 쓸 수 있고 부정은 'would rather not + 동사원형'을 쓴다.
> I'd **rather** sit on the floor.
> = I'd **prefer** to sit on the floor.
>
> ▶ 'would rather A than B'는 'B보다 차라리 A가 좋다'의 뜻으로 'prefer A to B'와 의미가 같은데 A와 B 자리에는 명사나 동명사를 써야 한다.
> I'd **rather** play soccer **than** (play) basketball.
> = I **prefer** playing soccer to playing basketball.
> = I like playing soccer **better than** playing basketball.

Unit 5 • 허락 (asking for permission)

Formal

May I use your dictionary? 당신 사전을 써도 될까요?
(They don't know each other.)

Could I use your dictionary? 당신 사전을 써도 될까요?
(They might or might not know each other.)

Informal

Can I use your dictionary? 당신 사전을 써도 될까요?
(They have been speaking together or they know each other.)

① can과 may가 허락(give permission)을 나타낼 때 '~해도 좋다'의 뜻이다. 부정은 can과 may 뒤에 not을 붙여 만드는데 may not은 축약형을 쓰지 않는다. 강한 부정은 must not을 쓴다.

You **can** use my smartphone. 너는 내 스마트폰을 써도 좋다.
You **may** come whenever you have time. 시간 나면 언제든 와도 좋다.
You **can't/mustn't** park here. 당신은 여기에 주차하면 안 된다.

② 'I'를 주어로 써서 May I~? 또는 Could/Can I~?로 허락을 요청할 수 있다. May I~?가 가장 정중한 표현이고 친구나 가족과 같이 가까운 사이에는 Can I~?를 쓴다. 대부분의 상황에서 Could를 사용하는 것이 가장 좋다. 여기서 Could는 과거가 아니라 현재와 미래를 나타낸다. please를 문장 중간(본동사 앞)에 쓰거나 문장 맨 뒤에 덧붙이기도 한다.

Can I play with my friends after school, dad? 아빠, 방과 후에 친구들과 놀아도 될까요?
May I (please) hand in my homework tomorrow? 숙제를 내일 제출해도 되나요?
Could I speak to John, (please)? John과 통화할 수 있나요?

기본기 탄탄 다지기

1 각 문장의 밑줄 친 조동사를 능력, 가능성, 허락으로 구별하시오.

(1) He can't borrow my car; I need it today. _____

(2) That's dangerous! He may fall! _____

(3) May I use your computer? _____

(4) She can run 100 meters in 11 seconds. _____

(5) Can I borrow your pen? _____

(6) You may not speak during the exam. _____

(7) May I see your tickets? _____

▶May(Could, Can) I ~?에 대해 자주 쓰이는 답변은 긍정인 경우 Yes, certainly. / Certainly. / Of course. / Yes, of course. / Sure. / Okay. 등이다. 부정인 경우 I'm sorry, but I can't. / Sorry, I can't. / No, I'm sorry. 등이다.

A: Could I have a look at that blue hat?
B: Yes. Of course.

A: Can I please borrow your eraser?
B: I'm sorry, but I need to use it myself.

Unit 6 • 부탁 (making requests)

Would you call me later?
나중에 전화 주실래요?

Can you shut the door? It's freezing.
문을 좀 닫아 줄래? 굉장히 춥다.

1 'you'를 주어로 하여 Can/Will/Could/Would you~?로 정중한 부탁(polite requests)을 할 수 있다. Could/Would는 잘 모르는 사람 또는 윗사람(선생님, 나이 든 사람 등)에게 쓰고 will과 can은 가족이나 친구와 같이 편안한 사이에 자주 쓴다. please를 덧붙이기도 한다.

Would you (please) close the window? 창문을 닫아 주시겠습니까?

Could you tell me how to get to the City Hall? 시청에 어떻게 가는지 알려줄 수 있나요?

Can/Will you turn off the TV, (please)? TV 좀 꺼 줄래(요)?

2 제안(offering)이나 초대(inviting)를 할 때 Would you like + 명사~? 또는 Would you like to + V~?를 쓴다. Do you want (to)~?보다 정중한 표현이다.

Would you like a cup of coffee? 커피 한잔 하실래요?
- Yes, please. 네, 좋아요.

Would you like to come to dinner tomorrow evening? 내일 저녁 식사하러 오실래요?
- Yes, I'd love to. 네, 정말 가고 싶어요.

기본기 탄탄 다지기

1 다음 빈칸에 informal은 Can/Will you~?, polite은 Would/Could you~?를 써서 빈칸을 완성하시오.

(1) _____ open the window? (informal)

(2) _____ turn on the light? (polite)

(3) _____ give me some information about Korea? (polite)

(4) _____ come to my office at 5 o'clock? (informal)

▶ Can/Will/Could/Would you~?에 자주 쓰이는 답변으로 긍정에는 Of course. / Yes, I'd love to. / Certainly. / Sure. / Okay. 등이다. 부정은 I'd like to, but I can't. / I'm sorry, but I can't. / I don't think so. 등이다.

Could you please open the door? – I'm sorry, I'd **like to** help, but my hands are full.

2 다음 빈칸에 Would you like와 Would you like to를 구별하여 쓰시오.

(1) _____ go to a movie with me?

(2) _____ some chocolate?

(3) _____ a glass of water?

(4) What _____ do this weekend?

서술형 기초 다지기 ②

1 다음 문장을 읽고 Could(Would) you ...? 또는 Can you ...?를 이용하여 문장을 완성하시오.

> Ask your teacher to help you with the exercise.
> ➡ Could(Would) you help me with the exercise? _____

(1) Ask your brother to help you with the exercise.

➡ _____

(2) Ask the lady to fasten her seatbelt.

➡ _____

(3) Ask your boss to open the door.

➡ _____

(4) Ask your friend to tell you the time.

➡ _____

(5) Ask the waitress to bring you some water.

➡ _____

2 주어진 상황을 읽고 보기와 같이 Could(May) I ...? 또는 Can I ...?를 이용하여 의문문을 완성하시오.

> You're speaking to your brother.
> Lend me your MP3 player.   ➡ (borrow) Can I borrow your MP3 player? _____

(1) You're speaking to a waiter.
I want a glass of water.   ➡ (have) _____

(2) You're speaking to your boss.
I'm leaving early today.   ➡ (leave) _____

(3) You're speaking to your younger brother.
I'm going to turn on the TV.   ➡ (turn on) _____

(4) You're speaking to a stranger.
I'll put my coat here.   ➡ (put) _____

(5) You're speaking to your teacher.
I want to have some more time to finish the homework.
➡ (have) _____

3 보기와 같이 should와 oughtn't to를 이용하여 문장을 완성하시오.

> Jane has got a terrible stomachache.
> ➡ She should take an aspirin. _____ (take / an aspirin)
> ➡ She oughtn't to go shopping. _____ (go shopping)

(1) Scott can never wake up early in the morning, so he's always late for work.

➡ _____ (use / an alarm clock)

➡ _____ (go to bed / late / at night)

(2) Jessica feels very tired.

➡ _____ (take a break)

➡ _____ (work / so hard)

4 보기와 같이 괄호 안의 말을 이용하여 'Would you like to …?'로 질문을 완성하시오.

> What would you like to watch on television?
> ➡ Would you like to watch the news? _____ (watch the news)

(1) Where would you like to go to study English?

➡ _____ (Oxford)

(2) What would you like to do in your free time?

➡ _____ (go to the movie theater)

5 주어진 상황을 읽고 괄호 안의 표현과 had better를 이용하여 빈칸을 완성하시오.

> The movie starts in five minutes.
> ➡ We had better hurry _____ . (hurry)

(1) Sandra can't find her credit card. She has no idea where it is.

➡ She _____ . (call / the credit card company)

(2) I asked Tiffany to marry me ten times. She said no every time.

➡ You _____ . (find / a new girlfriend)

(3) Eric is always coughing because he smokes too much.

➡ He _____ . (not smoke / any more)

Oral Test

Challenge 1 충고나 제안의 의미로 쓰이는 조동사는 무엇인가?

(1) 충고나 제안의 의미로 쓸 경우 '~하는 게 좋겠다, ~해야 한다'의 뜻으로 [   ]와 [   ]는 같은 뜻으로 사용된다.

   You **should** try to lose weight. 너는 살을 빼는 게 좋겠다.

   People **ought to** worry more about global warming. 사람들은 지구 온난화에 대해 더 걱정해야 한다.

(2) should 보다 더 강한 어감으로 경고의 메시지를 나타내는 '[   ]'은 우리말 '~하는 게 좋겠다/ 낫겠다'의 뜻이다. 부정은 '[   ]'으로 쓴다.

   You'**d better not** read this article. 너는 이 기사를 읽지 않는 게 좋겠다.

Challenge 2 허락의 의미로 쓰이는 조동사는 무엇인가?

(1) [   ]과 [   ]가 허락을 나타낼 때 '~해도 좋다'로 의미가 같다.

   You **can** use my dictionary. 너는 내 사전을 사용해도 좋다.

   You **may** go home now. 너는 지금 집에 가도 좋다.

(2) 상대방에게 허락을 구할 때 'I'를 주어로 써서 May I~? 또는 Could/Can I~?로 쓴다. [   ] I ~?가 가장 정중한 표현이고 [   ] I ~?는 가족이나 친구들처럼 격이 없는 사이에서 많이 쓴다.

   May I see your driver's license? 운전면허증을 보여주시겠습니까?

   Could I have your name, please? 성함을 알 수 있을까요?

   Can I borrow fifty dollars? 50달러만 빌려줄래?

Challenge 3 정중한 부탁은 어떻게 하는가?

(1) 상대방에게 정중한 부탁을 할 때 '[   ]'를 주어로 하여 Can/Will/Could/Would you ~?로 쓴다.

   Could/Would you send the report, please? 그 리포트를 보내 줄 수 있나요?

   Can/Will you come here for a second? 잠시 여기에 와 줄래?

(2) 제안(offering)이나 초대(inviting)를 할 때 Would you like + 명사 ~? 또는 Would you like to + V ~?를 쓴다.

   [   ] first class or economy class? 일등석으로 하시겠어요, 보통석으로 하시겠어요?

   [   ] try it on? 입어 보시겠어요?

Unit 7 ● 현재 추론 (making logical conclusions)

Preview

You haven't eaten anything all day. You **must be** hungry.
너는 종일 아무것도 먹지 않았다. 너는 배고픈 게 틀림없다.

You **can't be** hungry. You've just eaten.
너는 배고플 리가 없다. 너는 방금 식사를 했다.

---

1 100% 현재의 사실이라고 확신할 경우 현재형을 쓰고, 현재 상황에 대한 어떤 논리적인 이유나 근거가 있어 95% 확신하는 경우 must (be)를 쓴다. '~임에 틀림없다'의 뜻이다.

Jessica plays badminton with her mother. Jessica는 엄마와 함께 배드민턴을 친다. (100% sure)

Jessica plays badminton every day. She **must** like to play badminton. (95% sure)
Jessica는 매일 배드민턴을 친다. 그녀는 배드민턴 치는 것을 좋아하는 게 틀림없다.

He **must be** a silly billy to ask such stupid things. 그는 그런 어리석은 질문을 하다니 바보임에 틀림없다. (95% sure)

2 can't be는 '~일 리가 없다'라는 뜻으로 현재 상황에 대한 논리적인 이유나 근거가 있어 95% 이상(almost 100% sure) 확신하는 경우에 쓴다.

I saw Carl a minute ago, so he **can't be** at home. (almost 100% sure)
나는 방금 Carl을 봤기 때문에 그는 집에 있을 리가 없다.

You **can't be** tired. You've been sleeping for ten hours. (almost 100% sure)
너는 피곤할 리가 없다. 너는 10시간 동안 잤다.

기본기 탄탄 다지기

1 다음 괄호 안의 표현과 알맞은 조동사를 이용하여 문장을 완성하시오.

▶couldn't도 '~일 리가 없다'의 뜻으로 can't 대신 쓸 수 있다. couldn't는 과거가 아닌 현재 상황에 논리적 이유가 있는 강한 확신(almost 100% sure)을 가질 때 쓴다.

She **can't be** in the park.
= She **couldn't be** in the park.

(1)

그녀는 피곤한 것이 틀림없다.
(she / be / tired)

_____

(2)

그들은 사무실에 있는 게 틀림없다.
(they / in the office)

_____

(3)

그것은 귀신일 리가 없다.
(that / a ghost)

_____

(4)

그는 집에 있을 리가 없다.
(he / at home)

_____

Preview

I wonder why Tiffany didn't answer the phone.

100% sure　　　She **was** asleep. 그녀는 자고 있었다.

95% sure　　　She **must have been** asleep. 그녀는 자고 있던 게 분명하다.

50% possibility　She **may/might have been** asleep. 그녀는 자고 있었을지도 모른다.

　　　　　　　= She **could have been** asleep. 그녀는 자고 있었을지도 모른다.

Scott passed me by on the street without speaking.

100% sure　　　　He **didn't see** me. 그는 나를 보지 못했다.

almost 100% sure　He **can't have seen** me. 그가 나를 봤을 리가 없다.

　　　　　　　　= He **couldn't have seen** me.

95% sure　　　　He **must not have seen** me. 그는 나를 못 본 게 틀림없다.

50% possibility　He **may not have seen** me. 그는 나를 못 봤을지도 모른다.

　　　　　　　= He **might not have seen** me.

(1) 100% 과거의 사실은 과거시제를 쓰고 과거 일에 대한 추론이나 가능성은 '조동사 + have + V-ed'를 쓴다. 부정은 조동사 뒤에 not만 붙이면 된다.

He **couldn't have driven** Ava to the airport. 그는 Ava를 공항까지 태워다 줬을 리가 없다.

She **must have overslept**. 그녀는 늦잠 잔 것이 틀림없다.

Kevin **may(might) have suffered** a bad headache. Kevin은 심한 두통으로 고생했을지도 모른다.

기본기 탄탄 다지기

1　우리말에 맞도록 괄호 안에서 알맞은 표현을 고르시오.

(1) 저 남자가 내 돈을 훔친 것이 틀림없다.

➡ That man (must / can't) have stolen my money.

(2) 너는 네 가방을 가게에 두고 왔을지도 모른다.

➡ You (might not / could) have left your bag in the store.

(3) 그녀는 공부를 충분히 열심히 하지 않았을지도 모른다.

➡ She (may not / must not) have studied hard enough.

(4) 어젯밤에 비가 온 것이 틀림없다.

➡ It (must / can't) have rained last night.

The fridge is empty.
냉장고가 비어있다.

I **should have done** the shopping yesterday. (I didn't do it and now I regret it.)
나는 어제 쇼핑을 했어야 했는데(하지 않았다).

① 'should have + V-ed'는 '~했어야 했는데(사실은 하지 않았다)'의 뜻으로, 과거 지나간 일에 대한 후회, 유감을 나타낸다. 'ought to have + V-ed'로 바꿔 쓸 수 있고 둘 다 과거의 행위나 동작을 하지 않았음을 내포하고 있다. 부정은 조동사 뒤에 not을 붙여 'should not have + V-ed, ought not to have V-ed'로 쓴다. '~하지 말았어야 했는데(했다)'의 의미로 과거의 행위나 동작이 실제 행해졌음을 내포하고 있다.

I **should have studied** harder when I was at school. 나는 학교 다닐 때 더 열심히 공부했어야 했는데(하지 않았다).

She **ought to have finished** high school. 그녀는 고등학교를 졸업했어야 했는데(하지 않았다).

She **shouldn't have bought** such an expensive bag. 그녀는 그렇게 비싼 가방을 사지 말았어야 했는데(샀다).

② 'must have + V-ed'는 '~이었음에/~했음에 틀림없다'라는 뜻으로, 과거의 행위나 동작을 실제 행하였음을 내포하고 있다. 부정은 조동사 must 뒤에 not을 쓴다.

Why isn't she here? She **must have missed** the train. 그녀가 왜 오지 않은 걸까? 그녀는 기차를 놓쳤음에 틀림없다.

The driver didn't stop at the intersection. He **mustn't have seen** the red light.
운전자는 교차로에서 멈추지 않았다. 빨간 신호를 못 본 게 틀림없다.

기본기 탄탄 다지기

1 다음 괄호 안의 말을 알맞게 배열하여 문장을 완성하시오.

(1) You (brought, have, should) an umbrella.

➡ _____

(2) He (not, driven, should, have) the car so fast.

➡ _____

(3) She (must, been, have) at home yesterday.

➡ _____

(4) I feel sick. I (not, to, ought, have, eaten) so much chocolate at the party last night.

➡ _____
_____

▶ought to는 부정문으로 거의 쓰지 않는다.
You oughtn't to have invited him to your party.

▶'need have + V-ed'는 '~할 필요가 있었는데(하지 않았다)'의 뜻이고 부정은 'need not have + V-ed'로 '~할 필요가 없었는데 (사실은 했다)'의 뜻이다. 이는 영국식 표현으로 미국식 영어에서는 잘 사용하지 않는다.
I need not have bought a car.

서술형 기초 다지기 ❸

1 다음 우리말과 같은 뜻이 되도록 괄호 안의 동사를 이용하여 빈칸을 완성하시오.

(1) 정부가 노숙자를 돕기 위해 더 많은 것을 했어야 했다.

➡ The government _____ more to help homeless people. (do)

(2) 그는 태국에 간 것이 틀림없다. 한동안 그를 보지 못했다.

➡ He _____ to Thailand. I haven't seen him for a while. (go)

(3) 그녀는 어젯밤 쇼핑을 갔을지도 모른다.

➡ She _____ shopping last night. (go)

(4) 그녀는 열쇠를 레스토랑에 두고 왔을지도 모른다.

➡ She _____ the key in the restaurant. (leave)

(5) 그는 할아버지 댁에 갔을 리가 없다.

➡ He _____ to his grandfather's. (go)

(6) 우리는 그 음식을 먹지 말았어야 했다.

➡ We _____ the food. (eat)

2 다음 두 문장이 같은 뜻이 되도록 빈칸에 알맞은 말을 쓰시오.

I am sure that she didn't see me.
➡ She _____ must not have seen _____ me.

(1) It is almost certain that she met her boyfriend in the subway.

➡ She _____ her boyfriend in the subway.

(2) I didn't listen to my teacher, but I regret it.

➡ I _____ to my teacher.

(3) It is not right that you worked until so late last night.

➡ You _____ until so late last night.

(4) It is almost certain that she has forgotten the promise.

➡ She _____ the promise.

3 다음 글을 읽고 must not 또는 can't를 이용하여 빈칸을 완성하시오.

(1) She was in Tokyo one hour ago when I spoke to her. She _____ here yet.

(2) Their car isn't outside their house. They _____ be home.

(3) They didn't want anything to drink. They _____ be thirsty.

(4) Jessica has already eaten four sandwiches. She _____ hungry already.

(5) Peter _____ working today. I just saw him at the gym.

(6) That restaurant _____ be very good. It's always empty.

4 다음 문장을 괄호 안의 조동사를 이용하여 보기와 같이 빈칸을 완성하시오.

> It is possible that he was in the museum. (may)
> ➡ He may have been in the museum _____.

(1) I'm certain they know each other. (must)

➡ They _____.

(2) I'm certain they go to bed early on Sunday nights. (must)

➡ They _____.

(3) It is possible Sandra is in her office. (may)

➡ Sandra _____.

(4) I'm sure Amy hasn't finished her homework. (can't)

➡ Amy _____.

(5) Perhaps Helen forgot to turn off the lights. (could)

➡ Helen _____.

(6) Perhaps she doesn't know about these changes. (might)

➡ She _____.

Oral Test

Challenge 1 현재를 추론할 때는 어떤 조동사를 사용하는가?

(1) 100% 현재의 사실이라고 확신하는 경우에는 현재형을 쓰지만 현재 상황에 대한 논리적 이유가 있는 강한 확신

(95%)을 갖는 경우에는 [   ]를 쓴다.

Sarah never stops talking about Steve. She must be in love with him! (95% sure)

Sarah는 Steve에 관한 얘기를 멈추지 않는다. 그녀는 사랑에 빠진 게 틀림없다.

(2) '~일 리가 없다'의 뜻으로 현재 상황에 대해 100%에 가까운(almost 100% sure) 확신을 하는 경우에는

[   ]를 쓴다.

Olivia can't be at home. I saw her leave 10 minutes ago. (almost 100% sure)

Olivia는 집에 있을 리가 없어. 10분 전에 나가는 것을 봤거든.

Challenge 2 과거에 대한 추론과 가능성은 어떻게 나타내는가?

100% 과거의 사실은 과거시제를 쓰고 과거 일에 대한 추론이나 가능성을 나타낼 때 '조동사 + [   ] +

[   ]'를 쓴다.

She couldn't have sung in front of people.

그녀는 사람들 앞에서 노래를 불렀을 리가 없다.

I've lost one of my gloves. I must have dropped it somewhere.

나는 장갑 하나를 잃어버렸다. 어딘가에 떨어뜨린 것이 틀림없다.

Challenge 3 must have V-ed와 should have V-ed의 의미를 구별할 줄 아는가?

[   ]는 과거에 했어야 하는 일이나 행동에 대한 후회, 유감을 나타내고,

[   ]는 과거 사실에 대한 논리적 이유가 있는 강한 확신을 갖는 경우에 사용한

다.

You missed a great party last night. You ought to/should have come.

너는 지난밤 멋진 파티를 놓쳤다. 너는 파티에 왔어야 했다.

I feel sick. I shouldn't have eaten so much food.

속이 안 좋아요. 음식을 너무 많이 먹지 말았어야 했어요.

She looks tired. She must have stayed up all night.

그녀는 피곤해 보인다. 그녀는 밤을 꼬박 새운 것이 틀림없다.

Preview

Scott **used to** play soccer. = Scott **would** play soccer. Scott은 축구를 하곤 했었다.
➡ He played soccer regularly for some time in the past, but he doesn't play soccer now.

1 'used to + 동사원형'은 '~하곤 했(었)다'의 뜻으로 지금은 하지 않으나 과거에 했던 반복된 행동이나 상태를 나타낸다. used to 대신 would를 구별 없이 쓸 수 있지만 과거의 동작이 아닌 '상태나 존재했었던 것'에는 used to만 사용한다.

I **used to** wear glasses. = I **would** wear glasses. 나는 안경을 낀 적이 있었다.

There **used to** be a church near my house. 우리 집 근처에 교회가 있었다. (would 사용 불가능)

Kathy **used to** have very short hair. Kathy는 아주 짧은 머리를 하고 있었다. (would 사용 불가능)

2 '예전에는 ~하지 않았지만 지금은 ~한다'의 뜻인 used to의 부정은 didn't use(d) to 또는 never used to를 쓴다. 의문문은 'Did + 주어 + used(d) to ~?'로 쓴다.

She **didn't use(d) to** play tennis. 그녀는 테니스를 친 적이 없었다.
(➡ Once she didn't play tennis, but now she does.)

A: **Did** you **use(d) to** jog? 너는 조깅을 하곤 했니?
B: Yes, I did. / No, I didn't. 응, 그랬어. / 아니, 그렇지 않았어.

기본기 탄탄 다지기

1 다음 빈칸에 used to와 would를 구별해서 쓰시오. 둘 다 가능한 경우 모두 쓰시오.

(1) Most people _____ walk or ride a horse. Today they drive cars.

(2) They _____ wash clothes by hand.

(3) She _____ be a long distance runner.

(4) Nancy _____ have very long hair when she was a child.

(5) There _____ be two movie theaters in town.

(6) I _____ watch TV a lot.

▶실제 원어민조차 규칙적인 것과 불규칙적인 것을 구별하기 애매하기 때문에 과거의 습관, 특히 동작에 대해서는 used to와 would를 구별 없이 쓰고 상태인 경우에만 would를 쓰지 않고 used to만 쓴다.

▶'be/get used to + V-ing'는 'V-ing하는 데에 익숙하다'라는 뜻이다. 'be accustomed to + V-ing'도 같은 의미로 사용된다.
'used to + 동사원형'과는 의미가 전혀 다르므로 해석에 주의한다.
I am used to living alone.
나는 혼자 사는 데 익숙하다.
Lisa is accustomed to eating Kimchi.
Lisa는 김치 먹는 데 익숙하다.

1 다음과 같이 used to의 의문문을 만들어 보시오.

> I know she doesn't smoke now, but <u>did she use to smoke</u>   ?

(1) I know he doesn't play the violin now, but _____ ?

(2) I know she isn't very rich now, but _____ ?

(3) We know she doesn't dance these days, but _____ ?

(4) We know she doesn't wear a mini skirt now, but _____ ?

(5) I know he doesn't eat vegetables now, but _____ ?

2 주어진 표를 참고하여 보기와 같이 used to 또는 didn't use to를 이용하여 문장을 만드시오.

	Stella		Bob	
	Past	Present	Past	Present
ride a bicycle to work	O	X	X	O
go to the movies very often	X	O	O	X
wear fashionable clothes	X	O	O	X
watch cartoons on TV	O	X	X	O

> Stella used to ride a bicycle to work, but she doesn't now.
> Bob didn't use to ride a bicycle to work, but he does now.

(1) _____

(2) _____

(3) _____

(4) _____

(5) _____

(6) _____

1 밑줄 친 우리말에 해당하는 표현을 고르시오.

> "Look at the water. It's dark, isn't it? All the fish <u>죽었음에 틀림없다</u> or fled."

① must have die
② must have died
③ must has die
④ must have dead
⑤ have to die

2 다음 빈칸에 알맞은 시제를 고르시오.

> A: How did you use to go to school?
> B: I _____ my bicycle to school, but now I take the school bus.

① used to ride
② rode
③ used
④ am used to riding
⑤ didn't use to ride

3 다음 표지판의 의미로 알맞은 것을 고르시오.

① You may use your phone here.
② You must use your phone here.
③ You mustn't use your phone here.
④ You don't have to use your phone here.
⑤ You must have used your phone here.

4 다음 두 문장이 같은 뜻이 되도록 빈칸에 알맞은 말을 넣으시오.

> You don't have to come to the meeting.
> ➡ You _____ _____ come to the meeting.

[5–6] 다음 빈칸에 알맞은 것을 고르시오.

5

> Sunny got the best grades. She _____ be very happy.

① should
② would rather
③ had better
④ ought to
⑤ must

6

> A: I was surprised that Nancy wasn't at the party.
> B: She _____ about it.

① may not know
② doesn't know
③ might not have known
④ may have known
⑤ can't know

7 다음 중 밑줄 친 단어의 의미가 <u>다른</u> 하나는?

① The girl <u>can't</u> find her smartphone.
② You <u>can't</u> play the piano, can you?
③ We <u>can't</u> get to the airport in ten minutes.
④ Are they still alive? It <u>can't</u> be possible.
⑤ You can store water in a glass jar, but you <u>can't</u> store it in a paper bag.

8 다음 대화의 빈칸에 알맞은 것은?

> A: Did you call Cindy last night?
> B: No, I didn't. I _____ have called her and said sorry to her.

① should
② must
③ may
④ might
⑤ would

9 다음 우리말을 바르게 영작한 것을 고르시오.

> 너는 어젯밤 그 파티에 가지 말았어야 했다.

① You shouldn't have gone to the party last night.
② You ought to have gone to the party last night.
③ You shouldn't go to the party last night.
④ You must not have gone to the party last night.
⑤ You'd better not go to the party last night.

10 다음 우리말에 맞게 빈칸에 공통으로 들어갈 영어를 쓰시오. (두 단어)

> • My grandfather _____ _____ live in Pyong-yang.
> 할아버지는 예전에 평양에 사셨다.
>
> • Kevin _____ _____ visit Susan every Saturday.
> Kevin은 전에 매주 토요일마다 Susan을 방문하곤 했다.

11 밑줄 친 부분의 뜻이 나머지와 다른 하나를 고르시오.

① You may use my car if you want to.
② Jessica may not go out tonight. She isn't feeling well.
③ Tom may visit me if he'd like to.
④ You may go to bed when you are sleepy.
⑤ You may not smoke here.

12 다음 두 문장의 뜻이 서로 다른 것은?

① It's summer now. My friends and I can play tennis outdoors.
= It's summer now. My friends and I are able to play tennis outdoors.
② You shouldn't go to bed late at night.
= You oughtn't to go to bed late at night.
③ It is probable that she revealed the secret.
= She might have revealed the secret.
④ It is necessary for us to study English.
= We should study English.
⑤ It is possible that Julie has done the work by herself.
= Julie can't have done the work by herself.

서술형 대비 문제

1 다음 글을 읽고 괄호 안의 동사를 이용하여 알맞은 표현을 쓰시오.

> We had a test in class yesterday. Charles, who rarely studies and usually fails the tests, got a score of 95% this time.

➡ He _____ (study) for the test.

2 다음 문장의 밑줄 친 부분을 어법에 맞게 고쳐 쓰시오.

> I heard a loud crash in the next room. When I walked in, I found a brick on the floor, and the window was broken. Someone <u>must throw</u> the brick through the window.

➡ _____

[3–4] 다음 우리말에 맞게 괄호 안의 동사를 이용하여 빈칸을 채우시오.

3
> 너는 그 장면을 보지 말았어야 했는데.

➡ You _____ the scene. (see)

4
> 나는 그녀를 같은 장소에서 만났을지도 모른다.

➡ I _____ her at the same place. (meet)

5 다음 빈칸에 공통으로 들어갈 단어를 쓰시오.

> A: _____ you like to go to the movies tonight?
> B: I _____ rather stay home tonight. I'd prefer not to go out.

Grammar in Reading

해외 갔다 왔더니 시차적응이 안돼! 어디 갔다 왔는데? 제주도!

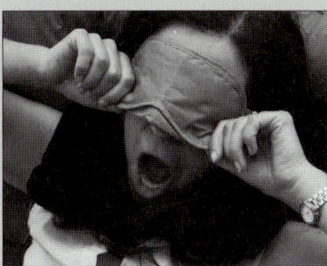

Have you ever felt sick, sleepy, or very tired after a long hour flight? Especially, flying east to west or west to east, you will definitely have <u>this</u> problem. <u>This</u> is a combination of fatigue and other symptoms caused by traveling across different time zones. <u>This</u> happens because of the alteration of your circadian rhythm. There are numerous symptoms that _____ with <u>this</u>. For example, traveling across a time zone confuses your physiological clock, which results in fatigue. Sometimes, you may feel so disoriented that you won't feel like doing anything. You may also get headaches and notice that you have eating and sleeping disorders. These are all general symptoms of <u>this</u>. Below is presented some information about how to meet and manage <u>this</u>.

circadian rhythm 24시간 주기 리듬 disorient 혼란시키다

Chapter 5

---

1 Choose an expression to replace the underlined words 'this'.

① a vertigo   ② chronic insomnia   ③ a nervous breakdown
④ jet lag   ⑤ brain and nervous system

2 이 글 바로 뒤에 올 수 있는 내용으로 가장 알맞은 것은?

① Directions of top hospitals in the west or east area
② Tips to avoid this sickness or problem
③ Reasons for suffering from this problem
④ Suggestion for an operation to prevent this problem
⑤ Survey of people's opinions about this problem

3 글의 흐름상 빈칸에 들어갈 말로 알맞은 것은?

① may occur   ② may have occurred   ③ should occur
④ must have occurred ⑤ ought to occur

A 보기와 같이 조동사 may/might를 이용하여 묻고 답하는 형식으로 말하기 연습을 하세요. 연습이 한 번 끝난 후 서로 역할을 바꿔 다시 말하기 연습을 하세요.

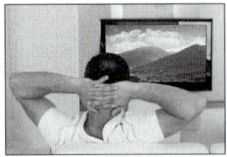

Frank / him / ?

➡ at home / watch TV now

A I can't find Frank. Have you seen him?

B He might be at home. He may be watching TV now.

1

Tiffany / her / ?

➡ in the tennis court / play tennis now

2

Kathy / her / ?

➡ in her room / do her homework now

B 보기와 같이 조동사 had to를 이용하여 묻고 답하는 형식으로 말하기 연습을 하세요. 연습이 한 번 끝난 후 서로 역할을 바꿔 다시 말하기 연습을 하세요.

Alice / call the babysitter / ?

➡ attend a meeting

A Why did Alice call the babysitter?

B Because she had to attend a meeting.

1

Peter / buy a dictionary / ?

➡ translate a novel

2

Ava / go to a restaurant / ?

➡ entertain her client

출제의도 | 과거의 일에 대해 후회, 유감 나타내기

평가내용 | should have + 과거분사

서술형 유형	10점
난이도	하

Chapter 5

 보기와 같이 괄호 안의 말을 이용하여 과거의 일에 대한 후회하는 문장을 만드시오. (주어는 we를 쓸 것.)

> **보기** A: Hurry up. We are late for the meeting again.
>
> B: We should have got(= gotten) up earlier. _____ (get up earlier)

1 A: We watched a movie last night, but it was a waste of time and money.

B: _____ (go to the movies)

2 A: It was unlucky that we failed in the exam.

B: _____ (study for it)

3 A: I didn't go to college. Now I'm unhappy with my job.

B: So did I.

A: _____ (go to college)

4 A: It's raining outside, but we don't have any umbrella.

B: _____ (bring umbrellas)

5 A: We got up late again.

B: _____ (use an alarm clock)

평가영역	채점기준	배점
유창성(Fluency) & 정확성(Accuracy)	5개의 문장을 모두 올바른 표현과 함께 정확하게 완성한 경우 (문법, 철자가 모두 정확한 경우)	5×2 = 10점
	should have + 과거분사를 만들지 못하였거나 문법, 철자가 1개씩 틀린 경우	문항당 1점씩 감점
	내용과 전혀 일치하지 않거나 답을 기재하지 못한 경우	0점

출제의도	현재와 미래에 있을 가능성 나타내기	서술형 유형	12점
평가내용	현재진행형 / 조동사 may(might)	난이도	하

B 다음은 Alice의 다음 주 월요일 스케줄이다. 그녀는 확실하지 않은 항목에 물음표(?)를 써 놓았다. 보기와 같이 이미 예정된 일에는 현재진행형을 쓰고 확실하지 않은 가능성이 있는 일에는 may(might)를 써서 문장을 완성하시오.

MONDAY	
call William at 9:00	go to work at 1:00
buy some notebooks before class?	go shopping after work?
go to the meeting with Sunny at 11:00	take the 6:00 train?
have coffee with Susan after class?	eat dinner with Eric?

보기 Alice is calling William at 9:00.

She may/might buy some notebooks before class.

1 _____

2 _____

3 _____

4 _____

5 _____

6 _____

평가영역	채점기준	배점
유창성(Fluency) & 정확성(Accuracy)	6개의 문장을 모두 올바른 표현과 함께 정확하게 완성한 경우 (문법, 철자가 모두 정확한 경우)	6×2 = 12점
	조동사, 현재진행형을 만들지 못하였거나 문법, 철자가 1개씩 틀린 경우	문항당 1점씩 감점
	내용과 전혀 일치하지 않거나 답을 기재하지 못한 경우	0점

출제의도 | 실생활에서 쓰이는 허락을 요청하기

평가내용 | May I ~? / Can I ~? / Could I ~?

서술형 유형	10점
난이도	중

C 주어진 상황을 읽고 보기와 같이 May I, Can I, Could I 중 가장 알맞은 표현과 함께 문장을 완성하시오.

> **보기** You are a teenager. You want to go to a party tonight. Ask your dad.
>
> ➡ Can I go to a party tonight please, Dad?

1 You work in an office. You want to speak to your boss for a moment. Ask your boss.

➡ _____

2 Your teacher is carrying a lot of books. Ask if you can help.

➡ _____

3 You're an attendant at the theater. You want to see a person's ticket. Ask the person.

➡ _____

4 You are a customer in a restaurant. You do not have a spoon to eat with. Ask the waiter.

➡ _____

5 You want to borrow your friend's smartphone. What would you say to him or her?

➡ _____

평가영역	채점기준	배점
유창성(Fluency) & 정확성(Accuracy)	5개의 문장을 모두 올바른 표현과 함께 정확하게 완성한 경우 (문법, 철자가 모두 정확한 경우)	5×2 = 10점
	조동사를 바르게 사용하지 못하였거나 문법, 철자가 1개씩 틀린 경우	문항당 1점씩 감점
	내용과 전혀 일치하지 않거나 답을 기재하지 못한 경우	0점

Chapter **5**

MEMO

Chapter 6
수동태

The Eiffel Tower **was built** in 1889.   It **was designed** by Gustave Eiffel.

에펠 타워는 1889년에 지어졌다.   그것은 Gustave Eiffel에 의해 디자인되었다.

1 주어가 동작을 직접 행하여 목적어에 그 영향을 끼치는 경우가 아닌, 주어가 동작을 받는(당하는) 대상이 되어 무슨 일이 일어났는지에만 관심을 두는 문장을 수동태(passive voice)라고 한다.

능동태 (주어가 직접 ~하다)	수동태 (주어가 ~당하다/되다/받다)
Someone **stole** my Galaxy S4. 누군가 내 갤럭시 S4를 훔쳐갔다. Shakespeare **wrote** Hamlet. 셰익스피어가 햄릿을 썼다.	My Galaxy S4 **was stolen** yesterday. 내 갤럭시 S4는 어제 도난당했다. Hamlet **was written** by Shakespeare. 햄릿은 셰익스피어에 의해 쓰여졌다.
행위자가 중요해서 능동태 문장을 쓴다. 능동태 문장은 동작이 전달되는 대상(목적어)이 반드시 있어야 한다.	수동태는 누가 그것을 했는가보다는 행위 자체에 중요성을 둔다. 주어가 행위를 받는 대상에만 관심이 있기 때문에 행위가 전달되는 목적어가 존재하지 않고, 보통 'by + 행위자(목적격)'가 없는 경우가 많다.

기본기 탄탄 다지기

1 다음 괄호 안에서 알맞은 것을 고르시오.

(1) She (studied / are studied) English literature at university.

(2) My father (ticketed / was ticketed) for speeding.

(3) This house (was built / built) in 1988.

2 다음 우리말과 같도록 괄호 안의 말을 이용하여 문장을 완성하시오.

(1) 많은 나무들이 파괴되었다. (destroy)

➡ A lot of trees ＿＿＿＿＿ ＿＿＿＿＿.

(2) 로마는 하루아침에 이루어지지 않았다. (not, build)

➡ Rome ＿＿＿＿＿ ＿＿＿＿＿ ＿＿＿＿＿ in a day.

(3) 그 잡지는 수백만 명의 사람들에 의해 읽혀진다. (read)

➡ The magazine ＿＿＿＿＿ ＿＿＿＿＿ by millions of people.

▶실제 원어민들도 행위자를 중심으로 할 때는 능동태를 선호하지만 수동태 문장이 효과적인 의미를 전달하는 경우에는 수동태를 쓴다.

1) 어떤 행위를 누가 했는지 모르거나, 누가 했는지 안다고 해도 중요하지 않은 경우 by + 행위자(목적격)를 쓰지 않는다.

My car **was made** in Korea.

2) 행위자가 일반인이거나, 언급하지 않아도 뻔히 아는 경우에도 'by + 행위자(목적격)'를 쓰지 않는다. 실제 수동태 문장 중 약 80%는 행위자를 쓰지 않는다.

English **is spoken** almost all over the world.

Rice **is grown** in Asia.

▶목적어를 갖지 못하는 자동사나 목적어를 갖는다 하더라도 상태 동사인 have, resemble, fit, suit, lack 등은 수동태로 쓰지 못한다.

He **has** an expensive car.

→ An expensive car is had by him. (X)

Unit 2 ● 수동태의 시제

Preview

The movie **is being made** in Hollywood.
그 영화는 할리우드에서 제작되고 있다.
The classroom **has not been cleaned** by them.
그 교실은 그들에 의해 청소되지 않았다.

① 수동태의 시제는 'be동사 + 과거분사(V-ed)'에서 과거분사는 그대로 두고 be동사만 바꾼다.

시제	능동태	수동태
현재시제	She **paints** the house.	The house **is** **painted** by her.
현재진행	She **is painting** the house.	The house **is being** **painted** by her.
현재완료	She **has painted** the house.	The house **has been** **painted** by her.
과거시제	She **painted** the house.	The house **was** **painted** by her.
과거진행	She **was painting** the house.	The house **was being** **painted** by her.
과거완료	She **had painted** the house.	The house **had been** **painted** by her.
미래시제 will	She **will paint** the house.	The house **will be** **painted** by her.
미래진행 be going to	She **is going to paint** the house.	The house **is going to be** **painted** by her.
미래완료	She **will have painted** the house.	The house **will have been painted** by her.

Chapter 6

기본기 탄탄 다지기

1 주어진 문장을 수동태로 고칠 때 빈칸에 알맞은 것을 쓰시오.

(1) We were building the small cottage.
  ➡ The small cottage _____ by us.

(2) Somebody has stolen my phone.
  ➡ My phone _____ .

(3) Graham Bell invented the telephone in 1876.
  ➡ The telephone _____ in 1876.

(4) The girls are going to eat the pizza.
  ➡ The pizza _____ by the girls.

▶미래진행형, 현재(과거/ 미래)완료
진행은 수동태로 쓰지 않는다.

cottage n. 오두막

Unit 3 ● 조동사가 있는 수동태 / get + 과거분사

Preview

This letter **must be sent** at once.
이 편지는 즉시 보내져야 한다.
The space shuttle **will be launched** soon.
그 우주왕복선은 곧 발사될 것이다.

① 조동사 뒤에는 반드시 동사원형을 써야 하므로 be동사의 원형인 be를 조동사 뒤에 써서 '조동사 + be + 과거분사(V-ed)'로 수동태를 만들면 된다.

Decisions **shouldn't be made** too quickly. 결정은 너무 빨리 이루어지면 안 된다.

Our car **has to be fixed**. 우리 차는 고쳐져야 한다.

The village **could be destroyed** if the river floods. 그 강이 범람하면 마을은 파괴될지도 모른다.

② be동사 대신에 get을 쓸 때에는 주로 대화체에서 계획되지 않았거나 예상치 못 한 일, 그리고 불공평한 행위를 강조하기 위해 사용한다.

The vase **got broken** when I bumped into the table. 내가 테이블에 부딪혔을 때 그 꽃병이 부서졌다. (accidentally)

She **got awarded** a big prize. 그녀는 큰 상을 받았다. (unexpectedly)

I **got blamed** for losing the money. 나는 그 돈을 잃어버린 것에 대해 비난을 받았다. (unfairly)

※ get(got) 대신 be동사를 써도 모두 상관없다.

기본기 탄탄 다지기

1 다음 괄호 안의 표현 중 알맞은 것을 고르시오.

(1) It is (going to be launched / going to launch) very soon.

(2) The work (might give / might be given) to us.

(3) The new drug (may be tested / must test) on patients this year.

(4) People (should be saved / should save) energy.

2 괄호 안의 단어를 이용하여 'get + 과거분사'의 문장을 완성하시오.

(1) The cup _____ when Morgan moved. (break)

(2) Our puppy _____ over by a car last Saturday. (run)

(3) Lots of postmen _____ by dogs. (bit)

▶get이 형용사나 과거분사와 함께 쓰일 경우 get은 become(~되다)의 뜻으로 많이 쓰인다.
I got(= became) hungry by eleven in the morning.

▶과거분사도 형용사와 같은 역할을 한다. 주로 상태나 감정을 나타내는 과거분사로 온다.
They are **getting married** next month.
I got **worried** because she was two hours late.

▶get은 주로 대화체에서 쓰고, 형식적인(formal) 말하기와 쓰기에서는 자주 사용하지 않는다.
She gets **bored** by long movies.

서술형 기초 다지기 ❶

1 다음 능동태 문장을 수동태로 바꿔 쓰시오.

> Thomas Edison invented the electric light bulb.
> ➡ The light bulb was invented by Thomas Edison.

(1) Lisa is painting the door.

➡ _____

(2) He has repaired the car.

➡ _____

(3) Kevin must send an e-mail in advance.

➡ _____

(4) You should not forget the deadline for reports.

➡ _____

(5) She is going to wash the dirty plates and bowls.

➡ _____

2 주어진 문장을 수동태로 고치고 'by + 행위자'는 필요한 경우에만 쓰시오.

(1) Someone built this ship in 1920.

➡ _____

(2) The police arrested the escaped prisoner.

➡ _____

(3) A famous architect designed the building.

➡ _____

(4) They grow the plants in Brazil.

➡ _____

(5) Someone broke the mirror last night.

➡ _____

3 주어진 문장을 능동태는 수동태로, 수동태는 능동태 문장으로 바꿔 쓰시오.

(1) We must not throw waste from factories into the sea.

➡ _____

(2) They built the pyramids around 400 A.D.

➡ _____

(3) The forests should not be cut down by us.

➡ _____

(4) Animals in danger ought to be protected by us.

➡ _____

(5) We will destroy our planet.

➡ _____

4 보기의 단어 중 알맞은 것을 골라 'get + 과거분사'의 문장으로 빈칸을 채우시오.

marry	hit	fire	ask	hurt

(1) She _____ in the head by a hockey puck.

(2) People always want to know what my job is. I often _____ that question.

(3) His thumb _____ when using the stapler.

(4) If you don't do your best, you might _____.

(5) Tom and Sue _____ last year. Sue is going to have a baby next month.

Oral Test

Challenge 1 언제 수동태를 사용하는지 알고 있는가?

수동태는 행위의 주체에 관심이 있는 것이 아닌, 행위를 받는 대상에 중요성을 두기 때문에 행위가 전달되는 [ ]가 존재하지 않는다. 행위를 받는 목적어가 문장의 중심(주어)이 되어 이를 주어로 쓰고 동사를 [ ]로 고쳐 쓴다.

Taxes **are collected** by the government. 세금은 정부에 의해서 걷힌다.

Our mail **is delivered** by Scott. 우리의 메일은 Scott에 의해 전해진다.

Challenge 2 수동태를 이용하여 시제를 나타낼 수 있는가?

시제	능동태	수동태
현재시제	She **fixes** the radio.	The radio [ ] by her.
현재진행	She **is fixing** the radio.	The radio [ ] by her.
현재완료	She **has fixed** the radio.	The radio [ ] by her.
과거시제	She **fixed** the radio.	The radio [ ] by her.
과거진행	She **was fixing** the radio.	The radio [ ] by her.
과거완료	She **had fixed** the radio.	The radio [ ] by her.
미래시제 will	She **will fix** the radio.	The radio [ ] by her.
미래진행 be going to	She **is going to fix** the radio.	The radio [ ] by her.
미래완료	She **will have fixed** the radio.	The radio [ ] by her.

Challenge 3 조동사가 있는 문장을 수동태로 고칠 수 있는가?

조동사가 있는 문장을 수동태로 고칠 때 조동사 뒤에는 반드시 동사원형을 써야 하므로 '[ ]' 로 수동태를 만든다.

Bottles and paper **should be recycled**. 병과 종이는 재활용되어야 한다.

This book **must be returned** to the library today. 이 책은 오늘 도서관에 반납되어야 한다.

Unit 4 • 4형식 문장의 수동태

Preview

I **was given** a nice mountain bike by my dad.
나는 아빠에게서 멋진 산악자전거를 받았다.
A nice mountain bike **was given to** me by my dad.
멋진 산악자전거가 아빠에 의해 내게 주어졌다.

① 4형식은 두 개의 목적어가 존재하므로 2개의 수동태 문장이 가능하다. 주로 사람을 나타내는 간접목적어를 주어로 사용하고, 직접목적어를 수동태의 주어로 쓰는 경우 간접목적어 앞에 to를 쓴다. 단, buy, make, get, find, build는 for를 쓴다. 영국식 영어에서는 to나 for를 생략해서 쓰기도 한다.

He gave *me a thank-you note*. ➡ *I* **was given** a thank-you note by him.
     I.O.   D.O.   나는 그에게 감사편지를 받았다.
(간접목적어) (직접목적어) ➡ *A thank-you note* **was given (to)** me by him.
                                 감사편지가 그에 의해 나에게 주어졌다.

② buy, make, write, cook, read, sell, send, hand는 직접목적어를 주어로 하는 수동태만 가능하다. 간접목적어를 주어로 쓰면 어색한 문장이 되기 때문이다.

She cooked me *a delicious dinner*. 그녀는 나에게 맛있는 저녁을 요리해 주었다.
➡ *A delicious dinner* **was cooked (for)** me by her.

My husband bought me *a gold ring*. 내 남편이 내게 금반지를 사줬다.
➡ *A gold ring* **was bought (for)** me by my husband.

기본기 탄탄 다지기

1 다음 괄호 안에서 알맞은 것을 고르시오.

(1) A letter (sent / was sent) (to / for) us by my father.

(2) A striped shirt (was bought / bought) (for / to) her by John.

(3) I (was shown / shown) (to / X) Van Gogh's paintings by Catherine.

(4) Jason (was given / gave) her a postcard.

(5) Life vests weren't (bring / brought) (to / for) us by the woman.

(6) Some aspirin (was given / gave) (for / to) Alexander by the nurse.

(7) She (was shown / showed) (X / to) the bill by the waiter.

▶explain, suggest는 3형식 동사로만 사용되기 때문에 간접목적어가 없다. 따라서 (직접)목적어만을 주어로 하는 수동태를 만든다.
 · He explained the project to the workers.
➡ The project **was explained** to the workers.
 · They suggested a simple solution to us.
➡ A simple solution **was suggested** to us.

▶직접목적어를 주어로 하여 수동태로 바꿀 때 전치사 of를 쓰는 동사 ask, beg, inquire, require
 · She **asked** me a favor.
➡ She **asked** a favor **of** me.

Preview

She **was made** a soccer player by her parents.
그녀는 부모님에 의해 축구선수가 되었다.

My son **was made to** wash my car by me.
나는 내 아들에게 차를 세차하게 했다.

1 5형식 문장은 목적어가 한 개이므로 목적어를 주어로 써서 수동태를 만든다. 이때 목적격 보어 자리에 있는 명사, 형용사, to부정사, 분사 등은 수동태 'be + V-ed' 뒤에 그대로 이어서 쓴다.

- He considered <u>his daughter</u> *a pretty girl*.
              O   O.C.
         (목적어) (목적격 보어)

  ➡ His daughter **was considered** *a pretty girl* by him. 그의 딸은 그에 의해 예쁜 소녀로 여겨진다.

- The teacher allowed <u>me</u> *to go home*.
                O   O.C.
         (목적어)(목적격 보어)

  ➡ I **was allowed** *to go home* by the teacher. 나는 선생님에게 집에 가는 것을 허락받았다.

2 지각동사나 사역동사가 쓰인 5형식 문장이 수동태로 전환될 때 목적격 보어 자리에 있는 동사원형은 'to부정사'로 바뀐다. let은 그대로 수동태 문장의 동사로 쓰지 않고 'be allowed to'를 이용하여 수동태로 만든다.

We **saw** Arthur *come* out of the office.
➡ Arthur **was seen to** *come* out of the office by us. Arthur가 우리에 의해 사무실에서 나오는 것이 목격되었다.

They **let** us go home.
➡ We **were allowed to** *go* home. 우리는 집에 가도록 허락받았다.

기본기 탄탄 다지기

1 다음 괄호 안에서 알맞은 것을 고르시오.

(1) John was made (repair / to repair) the roof by me.

(2) I (was asked / asked) to go out by her.

(3) I was told (to turn / turned) off the TV by my mother.

(4) He (elected / was elected) their captain by them.

(5) Peter was seen (walk / to walk) with a ghost at the park.

(6) Ava (persuaded / was persuaded) to donate some money.

> **repair** v. 수리하다
> **roof** n. 지붕
> **ask someone to go out** ~에게 데이트 신청하다
> **elect** v. 선출하다, 뽑다
> **persuade** v. 설득하다
> **donate** v. 기부하다

Chapter **6**

Preview

The dog **was looked after** by my sister.
그 개는 내 여동생에게 보살핌을 받았다.

Nick **was looked down on** by his girlfriend.
Nick은 그의 여자 친구에게서 무시를 당했다.

1 동사가 부사나 전치사와 함께 하나의 동사 역할을 하는 것을 동사구라고 한다. 이를 수동태로 고칠 때 동사구를 하나의 동사처럼 취급하여 동사만 'be + V-ed'로 고치고 부사나 전치사는 분리하지 않고 그대로 연결해서 수동태의 문장을 만든다.

The babysitter **takes good care of** my baby.
➡ My baby **is taken good care of** by the babysitter. 내 아기는 베이비시터가 잘 돌봐준다.

The woman **is laughing at** the girl.
➡ The girl **is being laughed at** by the woman. 소녀는 여자에 의해 비웃음을 받고 있다.

기본기 탄탄 다지기

1 다음 문장을 수동태로 바꾸어 쓸 때, 빈칸에 알맞은 말을 쓰시오.

(1) The children laughed at the clown.
　　➡ The clown ＿＿＿＿ ＿＿＿＿ ＿＿＿＿ by the children.

(2) Cindy put off our meeting.
　　➡ Our meeting ＿＿＿＿ ＿＿＿＿ ＿＿＿＿ by Cindy.

(3) The government must look after homeless children.
　　➡ Homeless children ＿＿＿＿ ＿＿＿＿ ＿＿＿＿ ＿＿＿＿ by the government.

(4) The boys are making fun of the poor girl.
　　➡ The poor girl ＿＿＿＿ ＿＿＿＿ ＿＿＿＿ ＿＿＿＿ by the boys.

> ▶자주 사용되는 동사구
> take care of ~을 돌보다
> run over ~을 치다
> take off ~을 벗다
> send for ~을 부르러 보내다
> put on ~을 입다
> carry out ~을 수행하다
> turn off ~을 끄다
> catch sight of ~을 보다
> turn on ~을 켜다
> look after ~을 돌보다
> catch up with ~을 따라잡다
> put up with ~을 참다
> depend/rely on ~을 신뢰하다
> pay attention to ~에 주의를 기울이다
> do away with ~을 제거하다

서술형 기초 다지기 ❷

1 주어진 문장을 수동태로 고치고 2개의 수동태가 가능한 경우 모두 쓰시오.

> My father bought me a new laptop computer.
> ➡ A new laptop computer was bought (for) me by my father.
> ➡ _____

(1) We gave the police the information.

➡ _____

➡ _____

(2) I sold her my old car for $500.

➡ _____

➡ _____

(3) My wife wrote me a long letter.

➡ _____

➡ _____

(4) Mrs. Smith teaches us French.

➡ _____

➡ _____

(5) He explained the reason to the customers.

➡ _____

➡ _____

2 다음 5형식 문장을 수동태로 바꿔 써 보시오.

(1) He made his children happy.

➡ _____

(2) They elected her the first female president of Korea.

➡ _____

(3) We saw a ghost go into the house.

➡ _____

(4) I won't let you do such a thing.

➡ _____

3 다음 동사구가 있는 문장을 수동태 또는 능동태로 바꾸어 쓰시오.

(1) A black car ran over my poor cat.

➡ _____

(2) The silverware were taken away last night by someone.

➡ _____

(3) Our bank was taken over by a foreign company.

➡ _____

(4) They looked up to the nurse.

➡ _____

(5) Lucy must put up with this unfortunate marriage.

➡ _____

4 다음 우리말과 의미가 같도록 괄호 안의 단어를 바르게 배열하여 빈칸에 쓰시오.

(1) 우유 한잔을 엄마가 내게 가져다주셨다.

➡ A glass of milk _____ by my mom. (me, brought, was, to)

(2) 우리는 별이 하늘을 가로질러 떨어지는 것을 봤다.

➡ Stars _____ across the sky by us. (fall, seen, to, were)

(3) 청중이 그녀로 인해 당황했다.

➡ The audience _____ by her. (made, was, embarrassed)

5 주어진 수동태 문장을 능동태로 고쳐 쓰시오.

(1) He was advised not to eat fatty food by the doctor.

➡ _____

(2) Jessica was made to clean her room by him.

➡ _____

(3) Their classmate was seen to get roughed up by them with folded arms.

➡ _____

Oral Test

Chapter 6

Challenge 1 4형식 문장을 수동태로 만들 수 있는가?

(1) 4형식은 두 개의 목적어, 즉 간접목적어와 직접목적어가 있으므로 수동태도 대부분 두 가지가 가능하다.
⬚⬚⬚ 목적어를 수동태의 주어로 쓸 경우 대부분 간접목적어 앞에 to를 쓰지만 buy, make, get, find, build는 ⬚⬚⬚ 를 쓴다.

- She gave John a birthday present.
  ➡ John **was given** a birthday present by her. John은 그녀에게서 생일선물을 받았다.
  ➡ A birthday present **was given** ⬚⬚⬚ John by her. 생일선물이 그녀에 의해 John에게 주어졌다.
- My dad made me a wooden toy car.
  ➡ A wooden toy car **was made** ⬚⬚⬚ me by my dad. 나무 장난감 자동차는 나를 위해 아빠에 의해 만들어졌다.

(2) make, write, cook, read, sell, buy, explain, suggest는 ⬚⬚⬚ 목적어만을 주어로 하는 수동태만 가능하다.

He bought me **a new dress**.
➡ **A new dress** was bought for me by him. 그가 나에게 새 드레스를 사주었다.

Challenge 2 5형식 문장을 수동태로 만들 수 있는가?

5형식 문장의 수동태는 목적어를 수동태의 주어로 하고, ⬚⬚⬚ 인 명사, 형용사, to부정사, 분사 등은 동사 뒤에 그대로 쓴다. 지각동사나 사역동사가 쓰인 5형식 문장에서 목적격 보어인 동사원형은 수동태로 전환될 때 ⬚⬚⬚ 로 바뀐다.

- The manager forced us **to work** over time every day.
  ➡ We *were forced* **to work** over time every day by the manager. 우리는 매일 야근을 하도록 매니저에게 강요받았다.

- The health inspector made the waiter **bring** him a cup of water.
  ➡ The waiter *was made* **to bring** him a cup of water by the health inspector.
  그 웨이터는 위생검사원에 의해 물 한 잔 가져오라는 요구를 받았다.

Challenge 3 동사구가 있는 문장을 수동태로 바꿀 수 있는가?

동사와 부사나 전치사가 이어진 동사구를 하나의 동사처럼 취급하여 ⬚⬚⬚ 만 'be + V-ed'로 고치고 부사나 전치사는 그대로 쓴다.

I'll **catch up with** you in a few minutes.
➡ You will **be caught up with** in a few minutes by me. 너는 나에 의해 몇 분 내에 따라 잡힐 거야.

People believe that she is a genius. 사람들은 그녀를 천재라고 믿는다.
→ **It is believed that** she is a genius. → **She** *is believed* **to be** a genius.

① 동사(think, say, believe, hope, suppose, consider, know)의 목적어가 명사절일 경우 가주어 it을 사용하여 수동태로 만들고 that 이하의 내용은 그대로 쓴다. that절 안의 주어를 문장의 주어로 써서 수동태를 만들 경우 that절 안에 있는 동사는 to부정사로 바뀐다.

People say that he is a billionaire. 사람들은 그가 억만장자라고 말한다.
➡ **It is said that** he is a billionaire. 그는 억만장자라고 말해진다.
➡ **He** *is said* **to be** a billionaire. ➡ that절 안의 주어를 문장의 주어로 쓴 경우 is는 to be로 쓴다.

We expect that the strike will end soon. 우리는 그 파업이 곧 끝날 거라고 기대한다.
➡ **It is expected that** the strike will end soon. 그 파업이 곧 끝날 거로 기대된다.
➡ **The strike** *is expected* **to end** soon. ➡ will end를 to end로 쓴다.

② that절 안의 동사 시제가 주절의 시제보다 더 과거인 경우 완료부정사 'to have + V-ed'를 쓴다.

People **believe** that Jane **was** a computer programmer. 사람들은 Jane이 컴퓨터 프로그래머였다고 생각한다.
➡ **It is believed that** Jane **was** a computer programmer.
➡ **Jane** *is believed* **to have been** a computer programmer.
➡ was는 believe 현재보다 더 과거이므로 'to have been'으로 쓴다.

기본기 탄탄 다지기

1 주어진 두 문장의 뜻이 같도록 빈칸에 알맞은 말을 쓰시오.

publish v. 출판하다
burglar n. 도둑
break into 침입하다
deal with 대처하다, 처리하다

(1) It is said that the book will be published soon.
　➡ The book ＿＿＿＿＿ ＿＿＿＿＿ ＿＿＿＿＿ ＿＿＿＿＿ ＿＿＿＿＿ soon.

(2) They said that a burglar broke into the office.
　➡ ＿＿＿＿＿ ＿＿＿＿＿ ＿＿＿＿＿ ＿＿＿＿＿ a burglar broke into the office.

(3) Laura is believed to have the ability to deal with it.
　➡ ＿＿＿＿＿ ＿＿＿＿＿ ＿＿＿＿＿ ＿＿＿＿＿ Laura has the ability to deal with it.

(4) Love is believed to be the most important thing in life.
　➡ People ＿＿＿＿＿ that ＿＿＿＿＿ ＿＿＿＿＿ the most important thing in life.

I **got** *the repairman* **to fix** the refrigerator.
나는 수리기사가 그 냉장고를 고치게 했다.
I **got** *the refrigerator* **fixed** by the repairman.
나는 수리기사에 의해 그 냉장고를 고쳐지게 했다.

1 have와 get은 그 자체로 수동태를 만들 수 없어 'have(get) + 목적어 + V-ed'로 수동의 뜻을 나타낸다. 행위자 (사람)를 목적어 자리에 쓸 경우 get은 목적격 보어 자리에 to부정사를 쓰고, have는 동사원형을 쓴다. 사물이 나 대상을 목적어 자리에 쓸 경우 목적격 보어 자리에 과거분사(V-ed)를 쓴다.

I'll **have** *my husband* **paint** the door. 나는 남편에게 그 문을 칠하게 할 것이다.
➡ my husband가 행위의 주체이므로 동사원형 paint를 쓴다.

I'll **have** *the door* **painted** by my husband. 나는 그 문이 남편에 의해 칠해지게 할 것이다.
➡ the door는 행위를 받는 대상이 되므로 과거분사 painted를 쓴다.

2 have와 get 동사로 수동의 의미를 나타낼 때 행위자는 꼭 필요한 경우에만 'by + 행위자'를 쓰고 중요하지 않 거나 누가 했는지 모를 경우 'by + 행위자'를 쓰지 않는다. get은 일상 영어에서 자주 쓰고 격식을 갖춘 글에는 잘 쓰지 않는다.

She **got(had)** *that coat* **cleaned** last week. 그녀는 저 코트를 지난주에 세탁하게 했다.
I **got(had)** *my car* **washed** by Lorenzo. 나는 Lorenzo에게 내 차를 세차하게 했다.

Chapter 6

기본기 탄탄 다지기

1 다음 괄호 안의 표현 중 알맞은 것을 고르시오.

(1) We didn't want to cook, so we got a pizza (deliver / delivered).

(2) Where did you have your hair (cut / to cut)?

(3) We're getting the architect (built / to build) a new house.

(4) You need to get your photo (taken / take) for your new passport.

(5) I had my smartphone (to steal / stolen) when I was on holiday.

(6) I got the man (painted / to paint) my bedroom walls.

(7) John was made (repair / to repair) the roof by me.

▶get과 사역동사 have, make, let 중 make만 목적어 자리에 있는 행위자를 주어로 하여 'be + made' 형태의 수동 태가 가능하다.
I **made** Bob repair the roof.
= Bob **was made** to repair the roof.
I **had(got)** Bob repair the roof.
= I **had(got)** the roof **repaired** by Bob.

▶let은 'let it be +V-ed' 또는 'be allowed to'로 수동태를 나타낸다.
She **let** me do it.
= I **was allowed to** do it by her.
= She **let** it be done by me.

Preview

I**'m interested in** arts so much. 나는 미술에 무척 관심이 많다.

He **is satisfied with** his mediocre income. 그는 평범한 수입에 만족하고 있다.

1 보통 수동태에서 행위자를 나타낼 때 by를 쓰지만 by 이외의 다른 전치사가 쓰이는 경우도 많으니 숙어처럼 외워두는 게 좋다.

be covered **with** : ~로 뒤덮이다	be married **to** : ~와 결혼하다
be filled **with** : ~로 가득 차 있다	be involved **in** : ~와 관련이 있다
be based **on** : ~에 근거를 두다	be known **to** : ~에게 알려져 있다
be known **for** : ~로 유명하다	be known **as** : ~로서 알려져 있다
be known **by** : ~을 보면 알 수 있다	be concerned **about** : ~에 대해 걱정하다
be engaged **in** : ~에 종사하다	be occupied **with/in** : ~에 종사하다
be absorbed/lost **in** : ~에 몰두(열중)하다	be devoted **to** : ~에 몰두(열중)하다
be made **of** : ~로 만들어지다(모양만 바뀜)	be made **from** : ~로 만들어지다 (성질이 바뀜)

This book **is known to** every student. 이 책은 모든 학생들에게 알려졌다.

The mountain **is covered with** snow. 그 산은 눈으로 덮여있다.

I don't want to **be involved in** this matter. 이 문제에 관여하고 싶지 않습니다.

The senator **is known as** a leading figure in politics. 그 상원의원은 정계의 거물로 알려져 있다.

기본기 탄탄 다지기

1 다음 빈칸에 들어갈 알맞은 말을 보기에서 골라 쓰시오.

with	by	from	about

(1) A man is known _____ the company he keeps.

(2) We are concerned _____ your safety.

(3) I was very satisfied _____ my student's answer.

(4) My shirt is made _____ cotton.

▶동사의 형태는 능동이지만 수동으로 해석되는 경우가 있다. 이 경우에는 보통 well, easily 등의 부사(구)와 함께 쓴다.

The book still **sells** well.
그 책은 아직도 잘 팔린다.

The poem **reads** well.
그 시는 술술 잘 읽힌다.

Jeju oranges **peel** well.
제주 감귤은 껍질이 잘 벗겨진다.

This bread doesn't **cut** easily.
이 빵은 쉽게 잘라지지 않는다.

서술형 기초 다지기 ❸

1 다음 문장을 It ~ that과 that절의 주어를 문장 전체 주어로 하는 두 개의 수동태 문장을 만드시오.

(1) We believe that Yu-na Kim will win the World Figure Skating Championships.

➡ _____

➡ _____

(2) They say that he was a brave soldier as a young man.

➡ _____

➡ _____

(3) We think that she was the right woman for the job.

➡ _____

➡ _____

(4) People say that stress causes headaches.

➡ _____

➡ _____

(5) We expect that this winter will be warmer than usual.

➡ _____

➡ _____

2 보기와 같이 'have + 목적어 + 과거분사'를 이용하여 문장을 완성하시오.

> Sally / clean / her car / every week
> ➡ Sally has her car cleaned every week. _____

(1) I / must / type / these letters / by / tonight

➡ _____

(2) Tiffany / always / do / her nails / at a beauty salon

➡ _____

(3) Nancy / dye / her hair / next week

➡ _____

(4) Sunny / check / her teeth / last week.

➡ _____

3 다음 괄호 안의 단어를 이용하여 수동태 문장이 되도록 빈칸을 완성하시오.

(1) The square is _____ _____ people. (crowd)

(2) My parents are _____ _____ my grades. (worry)

(3) Are you _____ _____ learning to play the drum? (interest)

4 주어진 수동태 문장을 능동태 문장이 되도록 빈칸을 완성하시오.

(1) It is expected that John will win the race.

➡ We all _____.

(2) Kevin is said to be responsible for what happened.

➡ People _____.

(3) A flat tire is believed to have caused the accident.

➡ Experts _____.

5 다음 글을 읽고 보기와 같이 동작에 대한 실제 행위자에 V 표시하시오.

I've had my computer upgraded.	I ☐	somebody else ☐

(1) Lisa has already had lunch.	Lisa ☐	somebody else ☐
(2) We had the windows cleaned yesterday.	We ☐	somebody else ☐
(3) We've planted a lot of flowers in our garden.	We ☐	somebody else ☐
(4) Sue is having her picture taken.	Sue ☐	somebody else ☐
(5) Our company is having a new computer system installed.	Our company ☐	somebody else ☐
(6) Sarah is having her hair cut.	Sarah ☐	somebody else ☐

Oral Test

Challenge 1 목적어가 명사절일 때 어떻게 수동태로 쓰는가?

(1) 목적어가 명사절일 경우, 가주어 it을 사용하여 'It + [　　　　　] + that ~'으로 수동태를 만든다. that절 안의 주어를 문장의 주어로 하여 수동태를 만들 경우 that절 안의 동사는 반드시 [　　　　　]로 바뀐다.

They say that Thomas is a brilliant boy. Thomas가 똑똑한 아이라고 하는군요.
➡ **It is said** that Thomas is a brilliant boy.
➡ **Thomas** *is said* **to be** a brilliant boy.

(2) that절 안의 시제가 문장의 시제, 즉 주절의 시제보다 한 시제 앞선 경우 '[　　　　　]'를 써서 더 이전에 있었던 일을 나타낸다.

They **say** that Thomas **was** a brilliant boy. Thomas가 똑똑한 아이였다고 하는군요.
➡ **It is said** that Thomas **was** a brilliant boy.
➡ **Thomas** *is said* **to have been** a brilliant boy.

Challenge 2 have와 get을 이용한 수동태를 만들 수 있는가?

have와 get은 그 자체로 수동태가 불가능하기 때문에 'have + [　　　　　] + [　　　　　]'의 형태로 수동의 의미를 표현한다.

Kevin **had** *the roof* **repaired** yesterday. Kevin은 어제 지붕이 수리되게 했다.

I'm going to **get** *my hair* **cut** at the new hairdresser's. 나는 그 새로 생긴 미용실에서 머리를 자를 거다.

Challenge 3 by 이외의 전치사를 쓰는 수동태를 알고 있는가?

수동태에서 행위자를 나타낼 때 'by' 이외의 다른 전치사를 쓰는 경우가 많으니 중요 표현들은 따로 암기해 두어야 한다.

The professor **is devoted** [　　　　　] astronomy. 그 교수는 천문학에 전념하고 있다.

We **weren't** very **satisfied** [　　　　　] the service in the restaurant. 우리는 그 식당의 서비스에 만족하지 못했다.

[1–2] 다음 문장의 빈칸에 가장 적합한 것을 고르시오.

1

> Many people are very _____ the
> destruction of rain forests.

① concerning   ② concerned to

③ concerned with   ④ concerned about

⑤ concerned by

2

> It is believed that he kept the promise.
> = _____ the promise.

① It is believed his keeping

② It was believed for him to keep

③ He is believed to have kept

④ He was believed to keep

⑤ He is believed to keep

3 다음 문장들을 수동태로 바꾼 것 중에 <u>틀린</u> 것은?

① Children can't open these bottles easily.
  ➡ These bottles can't be opened easily
    by children.

② The party will celebrate his parents'
  anniversary.
  ➡ His parents' anniversary will celebrated
    by the party.

③ When did you hear the bell ring?
  ➡ When was the bell heard to ring by
    you?

④ They think that the prisoner escaped by
  climbing over a wall.
  ➡ The prisoner is thought to have
    escaped by climbing over a wall.

⑤ Somebody has cleaned the office.
  ➡ The office has been cleaned.

4 다음 문장을 수동태로 바꿀 때 빈칸에 적절한 표현은?

> They are teaching taekwondo in an
> increasing number of high schools.
> ➡ Taekwondo _____ in an
> increasing number of high schools.

① will be taught   ② will teach

③ are teaching   ④ is being taught

⑤ is been teach

5 다음 빈칸에 들어갈 말이 바르게 짝지어진 것은?

> • I'm very interested _____ Korean
>   movies.
> • All the books here are made _____
>   recycled paper.

① of - from   ② in - from   ③ with - of

④ at - in   ⑤ in - of

6 다음 빈칸에 들어갈 말이 알맞게 짝지어진 것은?

> • Did you know that a lot of animals are
>   _____ killed each year because
>   people want to wear their skin?
> • Seven books have _____ sold for a
>   month.

① having - being   ② had - been

③ having - had   ④ been - being

⑤ being - been

7 다음 문장의 빈칸에 공통으로 알맞은 것은?

> • Germany was _____ into East and West.
> • Korea is _____ into North and South.

① unified   ② unify   ③ reunified
④ divide   ⑤ divided

8 다음 대화의 빈칸에 알맞은 것은?

> A: How long will it take to finish the work?
> B: Everything _____ by the end of next week.

① does   ② is done   ③ will done
④ was doing   ⑤ will be done

9 다음 밑줄 친 부분 중 어법상 어색한 것은?

> Sports ① are being played by increasing numbers of athletes. Moreover, great strides ② have made by athletes in recent years. In the past, years often ③ went by before new records ④ were set. But now records ⑤ are being broken at an ever faster pace by ever stronger and more focused athletes.

10 다음 밑줄 친 부분 중 어법상 어색한 것은?

① My new hair style <u>was laughed at</u> by my girlfriend.
② Our school <u>is known for</u> its soccer team.
③ The teacher <u>was looked up to</u> by the students.
④ Why don't you <u>get your winter coat dry-cleaned</u>?
⑤ Tom and Christina <u>had all their money steal</u> while they were on vacation.

11 다음을 수동태 문장으로 바꿀 때 괄호 안에 주어진 말 중 알맞은 것은?

> The university offered him the opportunity to study in Moscow.

➡ The opportunity to study in Moscow was offered (to him / for him) by the university.

12 다음 문장 중 어법상 어색한 것을 고르시오.

① This medicine must be taken as directed by your doctor.
② William was made to carry the luggage to the station.
③ The day after tomorrow, she will have her washing machine repair.
④ The hamburger was introduced to the United States by German immigrants.
⑤ A polka-dot tie was bought for me by my mother.

서술형 대비 문제

[1–2] 두 문장의 뜻이 같도록 빈칸에 알맞은 말을 쓰시오.

1

The teacher made us do our homework right away.

= We _____ _____ _____ _____ our homework right away by the teacher.

2

We believe that calcium builds strong bones and teeth.

= Calcium is believed _____ _____ strong bones and teeth.

3 다음 우리말과 뜻이 같도록 주어진 단어를 이용하여 빈칸에 알맞은 말을 쓰시오.

그 공포영화는 오늘 상영되지 않을 것이다.
(the scary movie, show)

➡ _____

4 다음 사진을 보고 사진과 일치하는 문장을 영작하시오.

The house _____ .

5 괄호 안의 단어를 활용하여 주어진 질문에 알맞은 답을 영작하시오.

Q: Who wrote the Harry Potter books?
A: _____
   (J.K. Rowling / write)

아직도 일기예보를 믿는 사람이 있어?

(a) Weather is very important to live our lives. (b) Meteorologists, scientists who study the weather, analyze the air, wind, and rain, etc and predict the weather in the near future. Pilots must know how airplanes might affect by the bad weather. (c) Bad weather can be problematic. In order to grow healthy crops, farmers need the sunlight and enough amount of rain. An early frost can ruin the whole crop if the harvest season hasn't come yet. (d) Thick fog can cause accidents for cars and boats. But for children, the bad weather can be fun. (e) On dry hot days, they can go swimming. On snowy and cold days, they can go skiing.

Chapter 6

1 Choose the sentence that best summarizes this paragraph.

① (a)   ② (b)   ③ (c)   ④ (d)   ⑤ (e)

2 According to the paragraph, why is weather so important?

① Because people rely on the weather each day.
② People can die from bad weather conditions.
③ Weather can influence humans in many ways.
④ Children need to have a suitable environment in which to play.
⑤ Meteorologists need to keep their honorable jobs.

3 윗글 밑줄 친 문장을 어법상 바르게 고쳐 쓰시오.

➡ _____

Super Speaking

 Pair work A 보기와 같이 수동태를 이용하여 묻고 답하는 형식으로 말하기 연습을 하세요. 연습이 한 번 끝난 후 서로 역할을 바꿔 다시 말하기 연습을 하세요.

the telephone / invent / Shakespeare / ?

No ➡ Alexander Graham Bell

> **A:** Was the telephone invented by Shakespeare?

> **B:** No, it wasn't. It was invented by Alexander Graham Bell.

1

The Mona Lisa / paint / Leo Tolstoy / ?

No ➡ Leonardo da Vinci

2

the light bulb / invent / Walt Disney / ?

No ➡ Thomas Edison

 Pair work B 보기와 같이 수동태를 이용하여 말하기 연습을 하세요. 연습이 한 번 끝난 후 서로 역할을 바꿔 다시 말하기 연습을 하세요.

Coffee / grow / in Italy

➡ it / Brazil

> **A:** Coffee is grown in Italy.

> **B:** Coffee isn't grown in Italy. It is grown in Brazil.

1

The world's first Olympic Games / hold / in Korea

➡ they / Greece

2

Romeo and Juliet / write / Vincent van Gogh

➡ it / Shakespeare

출제의도 | 수동태로 문장 나타내기
평가내용 | 4형식, 목적어가 절인 문장의 수동태

서술형 유형	10점
난이도	중

 주어진 문장을 보기와 같이 가능한 수동태를 만들어 보시오.

> 보기 Aston University offered Tom a scholarship.
>
> ➡ Tom was offered a scholarship by Aston University.
>
> ➡ A scholarship was offered to Tom by Aston University.

1 The company gave Alex a farewell present.

➡ _____

➡ _____

2 Everybody thinks that Cindy has moved abroad.

➡ _____

➡ _____

3 The girl asked me the direction to the City Hall.

➡ _____

➡ _____

4 They say that people spend too much time watching TV and don't read enough.

➡ _____

➡ _____

5 Scott bought his grandfather a striped shirt.

➡ _____

➡ _____

평가영역	채점기준	배점
유창성(Fluency) & 정확성(Accuracy)	5개의 문항을 모두 올바른 표현과 함께 정확하게 완성한 경우 (문법, 철자가 모두 정확한 경우)	5×2 = 10점
	수동태를 만들지 못하였거나 문법, 철자가 1개씩 틀린 경우	문항당 1점씩 감점
	내용과 전혀 일치하지 않거나 답을 기재하지 못한 경우	0점

Chapter 6

		서술형 유형	8점
출제의도 | 동사 have를 이용한 능동태, 수동태 문장 표현하기		**난이도**	중상
평가내용 | have + something + V-ed(과거분사)			

B 보기와 같이 사진 속 인물이 어떤 일을 직접 하는 경우에는 현재진행형을, 남에게 시키는 경우에는 'have + 목적어 + 과거분사'를 이용하여 문장을 영작하시오.

보기 Peter (repair / the laptop computer)　　　Jane (take / her picture)

➡ Peter is repairing the laptop computer. _____　　➡ Jane is having her picture taken. _____

1 Karen (fill / her tooth)

➡ _____

2  Susan (mop / the floor)

➡ _____

3 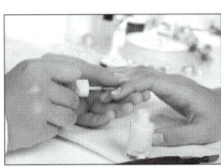 Jessica (paint / her nails)

➡ _____

4 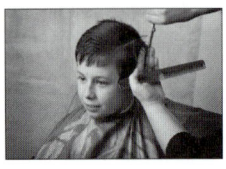 the boy (cut / his hair)

➡ _____

평가영역	채점기준	배점
유창성(Fluency) & 정확성(Accuracy)	4개의 문장을 모두 올바른 표현과 함께 정확하게 완성한 경우 (문법, 철자가 모두 정확한 경우)	4×2 = 8점
	have를 이용한 수동 표현을 사용하지 못하였거나 문법, 철자가 1개씩 틀린 경우	문항당 1점씩 감점
	내용과 전혀 일치하지 않거나 답을 기재하지 못한 경우	0점

출제의도 | 글을 읽고 수동태로 문장 전환하기
평가내용 | 다양한 형태의 수동태

서술형 유형	20점
난이도	상

C 주어진 글을 수동태를 이용하여 모두 다시 고쳐 써 보시오.

A few days ago, somebody stole Kevin's motorcycle. Kevin had left his motorcycle outside his house. Kevin reported the theft to the police. The police told him they would try to find his motorcycle. This morning, the police called Kevin and asked him to come to the police station. They had found his motorcycle. The thieves had painted it and then sold it to someone else. The new owner had parked the motorcycle outside the police station. The police arrested the thieves.

평가영역	채점기준	배점
유창성(Fluency) & 정확성(Accuracy)	모든 문장을 올바른 표현과 함께 정확하게 완성한 경우 (문법, 철자가 모두 정확한 경우)	20점
	수동태를 바르게 사용하지 못하였거나 문법, 철자가 1개씩 틀린 경우	문장당 2점씩 감점
	내용과 전혀 일치하지 않거나 답을 기재하지 못한 경우	0점

MEMO

Answer Key
정답

Unit 1 ● 기본기 탄탄 다지기   p.12
1 (1) To solve this problem   (2) to speak three languages
   (3) not to go out
2 (1) It is difficult to write a letter in English.
   (2) It is easy to understand why Jessica is angry.
   (3) It is a good idea to practice interview questions before going on an
     interview.

Unit 2 ● 기본기 탄탄 다지기   p.13
1 (1) Please tell me how to get to the City Hall.
   (2) He let me know what to say next.
   (3) Why didn't you ask me when to start?
   (4) Will you show me where to play this game?
   (5) I want to learn how I should drive a car.
   (6) I have no idea what I should do for her.

Unit 3 ● 기본기 탄탄 다지기   p.14
1 (1) to tell   (2) clean   (3) have   (4) shout
   (5) coming   (6) to make   (7) to light

서술형 기초 다지기 ❶   p.15
1 (1) It / to / eat   (2) It / to / learn   (3) It / to / learn
2 (1) Do you know what you should do next?
   (2) I don't know what I should give her for a birthday gift.
   (3) Do you know how you should go there?
3 (1) to have a baby this month   (2) to fill in this application form
   (3) to get a promotion this year   (4) To design a new house on the hill
4 (1) I saw him arrive early.
   (2) We watched her get out of the car.
   (3) We saw Susan and Paul having/have a date.
   (4) They let me telephone my lawyer.
   (5) The police officer had me empty my pockets.
5 (1) wants to help   (2) what to say   (3) to return some books
   (4) made him finish   (5) where to get

Oral Test   p.17
1 주어, 목적어, 보어 / 주어, 보어, 목적어
2 (1) 주어, 목적어, 보어
   (2) '의문사 + 주어 + should + 동사원형'
3 동작/행동, to eat
3 (1) make, have, let / to, 동사원형   (2) 동사원형 / 현재분사(V-ing)

Unit 4 ● 기본기 탄탄 다지기   p.18
1 (1) to live in   (2) person to tell
   (3) to help me   (4) way to contact
   (5) things to do   (6) something important to show

Unit 5 ● 기본기 탄탄 다지기   p.19
1 (1) 의무   (2) 예정   (3) 운명   (4) 의지   (5) 가능

Unit 6 ● 기본기 탄탄 다지기   p.20
1 (1) 원인   (2) 목적   (3) 결과
   (4) 형용사 수식   (5) 판단의 근거   (6) 조건

서술형 기초 다지기 ❷   p.21
1 (1) I was excited to eat such delicious food.
   (2) Dad was disappointed to find that I lied to him.
   (3) Tom grew up to become a movie director.
2 (1) I went to the library to borrow some books.
   (2) Some people need English to get a better job.
   (3) Jane is going to go to the nursing home to take part in volunteer work.
   (4) I hurried not to be late for school.
   (5) We arrived early to finish the given work.
   (6) She turned on the TV to watch the news.
3 (1) I need something cold to drink.
   (2) They're looking for a house to live in.
4 (1) to hear the news   (2) computer games to fix
   (3) to break up with   (4) to see
5 (1) to be held / 예정   (2) are to succeed /의지
   (3) are to come / 의무   (4) to be heard / 가능

Oral Test   p.23
1 (1) 뒤   (2) to부정사 / 전치사
2 예정 / 의무 / 가능 / 의지 / 운명
3 (1) 형용사   (2) 목적   (3) 원인   (4) 근거   (5) 조건   (6) 결과

Unit 7 ● 기본기 탄탄 다지기   p.24
1 (1) him to arrive   (2) of you to refuse   (3) to ask
   (4) for me to understand   (5) of her to do

Unit 8 ● 기본기 탄탄 다지기   p.25
1 (1) to have been   (2) to take   (3) to have been
   (4) to have been   (5) to go   (6) to have passed

Unit 9 ● 기본기 탄탄 다지기   p.26
1 (1) To tell the truth   (2) To make matters worse
   (3) so to speak   (4) not to mention

서술형 기초 다지기 ❸   p.27
1 (1) of   (2) for   (3) for   (4) of   (5) for
2 (1) To tell   (2) To say   (3) To be
   (4) no to mention   (5) To make
3 (1) She appears to have bought a new smartphone yesterday.
   (2) I am sorry to have bothered you so far.
   (3) The reporter seems to enjoy writing on her blog.
4 (1) for me to stay up until late at night
   (2) of her to make me kill the flies
   (3) of Jessica to give up her new job although it is hard to get another one
   (4) of them to make the same mistake
   (5) for children to sit still for a long time

5 (1) appeared / my girlfriend had stopped smoking

(2) seems / he studied hard

(3) seems / they worked together in the past

(4) seems / the accident happened when I was young

(5) seemed / Sarah had gained weight

Oral Test   p.29

1 (1) 주어 / 목적어

(2) for + 명사(목적격) / of + 명사(목적격)

2 (1) to + 동사원형   (2) to have + V-ed

3

to be frank with you	솔직히 말하면
to begin with	우선, 먼저, 무엇보다도
not to mention	~은 말할 필요도 없이
to make a long story short	간단히 말하면
to tell the truth	사실대로 말하자면
so to speak	말하자면, 소위
strange to say	말하기에 이상하지만
needless to say	말할 필요 없지만
to make matters worse	설상가상으로
to sum up	요약해서 말하면

Unit 10 ● 기본기 탄탄 다지기   p.30

1 (1) brave enough to   (2) too young to go

2 (1) too expensive (for me) to buy

(2) enough to buy whatever he wants

Unit 11 ● 기본기 탄탄 다지기   p.31

1 (1) have some coffee   (2) play the violin   (3) take a break

(4) meet Sally   (5) buy a new car   (6) take a taxi

(7) stay

Unit 12 ● 기본기 탄탄 다지기   p.32

1 (1) can   (2) could   (3) wouldn't

2 (1) it / to brush   (2) it / to break   (3) it / learn

서술형 기초 다지기 ❹   p.33

1 (1) The pizza was so hot that we couldn't eat it.

(2) Susan is so old that she can drive in Korea.

(3) Kevin is so stupid that he can't understand the situation.

(4) The water was so cold that I couldn't swim in it.

(5) The girl is so brave that she can speak in front of other people.

(6) The T-shirt is so small that you can't put it on.

2 (1) They bicycle is too expensive (for me) to buy.

(2) She is tall enough to reach the top branch of the tree.

(3) Jane was too sick to attend the meeting.

(4) Sunny is cool enough to forgive anybody.

(5) She was foolish enough to trust him.

(6) Her grades were high enough to get the license.

3 (1) see the pyramids   (2) take your dictionary

(3) watch the movie   (4) go out for dinner

(5) punch my brother on the forehead

4 (1) I make it a rule to have breakfast at seven.

(2) They believed it easy to answer the questions.

(3) Do you think it difficult to grow those plants in this land?

---

(4) The machinery will make it possible to increase productivity.

(5) The alphabet makes it possible for us to read and write thousands of words with only twenty-six different letters.

Oral Test   p.35

1 (1) 형용사(부사) / so / that / can't / couldn't

(2) enough / 앞 / so / that / can / could

2 to

3 목적어 / it

중간 · 기말고사   p.36

1 ④

2 ⑤

3 ②

4 how to play tennis

5 ①

6 ⑤

7 ③

8 ④

9 ⑤

10 ⑤

11 ④

12 ⑤

서술형 대비 문제

1 to understand → understand

2 My mother helped me to solve the problems.

3 a thief breaking(break) into the(a) house

4 (1) to have had   (2) enough to break

Grammar in Reading   p.39

1 ④

2 wake me up

3 ⑤

1980년에 3M이 미국 전역에 처음 포스트잇을 판매하기 시작했다. 오늘날, 포스트 잇은 세계에서 가장 많이 팔리는 사무용품 중 하나이다. 사람들은 많은 다른 용도로 포스트잇을 사용한다. 어느 한 남자가 포스트잇에 "저와 결혼해 줄래요?"라고 쓰 고 그것을 그의 여자 친구 컴퓨터 모니터에 붙여 놓았다. 그녀는 "네!"라고 쓰고 다 시 그의 모니터에 붙였다. 어느 한 여자는 멀리 여행을 떠나는 조카의 차 뒤에 메모 를 해 두었다. 4,500 킬로미터를 간 후에 그는 그의 차에서 메모를 발견했다. 그는 여전히 그 메모를 읽을 수 있었다. 어느 한 대학생이 버스로 여행을 하고 있었다. 그 녀는 버스정류장에서 기다리고 있었고 매우 지쳐있었다. 그녀는 잠이 들어 버스를 놓칠 것 같아 걱정이 되어서 온몸에 포스트잇을 붙이기로 했다. 그 메모 내용은 그 녀의 버스 시간에 깨워 달라는 것이었다. 그녀는 잠이 들었지만 아무도 그 메모지를 보지 못했고 그녀는 버스를 놓치고 말았다.

Super Speaking   p.40

A **1** A: What do you want to be in the future?

B: I'd like to be a soccer player like Ji-sung Park.

2 A: What do you want to be in the future?

B: I'd like to be a rhythmic gymnast like Yeon-jae Son.

B **1** A: Can Jane carry the heavy suitcase?

B: No, she can't. She isn't strong enough to carry the heavy suitcase.

2 A: Can you make people laugh?

B: No, I can't. I'm not funny enough to make people laugh.

Chapter 2
동명사

서술형 기초 다지기 ❸   p.61

1 (1) my(me) starting   (2) Jessica('s) buying

   (3) her dancing   (4) their(them) coming

   (5) Susan('s) falling

2 (1) was busy working   (2) worth watching

   (3) It is no use learning   (4) has difficulty in talking

   (5) is used(accustomed) to sleeping

3 (1) 동물원에서 일하는 것 / 동명사   (2) TV를 보고 있다 / 현재분사

   (3) 침낭 / 동명사   (4) 경주용 자동차 / 동명사

   (5) 세탁기 / 동명사   (6) 웃고 있는 소녀 / 현재분사

4 (1) isn't worth reading   (2) is worth visiting

   (3) isn't worth repairing   (4) is worth discussing

5 (1) difficulty finding a place to live in   (2) difficulty making good friends

   (3) difficulty getting a ticket for the movie

Oral Test   p.63

1 (2) 소유격

2

on(upon) + V–ing	~ 하자마자
be busy + V–ing	~하느라 바쁘다
look forward to + V–ing	~하기를 고대하다
be accustomed(used) to + V–ing	~하는데 익숙하다
There's no use + V–ing	~하는 것은 불가능하다
be good at + V–ing	~하는 것을 잘하다
object to + V–ing	~에 반대하다
far from + V–ing	전혀 ~아닌
cannot help + V–ing	~하지 않을 수 없다
It's no use + V–ing	~해도 소용없다
be worth + V–ing	~할 가치가 있다
keep(prevent) ~ from + V–ing	~가 ...하지 못하게 하다
feel like + V–ing	~하고 싶다
have difficulty (in) + V–ing	~하는데 어려움을 겪다
not/never ~without + V–ing	~하면 반드시 ...하다
above + V–ing	결코 ~하지 않는

3 (1) 현재분사, 동명사, 현재분사, 동명사 (2) 현재분사, 동명사, 현재분사, 동명사

중간 · 기말고사   p.64

1 ④

2 ②

3 ⑤

4 ④

5 ①

6 ④

7 ②

8 ⑤

9 her, screaming

10 his, daughter('s), leaving

11 ①

12 prevented(kept), from, going

서술형 대비 문제

1 I never see her face without laughing.

2 blame the police for not taking

3 am interested in volunteering for your project

4 feels like eating spaghetti

5 I am not good at drawing paintings.

Grammar in Reading   p.67

1 ①

2 ⓑ to perform → performing

당신은 한 가족의 구성원이고 지역 야구팀의 선수이며 그리고 당신 학교의 학생이다. 당신은 또한 당신의 나라의 한 시민이다. 요컨대, 당신은 복잡한 사회 구조에서 몇 가지 다른 지위를 차지하고 있다. 이것은 당신이 다양한 상황에서 많은 역할을 해야 한다는 것을 의미한다. 일반적으로, 당신은 자신에게 기대되는 것이 무엇인지 알기 때문에 당신의 각각의 역할을 수행하는 데 어려움을 거의 갖지 않는다. 이러한 지식은 당신의 일상적인 상호작용을 통해 당신을 지도한다. 그러나 때때로 당신은 어떤 갈등에 휘말리게 된다. 당신의 각각의 역할은 당신에게 몇 가지 요구를 하고 당신은 동시에 두 개나 그 이상의 역할을 하도록 요청받을 수 있다. 당신이 상충하는 여러 역할들을 요구받을 때, 당신은 아주 불편하게 느끼고 때때로 좌절감을 느낄 수 있다. 예를 들어, 당신의 가족이 이번 일요일에 소풍 갈 예정이라고 하자. 하지만 당신의 가장 친한 친구는 당신이 같은 날 자신의 생일 파티에 와 주기를 원한다. 그러한 역할 갈등이 일어날 때, 당신은 더 중요한 것들을 먼저 할 필요가 있다. 그래서 어떤 순서로 무엇을 할 것인지 결정할 능력은 중요한 기술이고, 당신이 여러 가지 사회적 역할을 수행하는 것을 도와줄 수 있다.

Super Speaking   p.68

A **1** A: Are you interested in cooking?

     B: No, I'm not, I prefer washing dishes. What about you?

     A: I'm not interested in washing dishes.

  2 A: Are you interested in reading novels?

     B: No, I'm not, I prefer taking pictures. What about you?

     A: I'm not interested in taking pictures.

B **1** A: What do you enjoy when you have free time?

     B: I enjoy traveling around the country. How about you?

     A: I like going fishing with my dad.

  2 A: What do you enjoy when you have free time?

     B: I enjoy making Korean food. How about you?

     A: I like eating fast food.

실전 서술형 평가 문제 (모범 답안)   p.69

A **1** about being late for the movie

  2 in finding a good job

  3 for making so much noise

  4 to seeing the famous actress

  5 about going to Disneyland

B **1** The thief denied stealing money.

  2 Tom (always) puts off doing his homework.

  3 Jane (has) stopped smoking.

  4 His family hope to travel to Egypt this summer.

  5 Kelly wants to be an English teacher.

  6 My mother finished cleaning the room.

  7 Peter forgot to turn off the television.

C **1** Sarah can remember crying on her first day at school.

  2 Sarah can remember going to Korea when she was eight.

  3 Sarah can't remember saying she wanted to be a math teacher.

  4 Sarah can't remember being bitten by a rattlesnake.

  5 Sarah can remember falling into a deep well.

Unit 1 ● 기본기 탄탄 다지기　　　　　p.74

1　(1) floating　　(2) fallen　　(3) sitting　　(4) sleeping
　　(5) waiting　　(6) painted　　(7) made　　(8) running

Unit 2 ● 기본기 탄탄 다지기　　　　　p.75

1　(1) barking　　(2) fixed　　(3) looking　　(4) standing
　　(5) written　　(6) running　　(7) lying

Unit 3 ● 기본기 탄탄 다지기　　　　　p.76

1　(1) surprised　　　(2) shocked　　　(3) disappointed
　　(4) frightened　　(5) exciting

서술형 기초 다지기 ❶　　　　　p.77

1　(1) Who is the girl wearing a blue cap?
　　(2) The cars made in Korea are nice.
　　(3) The woman injured in the accident was taken to the hospital.
　　(4) The story written by T. J. Johnson is very weird.
　　(5) The man surrounded by many female fans is a very famous actor.
　　(6) The student sitting in the front row is my cousin.
2　(1) sounds very interesting　　(2) beaten by some children
　　(3) sat reading the newspaper　　(4) heard my name called
　　(5) found her washing
3　(1) interesting / interested　　(2) excited / exciting
4　(1) who is / The girl waiting at the bus stop is my sister.
　　(2) that was / The information found on that Website was incorrect.
　　(3) who is / Do you know the man standing by the window?
5　(1) written　　(2) translated　　(3) satisfied　　(4) crying

Oral Test　　　　　p.79

1　동작
2　뒤, 현재분사, 과거분사
3　(1) 현재분사, 과거분사　　　(2) 현재분사, 과거분사
4　현재분사, 과거분사

Unit 4 ● 기본기 탄탄 다지기　　　　　p.80

1　(1) Walking　　(2) Being　　(3) Turning　　(4) Living　　(5) Working

Unit 5 ● 기본기 탄탄 다지기　　　　　p.81

1　(1) coming　　　(2) Walking　　　(3) finishing
2　(1) Arriving　　　(2) leaving

Unit 6 ● 기본기 탄탄 다지기　　　　　p.82

1　(1) 이유　　(2) 조건　　(3) 이유
2　(1) Because　　(2) If　　(3) If　　(4) Because

서술형 기초 다지기 ❷　　　　　p.83

1　(1) Turning around　　(2) Watching TV
　　(3) Playing tennis　　(4) Feeling confident
　　(5) Taking a shower　　(6) Finding her address
　　(7) Arriving at the station　　(8) Having a slight cold
　　(9) Not knowing her address　　(10) Having two jobs
　　(11) Opening the door　　(12) Being a foreigner
2　(1) Because she was poor　　(2) If you take this bus
　　(3) When I walked along the street
3　(1) (e) / Hearing the news, she jumped for joy.
　　(2) (d) / Getting up early, you will not be late for school.
　　(3) (b) / Studying very little, Tom got a bad grade at the mid-term test.
　　(4) (a) / Finishing her homework, she always watches TV.
　　(5) (c) / Not having a car any more, she has to use public transportation.

Oral Test　　　　　p.85

1　V-ing (동사원형 + -ing)
　　(1) 접속사　　　(2) 주어, 주어, 주어　　　(3) 시제, 시제, V-ing
2　(1) 시간, Getting, Upon getting, On getting
　　(2) 이유/원인, Being　　(3) 조건, Turning

Unit 7 ● 기본기 탄탄 다지기　　　　　p.86

1　(1) Being　　(2) Studying　　(3) Working
2　(1) Being　　(2) Having

Unit 8 ● 기본기 탄탄 다지기　　　　　p.87

1　(1) reading　　(2) singing　　(3) waiting　　(4) Walking　　(5) arriving

Unit 9 ● 기본기 탄탄 다지기　　　　　p.88

1　(1) Traveling　　(2) Having worked　　(3) Having studied
　　(4) Having　　(5) Having found

서술형 기초 다지기 ❸　　　　　p.89

1　(1) looking for an empty seat　　(2) Having dinner together
　　(3) arriving in New York at 11　　(4) smiling charmingly
　　(5) Eating the cheery pie
2　(1) Admitting what you say　　(2) Living on the seashore
　　(3) Being very sick　　(4) Knowing the answers
　　(5) Playing the game very hard
3　(1) Having eaten 8 slices of pizza　　(2) Driving carefully
　　(3) Watching the city through the window
　　(4) Having failed in the exam　　(5) Having slept all day long
4　(1) As I was tired, I didn't go to the party.
　　(2) After I had read the book, I threw it away.
　　(3) After Olivia had failed several times, she succeeded at last.
　　(4) Because she was not sick, she couldn't be absent from school.
　　(5) As I lost my cell phone, I have to buy a new one now.

Oral Test　　　　　p.91

1　Living
2　(1) 동시동작　　　(2) 연속동작
3　having V-ed, Having met

1 (1) Crossing   (2) Smiling   (3) Written   (4) Seen
   (5) Compared   (6) Not knowing   (7) Built

1 (1) It snowing   (2) It being
2 (1) Strictly speaking   (2) Judging from

1 (1) turned   (2) falling   (3) locked
   (4) covered   (5) standing   (6) ringing

1 (1) (Being) Injured in his leg
   (2) (Having been) Deceived by her sweet words
   (3) Finishing the work
   (4) (Having been) Built more than five thousand years ago
   (5) Not having met him before
   (6) (Having been) Printed in haste
2 (1) It becoming darker, we turned the light on.
   (2) It being fine, they went shopping.
   (3) There being many umbrellas, you can have one.
   (4) The class being over, the children left quickly.
   (5) Homework done, the girls rushed out.
3 (1) Having   (2) Not, having
   (3) Frankly, speaking   (4) Generally, speaking
   (5) Judging, from
4 (1) with the windows locked   (2) with her legs crossed
5 (1) with her head leaning   (2) with the radio turned on
   (3) with her eyes closed

1 being, having been, Being, Having been
2 (1) 분사, 독립 분사구문   (2) 비인칭 독립 분사구문
3 현재분사, 과거분사, folded, running

1 (1) Coming   (2) Not having
2 ⑤
3 Because
4 While
5 Though
6 ⑤
7 ①
8 ①, ②
9 ②, ③
10 ①
11 ②
12 exhausting, exhausted
13 boring, interesting
14 ⑤
15 giving
16 ④

서술형 대비 문제

1 (1) Frankly speaking   (2) Generally speaking

2 producing ordinary people
3 breaking → broken
4 The people waiting for the bus in the rain are getting wet.

1 Studying in the United States, you will be able to practice English both in and out of the classroom.
2 ④
3 ④

만일 외국어를 공부하기 위해 해외에 가기를 원한다면, 결정을 내리기 전에 고려해야 할 많은 것들이 있다. 우선 어떤 나라로 가기를 원하는지 결정해야 한다. 예를 들어, 최근에, 많은 아시아 학생들이 영어를 배우기 위해서 미국으로 가고 있다. 미국에서 공부하면 교실 안과 밖에서 영어를 연습할 수 있을 것이다. 게다가, 전 세계에서 온 사람들을 만날 수 있고, 그래서 하루 24시간 영어를 말하는 환경에 있게 된다. 또한 당신은 다른 문화에 대해 배울 기회도 가질 수 있다. 반면에 미국에 가는 것은 고액의 비용이 드는 단점도 있다는 것을 알아야 한다.

A **1** A: Do you know the girl standing over there?
     B: Yeah, she is a figure skater. She is famous enough to be known by every teenager in Korea.
   2 A: Do you know the man wearing sunglasses?
     B: Yeah, he is a superstar. He is famous enough to be known by every teenager in Korea.
B **1** A: Could you tell me how to get to the nearest bank?
     B: Go straight ahead for one block. Turning to the right, you can find it.
   2 A: Could you tell me how to get to the nearest convenience store?
     B: Go straight ahead for one block. Turning to the left, you can find it.

A **1** Judging from her appearance
   2 Written in easy English
   3 Living near the school
B **1** Eating spaghetti, Alice met (was meeting) her boyfriend at lunch time.
   2 Eating popcorn, Alice watched (was watching) a scary movie with her friends in the afternoon.
   3 Listening to the radio, Alice cleaned (was cleaning) the floor in the evening.
C **1** interesting
   2 interested
   3 exciting
   4 excited
   5 fascinating
   6 bored / confused
   7 boring / confusing
   8 interesting

Chapter 4
시제

Unit 1 • 기본기 탄탄 다지기   p.108
1 (1) will   (2) is going to   (3) begins
    (4) am going to   (5) will   (6) arrives

Unit 2 • 기본기 탄탄 다지기   p.109
1 (1) am meeting   (2) starts   (3) leave   (4) get
    (5) starts / ends   (6) finish   (7) are / taking   (8) will be

Unit 3 • 기본기 탄탄 다지기   p.110
1 (1) 경험   (2) 결과   (3) 완료   (4) 계속
2 (1) has learned   (2) has not fixed   (3) have lived   (4) has read

서술형 기초 다지기 ❶   p.111
1 (1) No, they aren't. They're going to watch a movie (this evening).
    (2) No, she isn't. She's going to go to Seoul (next week).
2 (1) present   (2) future   (3) present   (4) future
3 (1) Have, met / 경험   (2) have, searched / 완료
    (3) has, gone / 결과   (4) has, worked / 계속
4 (1) The meeting begins at 9 tomorrow morning.
    (2) There is a conference at 10:00 tonight.
5 (1) goes / will do   (2) get / will go
    (3) get / will go   (4) arrive / will put / walk
6 (1) has broken his leg   (2) has turned it on
    (3) has arrived
7 (1) He is going to order a meal.   (2) She is going to buy some fruit.

Oral Test   p.113
1 (1) be going to   (2) 현재시제
2 (1) 현재진행   (2) 현재시제, be about to
3 have(has) + V-ed, 경험, 완료, 계속, 결과

Unit 4 • 기본기 탄탄 다지기   p.114
1 (1) for   (2) since   (3) for   (4) since
2 (1) have not been / returned   (2) has studied / was
    (3) have known / met

Unit 5 • 기본기 탄탄 다지기   p.115
1 (1) have learned   (2) exploded   (3) haven't visited   (4) visited
    (5) has been   (6) read   (7) has studied

Unit 6 • 기본기 탄탄 다지기   p.116
1 (1) has been studying   (2) has been watching
    (3) has been raining   (4) have, been learning

서술형 기초 다지기 ❷   p.117
1 (1) Gina has been collecting stamps since high school.
    (2) Lisa has been sitting in the sun for two hours.
    (3) John has been traveling around the world since 2011.
    (4) They have been playing basketball for four hours.
2 (1) saw / have not seen   (2) Have, eaten / have eaten, ate
    (3) did, do / stayed   (4) Have, been / went
    (5) have known / did, meet
3 (1) My dad has studied Korean since 1999.
    (2) I have not seen Karen since she left for Singapore.
    (3) We have been in Paris since we were married.
    (4) My wife and I have known each other since we were in high school.
    (5) Alice has read three science books since Tuesday.
4 (1) How long has he been speaking on the phone?
      When did he start speaking on the phone?
    (2) How log has it been raining?
      When did it start raining?
    (3) How long has Peter been using this book?
      When did Peter start using this book?
    (4) How long has Jessica been learning the Present Perfect?
      When did Jessica start learning the Present Perfect?

Oral Test   p.119
1 since, for
2 과거, 현재완료
3 (1) 진행, have(has) been + V-ing   (2) 과거, 완료

Unit 7 • 기본기 탄탄 다지기   p.120
1 (1) had taken   (2) went   (3) had gone   (4) did
    (5) have had   (6) have eaten   (7) had

Unit 8 • 기본기 탄탄 다지기   p.121
1 (1) has been jogging   (2) have been studying   (3) has washed
    (4) has lost   (5) has been talking   (6) have gone
    (7) has just eaten

Unit 9 • 기본기 탄탄 다지기   p.122
1 (1) left   (2) had   (3) had   (4) arrived   (5) has   (6) had

서술형 기초 다지기 ❸   p.123
1 (1) had left / arrived   (2) got / had already gone
    (3) had sent / went   (4) had locked / went
    (5) went / had never seen   (6) had studied / moved
2 (1) How long have you been jogging?
    (2) It had been raining for several hours.
    (3) She had been working as a CEO for five years.
    (4) Nancy has been speaking on the phone since six o'clock.
    (5) Jessica has been visiting her aunt and uncle for the last three days.
3 (1) She had been watching TV.
    (2) They had been fighting.
    (3) They had been playing soccer.
    (4) Somebody had been smoking in the room.
    (5) She had been lying in the sun too long.
4 (1) The movie had already begun.   (2) She had gone out.
    (3) They had just finished their lunch.   (4) The train had just left.

중간 · 기말고사   p.126

1 has been in China
2 had been waiting
3 ①
4 ⑤
5 ⑤
6 ④
7 ③
8 ①
9 ①
10 ⑤
11 ②
12 ④
13 ②

서술형 대비 문제

1 Have you ever been to
2 have been married
3 has been learning
4 She has been learning magic for three years.
5 had been wearing her new shoes

Grammar in Reading   p.129

1 ④
2 ③
3 consider → had considered

우리의 후각은 오늘날에는 다양한 목적으로 사용되고 있다. 냄새가 특별한 성과를 보이고 있는 한 분야는 마케팅이다. 한동안 제조업자들은 더 많은 가정용품들을 팔기 위해 우리의 후각을 이용해 왔다. 그들은 향기가 소비자들이 브랜드를 인지하는 데 영향을 미친다고 믿기 때문에 알맞은 향기를 찾기 위해 수백만 달러를 쓴다. (게다가, 흰색으로 벽을 칠하는 것이 치과 대기실에 있는 환자를 진정시키도록 돕는 데에 효과적일 수 있다.) 한 조사에서, 사람들은 세제를 살 때 가장 고려하는 것이 무엇인지에 대해 질문을 받았다. 세제의 향기가 가장 중요한 요소라는 것이 밝혀졌다.

Super Speaking   p.130

A 1 A: Has Carl ever tried waterskiing?
　　B: Yes, he has. He tried it last week.
2 A: Have you ever eaten pepperoni pizza before?
　　B: Yes, I have. I ate it two years ago.
B 1 A: What are your plans for this evening?
　　B: I'm going to go to the Korean Conversation Club.
2 A: What are your plans for this evening?
　　B: I'm going to go to an ice hockey match.

실전 서술형 평가 문제 (모범 답안)   p.131

A 1 He has been to Bangkok. He went there in September, 2007.
2 He has been to New York. He went there in February, 2008.
3 He has been to Istanbul. He went there in April, 2008.
4 He has been to Seoul. He went there in March, 2009.
5 He has been to Shanghai. He went there in July, 2009.
6 He has been to Cairo. He went there in January, 2010.
7 He has been to Mexico City. He went there in December, 2010.

B 1 Marco has been frying potato chips for 4 hours.
　　He has fried 5 kilos of potato chips so far.
2 Dorothy has been preparing salads for 3 hours.
　　She has prepared 20 salads so far.
3 Paul has been taking orders for 5 hours.
　　He has taken 150 orders so far.
4 Kimberly and Tom have been cleaning tables for 2 hours.
　　They have cleaned 40 tables so far.

C 1 If the dress is expensive, Sarah won't buy it.
　　/ If the dress isn't expensive, Sarah will buy it.
2 If you take the subway, you won't be late for work.
　　/ If you don't take the subway, you'll be late for work.
3 If you write on the desk, you'll be in trouble.
　　/ If you don't write on the desk, you won't be in trouble.

Chapter 5
조동사

Unit 1 • 기본기 탄탄 다지기   p.136

1 (1) can　　(2) could　　(3) was able to　　(4) can
　　(5) are　　(6) will be able to　　(7) Could

Unit 2 • 기본기 탄탄 다지기   p.137

1 (1) possibility　　(2) possibility　　(3) ability　　(4) possibility
2 (1) 그것은 사실일지 모른다.
　　(2) 그녀는 아마 그녀의 사무실에 있을지 모른다.
　　(3) 금요일에 회의가 없을지도 모른다.

Unit 3 • 기본기 탄탄 다지기   p.138

1 (1) have to　　(2) has to　　(3) have to　　(4) have to
2 (1) mustn't　　(2) doesn't have to　　(3) don't have to

서술형 기초 다지기 ❶   p.139

1 (1) It's summer now. My friends and I are able to play beach volleyball.
　　(2) She is able to go hiking in the mountains.
　　(3) Are you able to speak any foreign languages?
　　(4) He was able to play the piano when he was five.
　　(5) She wasn't able to come to the party.
2 (1) may come tomorrow
　　(2) may get an invitation
　　(3) may visit me
　　(4) may go to the movie theater this weekend.
　　(5) may not come to the party
3 (1) I must study English tonight.
　　(2) You have to drive slowly through the school zone.
　　(3) To get a cheap ticket, you have to book in advance.
　　(4) Jennifer has got to walk to school.
　　(5) She can't go to the movie tonight because she must study for final exams.

4 (1) You mustn't touch pictures in the museum.

(2) You don't have to go to school today.

(3) You don't have to stay in your seat throughout the flight.

(4) You mustn't spend your time playing video games.

(5) You don't have to finish your homework by tomorrow.

Oral Test p.141

1 (1) 현재 / 미래 / could　　(2) be able to

2 현재형 / may / might / can / could / 현재 / 미래

3 (1) must / have to / has to / has got to

(2) must not(mustn't) / don't(doesn't) have to / don't need to / need not

Unit 4 ● 기본기 탄탄 다지기 p.142

1 (1) should　　(2) ought　　(3) ought not　　(4) shouldn't

2 (1) had better tell　　(2) had better not be

(3) had better park

Unit 5 ● 기본기 탄탄 다지기 p.143

1 (1) 허락　(2) 가능성　(3) 허락　(4) 능력　(5) 허락　(6) 허락　(7) 허락

Unit 6 ● 기본기 탄탄 다지기 p.144

1 (1) Can/Will you　　(2) Would/Could you

(3) Would/Could you　　(4) Can/Will you

2 (1) Would you like to　　(2) Would you like

(3) Would you like　　(4) would you like to

서술형 기초 다지기 ❷ p.145

1 (1) Can you help me with the exercise?

(2) Could(Would) you fasten your seatbelt?

(3) Could(Would) you open the door?

(4) Can you tell me the time?

(5) Could(Would) you bring me some water?

2 (1) Could(May) I have a glass of water?

(2) Could(May) I leave early today?

(3) Can I turn on the TV?

(4) Could(May) I put my coat here?

(5) Could(May) I have some more time to finish the homework?

3 (1) He should use an alarm clock. / He oughtn't to go to bed late at night.

(2) She should take a break. / She oughtn't to work so hard.

4 (1) Would you like to go to Oxford?

(2) Would you like to go to the movie theater?

5 (1) had better call the credit card company

(2) had better find a new girlfriend

(3) had better not smoke any more

Oral Test p.147

1 (1) should / ought to

(2) had better + 동사원형 / had better not + 동사원형

2 (1) can / may　　(2) May / Can

3 (1) you　　(2) Would you like, Would you like to

Unit 7 ● 기본기 탄탄 다지기 p.148

1 (1) She must be tired.　　(2) They must be in the office.

(3) That can't be a ghost.　　(4) He can't be at home.

Unit 8 ● 기본기 탄탄 다지기 p.149

1 (1) must　　(2) could　　(3) may not　　(4) must

Unit 9 ● 기본기 탄탄 다지기 p.150

1 (1) You should have brought an umbrella.

(2) He should not have driven the car so fast.

(3) She must have been at home yesterday.

(4) I feel sick. I ought not to have eaten so much chocolate at the party last night.

서술형 기초 다지기 ❸ p.151

1 (1) should(ought to) have done

(2) must have gone

(3) may/might/could have gone

(4) could/may/might have left

(5) couldn't/can't have gone

(6) shouldn't (/oughtn't to) have eaten

2 (1) must have met

(2) should have listened

(3) shouldn't (/oughtn't to) have worked

(4) must have forgotten

3 (1) can't be　　(2) must not　　(3) must not

(4) can't be　　(5) can't be　　(6) must not

4 (1) must know each other

(2) must go to bed early on Sunday nights

(3) may be in her office

(4) can't have finished her homework

(5) could have forgotten to turn off the lights

(6) might not know about these changes

Oral Test p.153

1 (1) must (be)　　(2) can't(cannot) be

2 have / V-ed

3 should have + V-ed, must have + V-ed

Unit 10 ● 기본기 탄탄 다지기 p.154

1 (1) used to / would　(2) used to / would　(3) used to

(4) used to　　(5) used to　　(6) used to / would

Unit 10 ● 기본기 탄탄 달래기 p.155

1 (1) did he use to play the violin　　(2) did she use to be rich

(3) did she use to dance　　(4) did she use to wear a mini skirt

(5) did he use to eat vegetables

2 (1) Stella didn't use to go to the movies very often, but she does now.

(2) Bob used to go to the movies very often, but he doesn't now.

(3) Stella didn't use to wear fashionable clothes, but she does now.

(4) Bob used to wear fashionable clothes, but he doesn't now.

(5) Stella used to watch cartoons on TV, but she doesn't now.

(6) Bob didn't use to watch cartoons on TV, but he does now.

<table>
<tr><td colspan="2">중간 · 기말고사</td><td align="right">p.156</td></tr>
</table>

중간 · 기말고사   p.156

1 ②
2 ①
3 ③
4 need not
5 ⑤
6 ③
7 ④
8 ①
9 ①
10 used to
11 ②
12 ⑤

서술형 대비 문제

1 must have studied
2 must have thrown
3 should not have seen
4 may/might have met
5 Would(would)

Grammar in Reading   p.159

1 ④
2 ②
3 ①

여러분은 장거리 비행 후에 아프거나 졸리거나 매우 피곤한 적이 있었는가? 특히, 동쪽에서 서쪽으로 또는 서쪽에서 동쪽으로 비행한다면 여러분은 분명히 이러한 문제를 겪게 될 것이다. 이것은 다른 시간대로 여행을 함으로써 생기는 피로와 다른 증상의 조합이다. 이것은 24시간 주기 리듬의 변화 때문에 일어나는 것이다. 이것과 함께 수많은 증상들이 나타날 수 있다. 예를 들면, 시간대를 넘어 여행하는 것은 생리 시계에 혼동을 주어 피로를 초래한다. 때때로, 여러분은 너무 감각을 잃어 그 어떤 일도 하고 싶지 않은 것이다. 또한 두통이 있을 수 있고, 음식 섭취 장애와 수면 장애를 겪는 것을 인지할지도 모른다. 이것들은 모두 이것의 일반적인 증상이다. 아래에는 이것을 어떻게 대처하고 관리하는지에 대한 정보가 제시된다.

Super Speaking   p.160

A
1 A: I can't find Tiffany. Have you seen her?
    B: She might be in the tennis court. She may be playing tennis now.
2 A: I can't find Kathy. Have you seen her?
    B: She might be in her room. She may be doing her homework now.

B
1 A: Why did Peter buy a dictionary?
    B: Because he had to translate a novel.
2 A: Why did Ava go to a restaurant?
    B: Because she had to entertain her client.

실전 서술형 평가 문제 (모범 답안)   p.161

A
1 We shouldn't have gone to the movies.
2 We should have studied for it.
3 We should have gone to college.
4 We should have brought umbrellas.
5 We should have used an alarm clock.

B
1 She is going to go to the meeting with Sunny at 11:00.
2 She may/might have coffee with Susan after class.
3 She is going to work at 1:00.
4 She may/might go shopping after work.
5 She may/might take the 6:00 train.

---

6 She may/might eat dinner with Eric.

C
1 May/Could I speak to you for a moment, (please)?
2 May/Could I carry those books for you?
3 May/Could I see your ticket, (please)?
4 May/Could I have a spoon, (please)?
5 Can I borrow your smartphone, (please)?

Chapter 6
수동태

Unit 1 • 기본기 탄탄 다지기   p.166

1 (1) studied   (2) was ticketed   (3) was built
2 (1) were, destroyed   (2) was, not, built   (3) is, read

Unit 2 • 기본기 탄탄 다지기   p.167

1 (1) was being built   (2) has been stolen
   (3) was invented   (4) is going to be eaten

Unit 3 • 기본기 탄탄 다지기   p.168

1 (1) going to be launched   (2) might be given
   (3) may be tested   (4) should save
2 (1) got broken   (2) got run
   (3) get bitten

서술형 기초 다지기 ❶   p.169

1 (1) The door is being painted by Lisa.
   (2) The car has been repaired by him.
   (3) An e-mail must be sent in advance by Kevin.
   (4) The deadline for reports should not be forgotten by you.
   (5) The dirty plates and bowls are going to be washed by her.
2 (1) This ship was built in 1920.
   (2) The escaped prisoner was arrested by the police.
   (3) The building was designed by a famous architect.
   (4) The plants are grown in Brazil.
   (5) The mirror was broken last night.
3 (1) Waste from factories must not be thrown into the sea.
   (2) The pyramids were built around 400 A.D.
   (3) We should not cut down the forests.
   (4) We ought to protect animals in danger.
   (5) Our planet will be destroyed.
4 (1) got hit   (2) get asked   (3) got hurt   (4) got fired   (5) got married

---

Oral Test   p.171

1 목적어, be동사 + V-ed
2 is fixed, is being fixed, has been fixed, was fixed, was being fixed,
   had been fixed, will be fixed, is going to be fixed, will have been fixed
3 조동사 + be + V-ed

Unit 4 • 기본기 탄탄 다지기 p.172

1 (1) was sent / to   (2) was bought / for   (3) was shown / X

(4) gave   (5) brought / to   (6) was given / to

(7) was shown / X

Unit 5 • 기본기 탄탄 다지기 p.173

1 (1) to repair   (2) was asked   (3) to turn

(4) was elected   (5) to walk   (6) was persuaded

Unit 6 • 기본기 탄탄 다지기 p.174

1 (1) was, laughed, at   (2) was, put, off

(3) must, be, looked, after   (4) is, being, made, fun, of

서술형 기초 다지기 ❷ p.175

1 (1) The police were given the information.

The information was given (to) the police.

(2) My old car was sold (to) her for $500 by me.

(3) A long letter was written (to) me by my wife.

(4) We are taught French by Mrs. Smith.

French is taught (to) us by Mrs. Smith.

(5) The reason was explained to the customers.

2 (1) His children were made happy by him.

(2) She was elected the first female president of Korea (by them).

(3) A ghost was seen to go into the house by us.

(4) You won't be allowed to do such a thing.

3 (1) My poor cat was run over by a black car.

(2) Someone took away the silverware last night.

(3) A foreign company took over our bank.

(4) The nurse was looked up to by them.

(5) This unfortunate marriage must be put up with by Lucy.

4 (1) was brought to me   (2) were seen to fall

(3) was made embarrassed

5 (1) The doctor advised him not to eat fatty food.

(2) He made Jessica clean her room.

(3) They saw their classmate get roughed up with folded arms.

Oral Test p.177

1 (1) 직접, for, to, for   (2) 직접

2 목적격 보어, to부정사

3 동사

Unit 7 • 기본기 탄탄 다지기 p.178

1 (1) is, said, to, be, published   (2) It, was, said, that

(3) It, is, believed, that   (4) believe, love, is

Unit 8 • 기본기 탄탄 다지기 p.179

1 (1) delivered   (2) cut   (3) to build   (4) taken

(5) stolen   (6) to paint   (7) to repair

Unit 9 • 기본기 탄탄 다지기 p.180

1 (1) by   (2) about   (3) with   (4) from

서술형 기초 다지기 ❸ p.181

1 (1) Yu-na Kim is believed to win the World Figure Skating Championships.

It is believed that Yu-na Kim will win the World Figure Skating Championships.

(2) He is said to have been a brave soldier as a young man.

It is said that he was a brave soldier as a young man.

(3) She is thought to have been the right woman for the job.

It is thought that she was the right woman for the job.

(4) Stress is said to cause headaches.

It is said that stress causes headaches.

(5) This winter is expected to be warmer than usual.

It is expected that this winter will be warmer than usual.

2 (1) I must have these letters typed by tonight.

(2) Tiffany always has her nails done at a beauty salon.

(3) Nancy is going to have(/ is having / will have) her hair dyed next week.

(4) Sunny had her teeth checked last week.

3 (1) crowded, with   (2) worried, about   (3) interested, in

4 (1) expect that John will win the race

(2) say that Kevin is responsible for what happened

(3) believe that a flat tire caused the accident

5 (1) Lisa   (2) somebody else   (3) we

(4) somebody else   (5) somebody else   (6) somebody else

Oral Test p.183

1 (1) be동사 + V-ed, to부정사   (2) to have + V-ed

2 목적어, V-ed(과거분사)

3 to, with

중간 · 기말고사 p.184

1 ④

2 ③

3 ②

4 ④

5 ⑤

6 ⑤

7 ⑤

8 ⑤

9 ②

10 ⑤

11 to him

12 ③

서술형 대비 문제

1 were, made, to, do

2 to, build

3 The scary movie will not be shown today.

4 is being painted by them

5 The Harry Potter books (/ They) were written by J. K. Rowing.

1 ①

2 ③

3 Pilots must know how airplanes might be affected by the bad weather.

날씨는 우리의 삶을 살아가는 데에 매우 중요하다. 날씨를 연구하는 과학자인 기상학자들은 공기, 바람, 비 등을 분석하고 가까운 미래의 날씨를 예측한다. 비행기 조종사는 나쁜 날씨에 의해 비행기가 어떻게 영향을 받는지 알아야 한다. 나쁜 날씨는 문제가 될 수 있다. 품질이 좋은 농작물을 기르기 위해서 농부들은 햇빛과 충분한 양의 비가 필요하다. 만약 아직 수확기가 되지 않았다면 이른 서리는 농작물 전체를 망칠 수 있다. 짙은 안개는 자동차와 배의 사고를 일으킬 수 있다. 하지만 아이들에게 나쁜 날씨는 재미있을 수도 있다. 건조하고 더운 날에 그들은 수영을 하러 갈 수 있다. 눈이 오고 추운 날에는 스키를 타러 갈 수 있다.

A 1 A: Was the Mona Lisa painted by Leo Tolstoy?

B: No, it wasn't. It was painted by Leonardo da Vinci.

2 A: Was the light bulb invented by Walt Disney?

B: No, it wasn't. It was invented by Thomas Edison.

B 1 A: The world's first Olympic Games were held in Korea.

B: The world's first Olympic Games weren't held in Korea. They were held in Greece.

2 A: Romeo and Juliet was written by Vincent van Gogh.

B: Romeo and Juliet wasn't written by Vincent van Gogh. It was written by Shakespeare.

A 1 Alex was given a farewell present by the company.

A farewell present was given to Alex by the company.

2 It is thought that Cindy has moved abroad.

Cindy is thought to have moved abroad.

3 I was asked the direction to the City Hall by the girl.

The direction to the City Hall was asked of me by the girl.

4 It is said that people spend too much time watching TV and don't read enough.

People are said to spend too much time watching TV and not to read enough.

5 A striped shirt was bought for his grandfather by Scott.

B 1 Karen is having her tooth filled.

2 Susan is mopping the floor.

3 Jessica is having her nails painted.

4 The boy is having his hair cut.

C A few days ago, Kevin's motorcycle was stolen. His motorcycle had been left outside Kevin's(his) house. The theft was reported to the police by Kevin. He was told by the police that they would try to find his motorcycle. This morning, Kevin was called by the police and was asked to come to the police station. His motorcycle had been found. It had been painted by the thieves and then it had been sold to someone else. The motorcycle had been parked outside the police station by the new owner. The thieves were arrested by the police.